PIMLICO

745

AFTER DAYBREAK

Ben Shephard was born in 1948 and
read History at Oxford University. He
was a producer on the television series
The World at War and *The Nuclear Age*
and has made numerous historical and
scientific documentaries for the BBC
and Channel Four. He is the author of
the critically acclaimed *A War of Nerves:
Soldiers and Psychiatrists 1914–1994*
(published by Jonathan Cape and
Pimlico). He lives in Bristol.

AFTER DAYBREAK

The Liberation of Belsen, 1945

BEN SHEPHARD

PIMLICO

Published by Pimlico 2006

2 4 6 8 10 9 7 5 3 1

Copyright © Ben Shephard 2005

Ben Shephard has asserted his right under the Copyright,
Designs and Patents Act 1988 to be identified as the author of this work

First published in Great Britain in 2005 by
Jonathan Cape

Pimlico edition 2006

Pimlico
Random House, 20 Vauxhall Bridge Road,
London SW1V 2SA

Random House Australia (Pty) Limited
20 Alfred Street, Milsons Point, Sydney,
New South Wales 2061, Australia

Random House New Zealand Limited
18 Poland Road, Glenfield,
Auckland 10, New Zealand

Random House (Pty) Limited
Isle of Houghton, Corner of Boundary Road & Carse O'Gowrie,
Houghton, 2198, South Africa

Random House UK Limited Reg. No. 954009

A CIP catalogue record for this book is available from the British Library

ISBN 9781844135400 (from Jan 2007)
ISBN 1844135403

Papers used by Random House UK Limited are natural, recyclable
products made from wood grown in sustainable forests. The manufacturing processes
conform to the environmental regulations of the country of origin

Printed and bound in Great Britain by Cox & Wyman Ltd, Reading, Berkshire

After Daybreak

The Liberation

of Belsen, 1945

CONTENTS

ILLUSTRATIONS

The main camp at Bergen-Belsen, ten days after the British arrival (*Imperial War Museum*).

German officers are led through British lines after negotiating a truce, 12 April 1945 (*Imperial War Museum*).

Josef Kramer is paraded in irons before being removed to the POW cage at Celle, 17 April 1945 (*Imperial War Museum*).

Lt. Colonel James Johnston, the British Army doctor in charge at Belsen, with Hadassah Bimko, Ruth Gutman and Captain 'Frosty' Winterbotham, 17 April 1945 (*United States Holocaust Memorial Museum*).

Luba Tryszynska, the 'Angel of Belsen', 26 April 1945 (*Imperial War Museum*).

Brigadier H.L. Glyn Hughes, mastermind of the Belsen relief effort (*Wellcome Library, London*).

A survivor picks over clothing, 17 April 1945 (*Imperial War Museum*).

The 'typhus hospital' at Belsen, 26 April 1945 (*Imperial War Museum*).

Inmates prepare a meal, 17 April 1945 (*Imperial War Museum*).

The overcrowded interior of one of the women's huts, 17 April 1945 (*Imperial War Museum*).

British soldiers supervise the distribution of food, 21 April 1945 (*Imperial War Museum*).

A bulldozer pushes bodies into a mass grave, 19 April 1945 (*Imperial War Museum*).

British Tommies force German soldiers to remove bodies of the dead (*Wellcome Library, London*).

Evacuation of the sick from Camp 1, 22 April 1945 (*Imperial War Museum*).

Women prisoners collect freshly baked bread, 24 April 1945 (*Imperial War Museum*).

Survivors being washed and disinfected by German nurses in the 'Human Laundry' (*Wellcome Library, London*).

Newly evacuated patients in a temporary 'ward' set up in one of the squares of the Panzer Training School, 27 April 1945 (*Imperial War Museum*).

A patient is treated in the new hospital, 25 April 1945 (*Imperial War Museum*).

Konrad Herschel, a thirteen year-old Czech boy, three months after the liberation, 20 July 1945 (*Imperial War Museum*).

A British soldier sprays a prisoner with DDT (*Photograph by George Rodger © Times Life Pictures/Getty Images*).

British medical students shortly before their return to England, 25 May 1945 (*Imperial War Museum*).

Burgomasters of the neighbouring towns watch a mass burial for the benefit of *Movietone News*, 24 April 1945 (*Imperial War Museum*).

Dr Fritz Klein, 'the mad doctor of Belsen', posed in one of the mass graves, 24 April 1945 (*Imperial War Museum*).

Rabbi Leslie Hardman reads the *kaddish* over a mass grave at Belsen, 21 April 1945 (*Imperial War Museum*).

The last hut in Camp 1 is ceremonially burnt, 21 May 1945 (*Imperial War Museum*).

Leslie Hardman conducts an open-air service in one of the squares of the Panzer Training School, soon to become 'Belsen Displaced Persons Camp', 19 May 1945 (*Imperial War Museum*).

Two former inmates weep over one of the Belsen mass graves, 14 April 1946 (*Imperial War Museum*).

ACKNOWLEDGEMENTS

Working on this book, I was conscious of treading in the footsteps of such Belsen scholars as Eberhard Kolb, E.E. Vella, Paul Kemp, Joanne Reilly, A.-E. Wenck, and Elly Trepman. I would also like to pay particular tribute to the staff of three institutions who guided me through the mass of Belsen material. At the Imperial War Museum, Stephen Walton and Simon Robbins in the Department of Documents, Margaret Brooks in the Sound Archive, David Bell in the Photographic Archive, and Paul Sargent and Toby Haggith in the Department of Film; at the Gedenkstätte Bergen-Belsen, Dr Thomas Rahe, Arnold Jürgens, Klaus Tätzler, Martina Staats and Karin Theilen; and at the Fortunoff Archive for Holocaust Video Testimonies, in Yale University Library, Joanne Rudof. It was an enormous privilege to be taken round the old Panzer Training School, now a NATO barracks, by Warrant Officer Graham Parmenter.

My thanks also to the American Friends Archive (Eleanora Golobic); BBC Archives; British Red Cross (Helen Pugh); JDC Archives, Jerusalem (Dr Sara Kadosh); JDC Archives, New York (Sherry Hyman and Shelley Helfand); London Library; Public Record Office/ National Archives; RAMC Museum (Alan Scadding); Somerville College, Oxford (Pauline Adams); the Tank Museum, Bovington; the United States Holocaust Memorial Museum; University of Bristol Library; Yad Vashem; YIVO Institute for Jewish History (Leo Greenberg).

For advice, recollections and permission to use material, I am indebted to Mrs Edith Baneth, Mr Victor Baneth, Mrs Anna Bergman, Dr Jonathan Bird, Professor David Cesarani, Dr Michael Coigley, Sir Richard Doll, Mrs Carolyn Drake, Mr John Edwards, Mrs Eva Fried, the Revd Chris Gonin, Sir James Gowans, Dr Peter Horsey, Mrs Anita Lasker-Wallfisch, Professor Paul A. Levine, Dr Alan MacAuslan, Ms Rowan MacAuslan, Mrs Mary Park, Dr Alex Paton, Mr Anthony Pitt-Rivers, Mr Menachem Z. Rosensaft, Dr John Seaman, Mrs Jean Smart and Dr Michael Wilson. Every effort has been made to trace and contact the copyright holders of all material used in this book. The author and publishers would be glad to rectify any omissions at the earliest opportunity.

On a project like this, friends' support matters. Peter Barham, Caroline Garland, Raye Farr, Hugh Freeman, Rhodri Hayward, Jemima Hunt, Kristina Jones, Chris Keil, Jair Kessler, Jerry Kuehl, Bernice Lerner, Catherine Merridale, Peter Romijn, Roger Smith, Derek Summerfield and Simon Wessely have all in different ways bolstered morale. Mark Harrison generously allowed me to see a copy of his *Medicine and Victory* prior to publication. Michaela Gigerl provided German translations. My research in Washington and London was made possible by the hospitality of Caroline Moser and Peter Sollis and Marylla and Julian Hunt. My children, Louisa and Joe Shephard, have coped genially with my obsessions.

My agent, Clare Alexander, has been a tower of strength; thanks too to Kate Shaw and Sally Riley.

At Jonathan Cape, I have benefited from Will Sulkin's forbearance and understanding, Ellah Allfrey's editorial skill and Richard Collins's calm efficiency.

The hardest thing, as always, is fully to express my debt to my wife, Sue. Suffice it to say that without her I could not have written this book.

INTRODUCTION

IN THE SECOND week of April 1945 a rumour reached the war correspondents attached to the British Army in Germany. A concentration camp had been found nearby, they learned, and was to be handed over to the British. Most of the journalists thought it would be just another prisoner-of-war camp, no different from those they had already seen liberated, and did not stir from the Press Centre bar. But one BBC reporter decided to go and look for himself.

In a famous broadcast made a few hours later, Richard Dimbleby described what he had found inside the camp: the piles of dead bodies; the huts full of the starving; the people who died in front of his eyes. And then he told of how he had entered one of the huts and picked his way over corpse after corpse in the gloom, until he 'heard one voice above the undulating moaning'.

I found a girl – she was a living skeleton – impossible to gauge her age, for she had practically no hair left on her head and her face was only a yellow parchment sheet with two holes left in it for eyes. She was stretching out her stick of an arm and gasping something. It was 'Englisch – Englisch

– medicine – medicine', and she was trying to cry but she had not enough strength.[1]

This girl was one of the survivors of Bergen-Belsen camp.

Today Belsen remains a byword for human evil and depravity, a benchmark in the moral history of the world. At the time, though, the camp represented something much more immediate: a humanitarian disaster, a challenge to the conscience of the world, a gauntlet thrown down to medicine. Inside the camp were some 60,000 people – more than half of them Jewish survivors of the Nazi's 'Final Solution' – still clinging to life and crying out to be saved. It fell to the British to help them. This book is about how they responded to that challenge.

For half a century the British regarded their conduct at Belsen as one of the great epics of medical history; 'perhaps never in the history of medicine has a more gallant action been fought against disease', a doctor wrote in 1947. The role played by ninety-six volunteers from the London medical schools who were sent to work in the 'Horror Camp' was singled out for special praise. But when historians looked at this episode again in the 1990s, they noticed several disturbing elements. Why were the British not prepared for what they found at Belsen? Why did it take so long (almost two weeks) to organise a proper medical response? Why were the medical teams sent to the camp so poorly equipped, with only aspirin and opium, and no surgical instruments and anaesthetics? Why, when specialists did arrive, did they get so much of the medicine wrong? Above all, was it inevitable that nearly 14,000 people should die at Belsen *after* it was liberated?[2]

Such doubts have hardened into a new, revisionist view, voiced at a conference in 2000 by the Chairman of the United States Holocaust Memorial Council. The 'mishandling' of the medicine of liberating the camps, argued Rabbi Irving Greenberg, 'reflected Allied ignorance and failure to plan, which in turn mirrored the democracies' lack of concern for the fate of the Jews'. 'The organized mass killing stopped,' he said, 'but the dying went on.'[3]

Where does the truth lie? Did the British make a mess of it? The answers can be found in contemporary military records, the diaries of those who worked at Belsen and the testimony of survivors. Together, these sources make it possible to reconstruct events in April and May of 1945 as they unfolded day by day. It is a moving story of brotherhood, a sad tale of human frailty and an illuminating case study. For, as we see today, when the military are asked to deal with civilian problems, they are not always comfortable in the role.

Almost sixty years ago, Derrick Sington, one of the first British soldiers to enter the camp, wrote in his book *Belsen Uncovered* that 'someday someone will tell the story of the vast medical problem that was Belsen'. Since then important specialist accounts of the medical relief effort in the camp have appeared, by E. E. Vella, Paul Kemp, Joanne Reilly, Elly Trepman and others. But there has been no attempt to make what was done at Belsen accessible to the general reader. And, paradoxically, it is only now, after sixty years, that we are able to get a clear sense of what went on in the camp day by day, because over the last decade a mass of new material has become available, diaries and letters written at the time by British nurses, doctors, soldiers and relief workers so overwhelmed by what they saw that they felt compelled to record it. Most then returned to England, got on with their lives and sat on the material (and their Belsen memories) for half a century. Only after their deaths in the 1990s have these valuable accounts surfaced.[4]

The result has been to fill in several blank patches in the canvas. For example, in the mid-1990s, even as the historian Joanne Reilly was bemoaning the fact that there are very few written accounts from Belsen by women in the public domain and speculating why women did not seem to write as men did, a stream of diaries and letters written by women was coming to light. Jean McFarlane, Effie Barker, Molly Silva Jones, Muriel Blackman, Jane Leverson and many others powerfully convey the impact of the place. Of course, serious imbalances in the sources remain.[5]

Occasionally, when I was researching this book, the question arose, 'Why go back?' Why return to this episode? Why not continue the British tradition of the 1950s and forget the unpleasantness? For two reasons. The Holocaust continues to cast a heavy shadow over the modern world and it is important to be very clear about what happened. But, beyond that, Belsen should be remembered not simply for the evil perpetrated there, but for the humane and life-affirming work that was also done. It was a place that brought out the best, as well as the worst, in human beings. As such, it still has invaluable lessons to teach us.

PROLOGUE

MANY THINGS HAPPENED on 12 April 1945. In the United States, President Franklin D. Roosevelt died suddenly at his winter retreat at Warm Springs, Georgia; and Hitler and Goebbels were momentarily persuaded that a miracle was at hand. Outside Berlin, the Red Army made final preparations for its assault on the German capital. In the Far East, US Marines continued their bloody fight for the island of Okinawa, while, offshore, Japanese kamikaze pounded their carriers and battleships.

The 11th British Armoured Division was in northern Germany that day, about twenty miles east of Bremen. Three weeks earlier, in a massive and meticulously planned operation, the River Rhine had been crossed. Since then, 11th Armoured's Sherman tanks had been moving steadily northeastwards across the north German plain, in the face of intermittently stiff German opposition, aiming to reach the Baltic before the Russians. On 5 April, after heavy fighting, 11th Armoured had crossed the River Weser and established a bridgehead across the next barrier, the River Aller. Rocket-firing Typhoon fighters had softened up enemy positions and the engineers had constructed a bridge allowing the division's 270 tanks to cross at 9 a.m. that morning. The next objective, the River Elbe, lay across a huge area of woodland

and heather used as an army training ground, the Lüneburg Heath.[1]

In the middle of the day, as if from nowhere, a large German Mercedes staff car appeared at the 159th Battalion's forward headquarters – a white flag fixed to its bonnet. Out stepped two Wehrmacht Colonels, incongruously dapper in their peaked caps and leather boots.

The Germans had an unusual offer to make. Directly across 11th Armoured's line of advance, at a place called Bergen-Belsen, they said, lay a concentration camp full of prisoners seriously ill with typhus. To prevent them from roaming the countryside and spreading the disease, the Germans were prepared to offer a local truce. If the British would avoid fighting around Belsen, they would offer them another bridge over the River Aller.

The two officers were blindfolded and sent back to 8 Corps Headquarters. The British were already worried about a possible epidemic of typhus in the rear of their advancing forces and were sympathetic to the proposal for a truce, but would not accept the geographical limits proposed by the Germans. Eventually it was agreed that the area round Bergen-Belsen itself would be treated as 'neutral' and no shots would be fired into or out of this zone. A battalion of German infantry and a Hungarian regiment of about 2000 men would remain in the camp to guard the perimeter and prevent any mass break-out, while about fifty SS men, acting in a purely administrative capacity, would await the British commandant, to hand over the camp. The Germans would withdraw by 1000 hours the following morning.[2]

On 13 April, British commanders earmarked troops for the job of entering the camp, while their medical colleagues held a hasty preliminary conference. But German resistance in the surrounding area remained strong, and it was not till the morning of Sunday 15 April that 11th Armoured fought its way to Belsen. The main body of tanks paused only briefly to approach the wire and then swept on.

Behind them, the occupying force moved towards the camp's gates. For Belsen's inmates, the long wait was finally over.[3]

1

The Approaching End

'WE ALL FEEL the end approaching,' Hanna Lévy-Hass wrote in her diary on 30 August 1944. 'We are gripped . . . by a mad delusion that all will soon be over.' A schoolteacher from Sarajevo, she had been rounded up by the Gestapo six weeks earlier and sent to Bergen-Belsen concentration camp; but now, with Allied armies victorious in Normandy and the Red Army advancing through Poland, she was hopeful that she would soon be liberated.[1]

Belsen was an unusual camp. Its origins went back to a meeting held in an ugly concrete bunker in East Prussia on 10 December 1942. On that day, Heinrich Himmler, the mild-mannered, bespectacled man in charge of organising the systematic murder of millions of people all over Europe, drove over from his own luxurious field headquarters nearby for one of his frequent conferences with the Führer, Adolf Hitler, at the Wolfsschanze.

They met at a pivotal moment in the war. On the Russian front, the 200,000 men of General Paulus's Sixth Army had just been cut off by a Soviet counterattack at Stalingrad and, although Hitler was choosing to believe Göring's assurances that they could be supplied from the air by the Luftwaffe, most of his entourage knew better and were bracing themselves for a disaster. The news from the Mediterranean Front was equally grim: in early November 1942, only a week after Field Marshal Rommel's defeat at El Alamein in Egypt, Anglo-American troops had landed in Algeria and Morocco; now they were heading towards Tunis. To those in the know, it was apparent that Hitler's bid to achieve a decisive victory before the military might of the United States could be deployed in the European theatre had failed; a shudder passed through Axis morale; the Italians buckled and needed stiffening.

The Führerhauptquartier had so many military concerns that day – organising von Manstein's counterattack at Stalingrad; sending reinforcements to Rommel; shoring up Italian morale – that it might seem surprising Hitler could find time to see Himmler at all. But he always had time for the Reichsführer, and the recent reverses had only strengthened his resolve to 'proceed ruthlessly against the Jews'.[2]

Himmler, moreover, could offer better news. The 'Final Solution' of the Jewish problem was proceeding very well; so well, in fact, that just over a year since the policy of systematic genocide had begun, over two million European Jews had already been exterminated. For all the vicious anti-Semitic rhetoric of Hitler's early memoir, *Mein Kampf*, and all the barbarous threats uttered in his speeches, the Nazis' road to genocide had been long and tortuous and the Führer had been careful to distance himself from most of it. Before the war, the emphasis had been on deporting the Jews from German territory and as late as 1940 there were still vague plans to send them to the Indian Ocean Island of Madagascar – which had to be abandoned when the invasion of Britain was postponed and mastery of the seas could not be achieved. When Hitler turned against his Soviet ally in June 1941, the plan was to send the Jews eastwards, into the vast empty Russian steppe, there to die of starvation and overwork. When, however, Operation Barbarossa began to falter in the late autumn of 1941, the Germans confronted once more the question of what to do with the large Jewish population in Eastern Europe. All this time, murderous Einsatzgruppen had been working behind the

Wehrmacht as it advanced into the Soviet Union, shooting Jews and Communists in their thousands, while all over occupied Eastern Europe local commanders had taken 'initiatives' against the Jews, knowing they would meet with approval in Berlin. But now, in the later months of 1941, the line between mass murder and organised genocide was crossed.

On 15 August 1941, in Minsk in the Ukraine, Himmler witnessed a mass execution for himself and saw at first hand what a messy business it was. That gruesome experience may have provided the catalyst which led him to look for more efficient methods of killing; but even before then he had decided to apply to a new purpose the expertise in the lethal use of poison gas developed in the 'mercy killing' of some 70,000 German mental hospital patients.

This programme was executed with breathtaking speed. Initially gassing vans were used, but in late November 1941 teams arrived at Belzec in Poland to advise on the building of gas chambers and, in the spring of 1942, two other extermination factories were created, at Sobibor and Treblinka; in July the enormous camp at Auschwitz-Birkenau began to function. By the end of that year, 'the overwhelming majority of Jews in the Central Government [of Poland] had been murdered, and the rest of Europe's Jews were set to follow them into the gas chambers'.[3]

In this context, it might seem odd that Hitler and Himmler talked about sparing Jewish lives at their meeting. 'I have asked the Führer with regard to letting Jews go abroad for ransom', Himmler's *aide-mémoire* records. 'He gave me full powers to approve cases like that, if they really bring in foreign currency in appreciable quantities from abroad,' But the impulse which led to the creation of Bergen-Belsen was not merciful; it fitted, rather, into a wider pattern of combining the extermination of the Jews with the extraction of their full economic potential. Just as some of the younger and fitter would be temporarily saved from the gas chambers, to work in labour camps for the German war effort, so it made sense to squeeze all the juice out of the richer and more prominent. Also, the German Foreign Office was interested in exchanging some Jews for German citizens interned by the Allies – there had already been one such exchange before December 1942; while the SS thought they might be useful as hostages. It may also be true that Himmler had another purpose in mind: that, even while supervising the death factories in Eastern Europe and devotedly serving his Führer, he could see the way the war was going and felt it might be useful to have counters with which to bargain with the Allies.[4]

Later the same month, the bureaucracy was mobilised. Himmler ordered the Head of the Gestapo, Heinrich Müller, to 'segregate Jews who had important connections abroad' and to establish a special transit camp where they would be held – they would work but, Himmler stated, 'be kept healthy and alive'. In the spring of 1943 further steps followed. The SS persuaded the army to hand over part of a prisoner-of-war camp near Celle, in northern Germany, Sturmbannführer Adolf Haas was appointed camp commandant and gangs of prisoners were sent from nearby concentration camps to bring the place up to the standard felt necessary for its new role. Then, on 10 May 1943, the establishment of 'Bergen-Belsen civilian internment camp' was officially announced, only for its title to be speedily changed to 'Bergen-Belsen detention camp' when it was realised that 'according to the Geneva convention, civil internment camps must be accessible for visits by international committees'. In the middle of July the first inmates arrived.[5]

The Germans variously estimated the number of potential 'exchange Jews' at between 10,000 and 30,000, but only about 7000 of them were ever sent to Belsen. This elite group was made up of those who held dual nationality, those thought worth exchanging and those who had been granted exemption by acquiring or being given a place on one of the 'lists', those rolls of names of people who had won exemption from bureaucratic genocide. Much the most valuable of these was thought to be the 'Palestine list' containing the names of those with certificates enabling them to emigrate to Palestine.

Over the next year, groups of survivors from the Jewish communities in Poland, Greece, Holland and Hungary were sent to Belsen. Most of the Poles were eventually transported to Auschwitz, many of the Hungarians were moved on; and, after protracted negotiations, some 250 Jews were eventually exchanged for German nationals, in July 1944. But, although Belsen continued to be a camp for 'exchange Jews', the SS also began to use the site to accommodate other populations as well. By the middle of 1944, Belsen consisted of five different camps containing 'exchange Jews', neutrals, 'criminals' and political prisoners, all kept separate. The character of the place was changing, as it was increasingly used by the SS as just another part of the vast concentration camp empire. One area became a 'recuperation camp' to which sickly prisoners could be sent from other camps, but the medical care was primitive and most of the prisoners were in the last stages of tuberculosis and died quickly. In addition, a large camp for women was established at Belsen in the summer of 1944.[6]

With their usual thoroughness, the Germans kept the different groups at Belsen entirely segregated from each other, behind barbed wire, and enforced strict hierarchies of privilege. The Hungarian Jews were the most fortunate, not having to work or attend endless roll calls and being permitted to wear civilian clothing, eat kosher food and give their dead decent funerals. The 'politicals' were treated worst.

Because of the camp's 'special' status, certain groups at Belsen were even allowed to run their own affairs and to keep diaries; and most of what we now know comes from inmates of the 'Star Camp' for 'exchange Jews', where nearly all the Dutch were sent. The prevailing note in these journals is of hunger and despair, a daily struggle for survival as starvation, overwork and brutality take their toll, and the conditions of existence gradually remove the decencies of civilised life – 'a wild uncontrollable jealousy can overcome a person for a spoonful of soup'. But there are also striking individual differences. For Hanna Lévy-Hass, an

Yugoslav Communist, the destruction of the bonds of solidarity and comradeship, the ease with which the Germans set the prisoners against each other, was the worst thing. 'Our hut is like a madhouse,' she wrote in September 1944. 'It is exactly what the Nazis intended – to humiliate us and reduce us to animals, to drive us out of our minds, to extinguish even the faintest memory we might still have that we were once human beings.' She clung to her faith that after the war the restructuring of society would transform human nature.[7]

Another diarist, the Amsterdam lawyer and Zionist Abel J. Herzberg, was mainly preoccupied with the need to maintain in the camp the forms and structure of Jewish law and self-government. He proudly described the workings of 'the investigation branch, the judiciary, the youth care service' and the 'magistrate and chief investigator' within the 'Star Camp'; only then to deplore their gradual collapse.[8]

By the end of 1944 such concerns had become irrelevant. As the Allied armies paused, Belsen took on its third and final role – as the terminus, the last station, of the Holocaust, to which prisoners from the death camps in the East in the path of the Soviet Army were evacuated. Among the thousands brought by trains from Auschwitz to Belsen in the late autumn were a young Dutch Jewish girl, Anne Frank; a French musician who played in the camp orchestra, Fania Fénelon; and a housewife from Cracow, Bertha Ferderber. 'They fear nobody will believe them and will put their stories down as the tales of lunatics,' Hanna Lévy-Hass wrote after talking to some of the new arrivals. She was surprised, however, that they all looked 'healthy and comparatively well'.[9]

By now Belsen was seriously overcrowded, and, at first, the newcomers had to sleep in makeshift tents erected on the windswept heath. Then new barracks were erected, only for those to fill up instantly. Three-tiered bunks were installed in the huts and prisoners made to sleep two to a bunk.

In December 1944, SS Hauptsturmführer Josef Kramer was sent from Auschwitz to be the new commandant of Belsen. A tough but limited man who had joined the SS as an unemployed electrician in 1932, Kramer was used to following orders; he imposed a strict but vicious regime, putting Aryan 'Kapos' in charge of each hut and terrorising the prisoners with endless roll calls. At the same time, more and more transports were sent to Belsen. The camp became yet more overcrowded, the population growing from 15,257 at the end of 1944 to 44,000 by the end of March 1945, even though some 18,000 people had died there in that month alone. 'We are engulfed in our own stinking sea of germs, lice and fleas, and everything around us is putrid and slimy,' Lévy-Hass wrote. 'We are literally lying on top of each other, we provide a perfect breeding-ground for the lice.' In February 1945, an epidemic of typhus broke out. There began to be reports of cannibalism among the inmates: of corpses being cut open and organs such as the liver extracted and eaten.[10]

By early March 1945, Belsen was subsiding into chaos. The food supply began to fail completely; Allied bombing nearby disrupted the water supply. All attempts to bury the dead were abandoned. According to a later account:

Until about March the dead had been cremated but during this month the mortality rate rose sharply and the crematorium could no longer cope. The dead were then gathered into piles and burned in the open but this was discontinued when military personnel in [the nearby] barracks objected to the smell. Large pits were then bulldozed out and the dead were dragged to them for burial. . . . But as the death rate and the physical incapacity of the internees increased, and this was most marked in the women's laager, the dead were simply dragged as far away from the huts as possible and dumped. As exhaustion increased, the distance the corpses were dragged diminished and the piles around the huts grew.[11]

Not everyone starved at Belsen; there were ways of surviving. For example, valuables could be traded for food, if you still had anything worth selling. Here 'exchange Jews', who had not passed through the death camps and lost all their possessions, had a great advantage over the new arrivals from the East. A young Dutch Jewish girl later recalled that for her seventh birthday, in January 1945, her father traded his wedding ring for 'a sandwich with chocolate sprinkles on top', which she and her brother ate for about six months.[12]

Sex was another commodity that could be traded. 'Many of the women have sold themselves,' Hanna Lévy-Hass wrote in February 1945. 'Without a moment's thought quite young girls, who know nothing of life and its principles, have seized the opportunity that the tragic situation offered them.' Lucien Duckstein, a young French boy, later recalled how two Parisian prostitutes in his hut slept with Germans and brought back food and cigarettes. Everyone was grateful but that did not stop them receiving abuse from some of the women.[13]

The camp regime allowed some latitude to medical personnel, which tough and resourceful people could exploit. In particular, several doctors and nurses sent to Belsen in November 1944 were given a degree of freedom to move around the camp – partly because of their work; partly because they were given the job of looking after a group of Dutch children whose parents had been sent away from Belsen but who were still regarded as special; and partly because of two remarkable, though very different, individuals. Luba Tryszynska was an uneducated Jewish girl from Poland, the wife of a farmer, who had had her son taken from her at Auschwitz, but was herself spared from the gas chambers because of her beauty. Despite having no medical training, she had managed to work in the hospital at Auschwitz; there she met and befriended a Slovakian Jewess called Hermina Krantz, and worked for a young Polish Jewish doctor called Hadassah Bimko.[14]

Dr Bimko came from a prosperous and solid Jewish family in the Polish town of Sosnowiec, had qualified in dentistry at Nancy in France and was an ardent Zionist. Her husband and son perished at Auschwitz but she was chosen to work in the camp's hospital and sent to Belsen by Dr Mengele in late 1944. There, Dr Bimko was put in charge of the inmates' hospital and supervised the 'children's home' created for the Dutch children a month later.[15]

Dr Bimko and Nurse Tryszynska worked in different but complementary ways. The educated dentist won the respect even of the SS for her courage and fierce authority, whereas Luba's aura was in part sexual. A Dutch child who accompanied her on a visit to the camp's kitchens in search of food noticed that 'Luba had a magic smile to which the SS guards responded favourably . . . what courage this little woman had to mesmerise these evil men'.[16]

Anne Frank and her sister Margot lacked such protectors; by the middle of March, both had typhus. Margot's condition quickly worsened and, seeking to rise from her bunk one day, she fell to the floor; the shock killed her. Anne lingered for a few more days. A friend remembered seeing her wrapped in a blanket: 'She told me that she had such a horror of the lice and fleas in her clothes that she had thrown all her clothes away.' Anne Frank died in late March 1945. The bodies of Anne and Margot were carried over to one of the mass graves where up to 10,000 corpses were buried. By then, darkness had descended. The supply of the water to the camp was cut off, the diet consisted only of turnip soup and unburied bodies lay everywhere.[17]

Anka Fischer, a Czech Jewess, arrived in Belsen in March 1945 after a six-week 'death march', and succumbed immediately to disease. 'The worst was when we were stricken with dysentery and we had no toilets,' she wrote later in the year. 'The sad fact is that we had no control over our bowel movements and were virtually drowning in our own faeces and urine . . . Then came the lice. I was covered with thousands of them and typhus raged and took over.' Assumed to be dead, she was put on a pile of corpses.[18]

Fania Fénelon, the French musician, later recalled how she caught typhus:

> The illness took me over entirely; my head was bursting, my body trembling, my intestines and stomach were agony and I had the most abominable dysentery. I was just a sick animal lying in its own excrement. From April 8 everything around me became nightmarish. I merely existed as a bursting head, an intestine, a perpetually active anus. One tier above me there was a French girl I didn't know; in my moments of lucidity, I heard her saying in a clear, calm, even pleasant voice, 'I must shit, but I must shit on your head, it's more hygienic!' She had gone mad; others equally unhinged guffawed interminably or fought. No one came to see us anymore, not even the SS. They'd turned off the water.[19]

On 1 March, Kramer finally wrote a letter of protest to his superiors, warning them that 'the reception of further consignments' was impossible 'not only from the point of view of accommodation due to lack of space, but particularly on account of the feeding question'. The camp already contained 42,000 people, he said, and a further 6200 were on the way, even though it had been agreed back in January that 35,000 was too much. What was more, he added, there was now typhus to consider: the death rate was running at 250–300 a day.[20]

The response to Kramer's letter was slow, but on 19 March 1945 Himmler's deputy, SS Obergruppenführer Oswald Pohl, visited Belsen, accompanied by several other high-ranking officers. They were 'frightened and shocked' by the conditions they saw and agreed to one of Kramer's requests – that all the 'exchange Jews' and their families should be transferred elsewhere, to make room for the new arrivals. This decision maintained the policy of keeping hold of Jews with some value as hostages; perhaps, too, it formed part of the SS fantasy of making a final stand in southern Germany.[21]

On 25 March, the Germans began to fumigate the 'exchange Jews' in preparation for transport, and on 6 April they took the first of them to the railhead; the trains left the following days. In all, there were four of these transports, involving most of the estimated 7000 'exchange Jews', including Hanna Lévy-Hass and Abel Herzberg. None of the trains reached their destination. One group was packed into trucks which were coupled to a goods train transporting ammunition and when it was bombed by the British they were blown up. The rest of the trains were stopped by the Russian and American armies. To the end, the 'exchange Jews' maintained their exclusiveness. Most of them survived.[22]

However, Pohl and his associates refused to agree to Kramer's other request – that the movement of prisoners to Belsen should be stopped. The transports continued to arrive. On 7 April 1945, Hedi Szmuk, a teenager from Sighet, Transylvania, reached Belsen. Three days later, a further 15,000 men were brought from the Dora labour camp near Nordhausen, where V2s were built. By now there really was no room in Belsen, so they were put in the nearby barracks of the Panzer Training School, a mile away.[23]

In early 1945, the fate of Belsen's survivors hung in the balance. Would they be allowed to live or would there be a final orgy of killing? With the end of the war clearly in sight, international organisations like the Red Cross, Jewish charities operating in neutral countries and neutral governments all renewed their efforts to save them.

The Nazi leadership was divided in its response. Hitler was adamant that no one should survive and that all evidence should be destroyed – a view shared by his deputy Bormann and by the senior SS officials Ernst Kaltenbrunner and Adolf Eichmann. However, the position of Himmler, the Reichsführer of the SS and the overlord of the camps, was more complicated. Even while supervising the torture and execution of those who conspired against Hitler, he had made several overtures to the Western Allies and, although all had been rebuffed and it had been made clear that his name stood near the top of the Allied roster of war criminals, the Reichsführer continued to believe that it might be possible to work his own passage to survival by brokering a separate peace with the Western Allies – a fantasy in which he was encouraged by his chief of Foreign Intelligence, Walther Schellenberg, and his personal masseur, Felix Kersten. The inmates of the camps featured in his plans, not so much for their own sake but as a way of establishing his credentials with the British and the Americans, and so saving his skin.[24]

Himmler was sending a clear signal to the Western Allies when, in January 1945, he responded to an overture from the Swiss politician Jean-Marie Musy and ordered the freeing of some 1210 Jewish prisoners at Theresienstadt. However, when Hitler was told about this by Kaltenbrunner, he flew into a rage and ordered that there should be no more such concessions. He then gave 'orders that the concentration camps at Buchenwald and Bergen-Belsen, and probably also Theresienstadt should be evacuated, and the prisoners compelled to cover a distance of about one hundred and ninety miles on foot'. At this time, thousands of lives were being lost in the 'death marches' from Auschwitz and other camps to the West.[25]

Hitler's action put Himmler in a delicate position. For the last four months of the war, he was in a lather of indecision, trying to find a way of remaining loyal to his Führer while simultaneously working his passage with the Allies. In the course of this period, he met four times with the Vice-President of the Swedish Red Cross and cousin of the King of Sweden, Count Folke Bernadotte, and held a clandestine meeting in Berlin with a representative of the World Jewish Congress. However, his most important contacts as far as the inmates of Belsen were concerned, were those with his personal masseur, Felix Kersten, who by this stage of the war was commuting to Berlin from his base in Stockholm and acting as an intermediary for groups in the Swedish capital. The problem in reconstructing their meetings is that

Himmler himself left no record of them, while Kersten's *Memoirs* are a tainted source.[26]

Kersten claims that on 5 March he informed Himmler of the outbreak of typhus at Belsen (about which he had, presumably, learned from the World Jewish Congress representative in Stockholm). The head of the SS appeared to have no knowledge of the medical emergency in the camp: 'At once I remonstrated with him and pointed out that he could not in any circumstances permit this camp to become a plague centre which would imperil all Germany; he had to take action quite apart from his feelings towards the camp's occupants.' As a Baltic German, Kersten would have been well aware that typhus had killed three million people in Russia at the end of the First World War and Himmler, for his part, would have shared the Nazi terror of the disease as an 'Eastern plague'. According to Kersten, Himmler then took 'immediate action', making use 'of the terms I had chosen in urging measures against the plague'.[27]

There then followed – says Kersten – several days of 'very exhausting discussions', at the end of which Himmler finally agreed to ignore Hitler's orders and spare the prisoners in the camps. Their agreement was sealed in a document which they both signed on 12 March.[28]

There is no evidence that all this signing of bits of paper in Berlin made much difference to the lives of prisoners in Belsen – there were no grounds at all for the 'the reassuring news' which on 21 March 1945 reached Felix Kersten, now back in Stockholm, 'that effective measures were being taken to combat the outbreak of spotted typhus in the Bergen-Belsen camp'. Equally, Himmler's authority was at this point by no means uncontested and events on the ground were developing their own momentum.[29]

On 2 April 1945, at his second meeting in Berlin with Count Folke Bernadotte, who had been negotiating on behalf of the Swedish government to secure the release of Scandinavian prisoners held in German concentration camps, Himmler told the Swedish aristocrat that concentration camps for Jews in Germany should

not be evacuated but left intact for the Allied military authorities. A letter from his adjutant stated that he had appointed a
special 'commissar' for Bergen-Belsen 'who had been given careful
guidelines'.[30]

On 6 April Himmler appointed SS Standartenführer Kurt
Becher Reich Special Commissar for the affairs of all Jewish and
political prisoners – 'in view of the difficult sanitary and accommodation situation'. Becher was, in SS terms, a moderate; after
a spell with the Einsatzgruppen in the East he had specialised
more in receiving stolen goods from rich Jews than in torture or
industrialised murder. He had also been closely involved in the
tortuous negotiations which had resulted in the saving of the
1600-odd Hungarian Jews, who stayed at Belsen between August
and December 1944.[31]

Becher immediately decided to go on a tour of inspection of
all concentration camps and arrived at Belsen on the late afternoon of 10 April 1945. There he was briefed by Kramer on the
terrible conditions in the camp: 1000 inmates were visibly ill with
typhus, no bread had been distributed for two weeks, there was
now only eight days' supply of turnips and potatoes and some
meat and 500–600 prisoners were dying each day.[32]

Becher and Kramer agreed that there was no alternative but to
hand the camp over to the British, and by the following morning
Becher had Himmler's authority to carry this decision out immediately. He then persuaded the Wehrmacht officers in the Panzer
Training School nearby to agree to seek a truce from the British,
something they were initially very reluctant to do. On the morning
of 12 April 1945, Colonel Schmidt and Lt. Colonel Bohnekamp,
accompanied by a medical officer and a translator, in a car bearing
a white flag, set forth for the English lines.

Three days later, on 15 April, at Belsen, Clara Greenbaum and
her daughter woke early as usual, ready to leap into action when
the Kapo came into their hut. But he did not come, and they slept
on. Eventually they went out, to the *Appellplatz*, the piece of
ground where they endured four-hour roll calls, and found

everyone else who could still walk out there also. Gradually, they heard a curious rumbling sound; the earth was shaking. British tanks were coming, someone said. Somewhat later, they saw soldiers in khaki come up to the wire. The soldiers looked into the camp and then, one after another, they threw up. Seeing this, the inmates became embarrassed and turned away. Clara's daughter began to cry, then Clara did herself. She had not cried for years.[33]

Liberation had come at last. But were the liberators prepared for their task?

2

What Was Known

EXACTLY A WEEK after the meeting between Hitler and Himmler which led to the creation of Belsen camp, the British Foreign Secretary rose to make a statement to Parliament. As a result of information received from Polish sources, Anthony Eden told the House of Commons on 17 December 1942, the British government had issued a statement in consultation with its allies. He then read it aloud.

There could no longer be any doubt, the statement declared, that the Germans were 'carrying into effect Hitler's oft-repeated intention to exterminate the Jewish people in Europe'.

From all the occupied countries Jews are being transported, in conditions of appalling horror and brutality, to Eastern Europe. In Poland, which has been made the principal Nazi slaughterhouse, the ghettoes established by the German invaders are being systematically emptied of all Jews except a few highly skilled workers required for war industries. None of those taken away are ever heard of again. The able-bodied are slowly worked to death in labour camps. The infirm are left to die of exposure and starvation or are deliberately massacred in mass executions. The numbers of

victims of these bloody cruelties is reckoned in many hundred
of thousands of entirely innocent men, women, and children.

The Allied governments, Eden continued, condemned in the
strongest possible terms this 'bestial policy of cold-blood extermination'. Such events only strengthened the determination of
freedom-loving peoples to 'overthrow the barbarous Hitlerite
tyranny'. They reaffirmed their solemn resolution to ensure that
those responsible for these crimes would not escape retribution
and to 'press on with the necessary practical measures to this
end'.[1]

Eden's 'eloquent and just denunciation' was warmly welcomed
by the Liberal MP James de Rothschild. It would cause a 'really
grateful feeling' to 'permeate the Jewish subjects of His Majesty's
Government in this country and throughout the Empire', he told
the House. He trusted that the proclamation would be given wide
publicity through the BBC so that it could 'give some faint hope
and courage to the unfortunate victims of torment and insult and
degradation'. Eden responded that the statement would indeed
be broadcast throughout Europe and assured Members that it
would be made clear to the German people that this was not war
but murder, for which they would be held responsible. As Eden
was concluding, a Member asked whether it was possible for the
House to stand in silence 'in support of this protest against
disgusting barbarism'. The Speaker said it was up to the House.
Members then rose and stood in silence for a minute.[1]

'It was fine moment, and my back tingled', the Conservative
MP Henry ('Chips') Channon wrote that evening. 'It had a far
greater dramatic effect than I had expected', Eden noted in his
diary. 'Lloyd George said to me later: "I cannot recall a scene
like that in all my years in Parliament."'[2]

It might, on the face of it, seem surprising that, only twenty-
eight months after this public display, the British should be unpre-
pared for what they found at Belsen. But things are not always
what they seem: the scene in the House of Commons was largely

a charade. Few subjects have been more thoroughly researched than British policy towards the destruction of the Jews and there is now general consensus that, in the words of one recent historian, the British government 'had many reasons for not acting to save Jews and detected no vital interest for Britain in doing so. Since the government did not regard this as a British problem, it tried to prevent it becoming one.' Even at the time, sceptics would have noticed Eden's vague and evasive answers to specific questions. When asked 'what constructive measures of relief' were 'immediately practicable', he spoke of 'immense difficulties', and, when a Member enquired whether people who managed to escape from occupied Europe would be welcomed in Allied territory, he referred to 'certain security formalities' which had to be considered and the 'immense geographical and other difficulties in the matter'.[3]

As early as September 1941 those in London with access to Enigma intelligence knew from decoded German Order Police signals that there was a systematic policy of slaughter of the Jews; but, to protect their source, they kept quiet about this until late 1942, when information from a German businessman and the Polish underground had made the 'Final Solution' more generally known. Although Churchill occasionally made warm-hearted rhetorical gestures towards the Jews, British policy was run by the Foreign Secretary, Eden, whose 'passive anti-Semitism' was obvious to those around him. 'I am sorry to bother you about Jews . . . I know what a bore this is,' his junior minister wrote in March 1943. Eden was fearful that any attempt to intervene on the Jews' behalf might result in Berlin 'calling our bluff' and leave the British with some 100,000 Jewish refugees to absorb; he repeatedly sought Washington's help in fending off 'the archbishops' and others who urged him to take a stronger line.[4]

By and large, Eden's stalling tactics found a sympathetic hearing at the State Department and, in particular, with Breckinridge Long, the official who was for much of this time in charge of US policy. In April 1943 the British and Americans called a special conference on the implications of Nazi policy for the refugee problem, in Bermuda – in order to be seen to be doing something; and then carefully made sure that nothing whatever emerged from it.[5]

The mood in Washington changed early in 1944, however. President Roosevelt responded to lobbying from Jewish groups, pressure from his Treasury Secretary, Henry Morgenthau, and the politics of an election year by creating the War Refugee Board, 'the only body ever established by any Allied government with the specific aim of rescuing Jews from the Nazis'. Run by intelligent, energetic and committed people, with access to some $20 million in funds provided by American Jewish charities, the Board took bold action to mitigate the effects of the Holocaust – for example, by helping to initiate the mission to Hungary of the Swedish businessman Raoul Wallenberg[6] – and has been sympathetically treated by historians understandably looking for glimmers of light in this dark tale; but it remains debatable whether by its efforts the Board actually saved 200,000 Jews, 20,000 Jews or no Jews at all and what it could have achieved had it been set up earlier. Moreover, the WRB's expertise lay in behind-the-scenes diplomacy in neutral and Axis satellite countries. It never operated in Germany itself.[7]

More importantly, the creation of the WRB did not shake Roosevelt's conviction that the best way to save the Jews of Europe was to win the war as soon as possible. His Administration considered numerous proposals for direct intervention from the representatives of American Jewry – including the bombing of the approaches to Auschwitz – and rejected them all, not simply as operationally impossible but as distractions from the main business of the military. As Europe was liberated, so Jews would be freed; which necessarily meant that it would fall to the military to handle the problem.

Was that the right decision? For decades, historians have asked whether more could have been done to save the Jews; a small library has been generated on the bombing of Auschwitz alone.

Most writers have argued that more could (and should) have been done; only William Rubinstein has insisted that nothing the Allies did could have made the slightest difference. But where Belsen is concerned, the issue is not about *rescue*; it is about *relief*, the provision of medical and other aid to survivors. The planning for the liberation of the camps – or the lack of it – can only be understood within the wider context of Allied humanitarian policy in general.[8]

We need first of all to rid ourselves of modern preconceptions – however difficult that may be. Take, for example, the 'Holocaust' itself. As the historian Peter Novick has pointed out, '"The Holocaust", as we speak of it today, was largely a retrospective construction, something that would not have been recognizable to most people at the time'. Novick insists that 'to speak of "the Holocaust" as a distinct entity . . . is to introduce an anachronism that stands in the way of understanding contemporary responses'. Certainly, most British people at the time could not begin to conceive of what was going on in occupied Europe. Of course, this may partly be because the British Foreign Office regarded the Declaration of December 1942 about German crimes in Europe as an exception to the general practice, and was usually very reluctant to identify the Jews as special targets of the Nazi terror. But it is also true that, while the Jews were the Nazis' main victims, they were not their only ones. The Hitler regime murdered millions of Jews, but it also took millions of other peoples into forced labour and allowed millions more to die in its prisoner-of-war camps.[9]

Confronted by an entire continent starving and uprooted, Allied planners did not single out the victims of the death camps for particular attention, but tried to devise strategies to help all 'displaced persons' – as they had become known by 1943. At the same time, Allied leaders also decided that the immense humanitarian and medical problems of a liberated Europe could best be dealt with by a specialist, intergovernmental body, and in October 1943 created UNRRA, the United Nations Relief and

Rehabilitation Agency. A great idea on paper, UNRRA proved a disaster in reality, for many reasons. The Allied military was suspicious of this new beast and preferred dealing with old-fashioned charities like the Red Cross; it proved difficult in wartime to recruit dynamic and experienced people to UNRRA; and the Agency failed properly to establish itself under the weak leadership of Governor Herbert Lehman. The result, organisationally, was an ill-defined division between the military, UNRRA and the traditional relief charities.[10]

UNRRA generated mountains of paper and layers of bureaucracy, but when the Allies invaded Europe in June 1944 it could only put into the field a few 'flying squads' with a vague preventive health-care brief. Usually comprising a dozen US civilians, loosely attached to the invading armies, the 'flying squads' sought to prevent a repetition of the 1943 Naples typhus epidemic by intercepting thousands of refugees on the roads and delousing them by puffing their clothes inside and out with DDT powder; but they never amounted to a serious, trained, emergency relief force. The International Red Cross in Geneva, which could perhaps have played such a role, had decided in October 1942 not to launch an international appeal on behalf of the Jews of Europe and continued almost to the end to prefer caution to action.[11]

And so responsibility for dealing with the 'displaced persons' problem fell mainly to the military. They saw 'DPs' primarily as obstacles, refugees who might get in their way – just as fleeing civilians had impeded the British Army in France in 1940 – and feared that 'a flooding east of the expected millions of slave workers and escapees' would spread infection and disease into the Western countries and exacerbate the feeding problems of Holland, Belgium and France. To prevent this, plans were drawn up to establish barrier zones at certain water obstacles including the Rhine and the Elbe and to hold civilians there until the end of the campaign. Similarly, the pamphlet on 'Germany' issued to British troops warned that they would 'encounter roving bands of freed slave workers, all probably undernourished and ill-clothed' but said nothing about concentration camps.[12]

Of course, Allied intelligence knew all about the camps: a document produced by Eisenhower's staff gives a long list of them, Belsen included, with rough map references for each and a perfectly adequate account of the development of the camps by the Nazis. But it was based on out-of-date information, and there is no trace in the surviving military files of any awareness of the humanitarian disaster unfolding at Belsen. Second Army's Medical Plan for Operation Eclipse in April 1945 lists the second task of the Medical Services, after 'Medical care of the British forces', as 'Medical Care of UN P[risoners of] W[ar]'.[13]

There were, however, officials in Whitehall who did know something about Belsen. Ever since 1941, the Colonial Office and the Foreign Office had been engaged in laborious negotiations with the Germans which eventually resulted in the exchange of a number of Germans resident in Palestine for European Jews who held certificates entitling them to emigrate to Palestine. When, however, it transpired that most of the Jews on the 'Palestine list' had already been murdered, Jewish organisations in Palestine managed to have them replaced by prominent Jews held in Belsen. In this way, British officialdom learned about the camp during the long negotiations which preceded the third exchange of Jews and Germans in July 1944.[14]

'We are anxious for more information about Bergen Belsen', A. G. Ponsonby of the Foreign Office's Refugees Department wrote on 14 July 1944. In the following month, his department built up a reasonably accurate picture of the camp based on information supplied by the British embassies in Lisbon and Berne and the Jewish charities, though it remained vague about its 'exact location'. Belsen was seen as primarily a 'transit camp to which all Jews eligible for repatriation are temporarily sent'. Later that year, British diplomats became concerned about people holding dual British and Dutch nationality held in Belsen and asked the Swiss – who represented their interests in Berlin – urgently to request a visit to the camp, particularly as the Red Cross had not been allowed into it. Two months later, at the end of February 1945, the German Foreign Office responded that 'a first inspection trip could be organized in about six weeks, that is towards the middle of April'.[15]

It is not clear when the British first became aware of Belsen's new role as a dumping ground for prisoners from other camps or of the collapse which took place there. They may have been kept informed by the Jewish agencies, though they tended to regard such information as unreliable. But by early April 1945, officials in London certainly knew what was happening in Belsen.

Two weeks earlier, on 19 March 1945, the Security Control Office in Liverpool had interviewed a Dr Rudolph Levy, one of a 'Jewish party from Bergenbelsen' that had just arrived at that port on the SS *Drottnigholm*. A Belsen prisoner holding Turkish nationality, Dr Levy had been released from the camp on 4 March with 104 others, and put on board the *Drottnigholm* in Stockholm, bound for Istanbul, via Liverpool. He gave the British official a clear account of what had happened recently in Belsen – the arrival of Kramer as commandant at the end of 1944, the overcrowding caused by evacuating the camps in the East and the outbreak of typhus. The report on Dr Levy reached the Prisoners of War division of the Foreign Office, via the War Office, on 2 April. The only written comment is 'unfortunately they do not appear to have got the exact location of the camp'.[16]

British officials therefore knew roughly what was happening in Belsen ten days before the Germans offered a truce there, but were still unsure of the camp's precise whereabouts. Dr Levy was questioned at the request of the Foreign Office, channelled through the War Office; and in both ministries, the POW department was involved. This suggests that Whitehall was trying to get news of British prisoners of war held in German camps. The information gleaned from Dr Levy may have been sent to specialist units like the Special Air Service, which were preparing to rush into German camps to seize British POWs, but it does not seem to have been generally communicated to units on the ground.[17]

And so the British came to Belsen – without a plan.

3

'You Are Free': 12–16 April 1945

THE FIRST THAT Lieutenant Derrick Sington knew of Belsen was on 12 April 1945; he was standing outside the divisional commander's caravan, on the road to Winsen in northern Germany, at the time. A staff officer explained that the Germans had offered a truce at Belsen. It was a concentration camp, he said, and there was a typhus epidemic there. They agreed it was all a bit odd.[1]

Then the war intervened. For the next thirty-six hours, Sington had other preoccupations – the column of tanks he was riding with was ambushed by a German anti-tank gun; the camp he spent the night in was stonked by mortars; he had to interrogate a German burgomaster. But on his return to Brigade Headquarters on the evening of 14 April he was told that 'division want you to go forward with your loud-speaker into this place, Belsen'.

Sington commanded a small 'Amplifier Unit', consisting of an armoured car equipped with a powerful battery of loudspeakers and three sergeants with a command of several European languages, designed for waging 'psychological warfare'. He was thirty-seven, Oxford-educated, a journalist in civilian life, and unusual among British soldiers in having a strong ideological commitment to the war and a passionate hatred of National Socialism; but then he was half-Jewish, descended through his father from a long line of German Jewish business people, and had followed German politics in the 1930s closely. During the war he had written a study of Goebbels's propaganda methods. But he still hadn't heard of Belsen.[2]

The following day he met up with Lt. Colonel Taylor, commander of the 63rd Anti-Tank Regiment, who seemed less than overjoyed at having been given the job of commandant of Belsen camp. Taylor's orders were to 'prevent the spread of disease and to prevent criminals breaking out'; Sington's were to drive into the concentration camp and tell the inmates that 'although they were liberated from the Germans, they must not leave the camp because of the danger of spreading typhus'. Some 2000 armed Hungarian guards would be maintained to keep them in, but food and medical aid would be rushed up as soon as possible. The two officers agreed to meet later in the day, and Taylor went off to make contact with the German Army.

Sington then drove forward, along the main road north-east, into thick fragrant woods being burnt by the British to flush out any snipers. After passing several boards declaring 'Danger Typhus', he rounded a bend and came to the camp entrance – 'a single pole across the roadway with wooden huts on either side'. There, waiting to greet him, was a group of German officers, including a stockily built SS Hauptsturmführer with a scar across one cheek, who turned out to be Josef Kramer, the camp commandant. He told Sington that Belsen contained homosexuals and professional criminals and some political prisoners, but cautioned against making any loudspeaker announcement. The camp was calm at the moment, he said, and it would be unwise to risk stirring up the inmates. At that point Colonel Taylor arrived from the Panzer Training School and confirmed the order to broadcast. So Sington commanded Kramer to get on the running board and drove the armoured car into Belsen.

They passed first through the now deserted area where the SS guards had lived and reached a 'high wooden gate with criss-cross wiring', which reminded Sington of the entrance to a zoo.

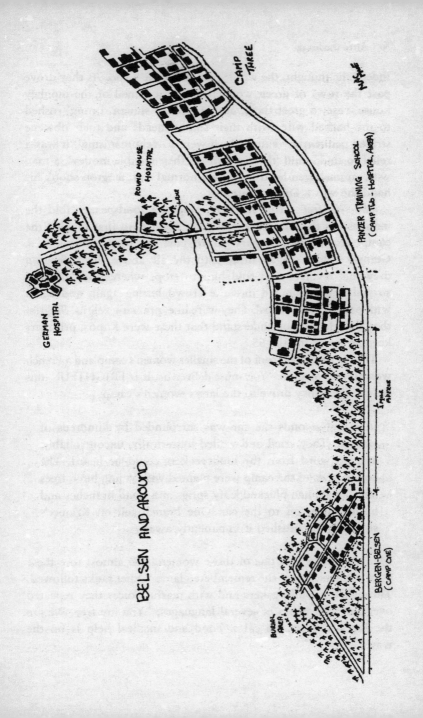

BELSEN AND AROUND

CAMP THREE

NAAFE

PANZER TRAINING SCHOOL
(CAMP TWO - HOSPITAL AREA)

ROUND HOUSE HOSPITAL

GERMAN HOSPITAL

1500 ACRES

BURIAL AREA

BERGEN-BELSEN (CAMP ONE)

Indeed, he thought, the whole place was like a zoo. As they drove past the rows of green wooden huts, the 'smell of the monkey house' rose to greet them, and 'a strange simian throng' rushed to the barbed wire 'with their shaven heads and their obscene striped penitentiary suits, which were so dehumanising'. It was a relief to find, amid 'these clowns in their terrible motley', a man with an unshaven head wearing a normal suit. Sington shook his hand; he was a Dutch journalist.

'*Ihr seid frei*': 'You are free', Sington's loudspeaker told the inmates. As the car drove along the main road that divided the camp, crowds of prisoners surged past the wire towards it. A German soldier began firing into the air above them. Sington drew his revolver and told him to stop, whereupon 'a dozen striped figures jumped into the crowd hitting again and again with packing case strips'. They were like 'prancing zebras' Sington thought. He did not understand that these were Kapos, prisoners keeping order for the SS.[3]

The car paused in front of the smaller women's camp and a French woman told Sington, 'You must deliver us. It is FRIGHTFUL, this camp.' Then they drove to the larger women's camp:

In a few seconds the car was surrounded by hundreds of women. They cried and wailed hysterically, uncontrollably, and no word from the loudspeakers could be heard. The compounds of the camp were planted with young birch trees and the women plucked leafy sprigs and small branches and hurled them on to the car. One branch fell on Kramer's shoulder. He brushed it impatiently away.

Mania Salinger was one of those women. 'We almost tore these poor soldiers apart,' she remembered later. 'Other tanks followed. Through the loudspeakers and with tearful voices they repeated over and over again in several languages, "You are free. We are the English Army. Be calm. Food and medical help is on the way".'[4]

In the middle of the afternoon, Sington was joined in Camp 1 by Colonel Taylor and several officers from 8 Corps Headquarters, sent forward as a reconnaissance party to check the place out. They cross-questioned Kramer in his office and learned that all Belsen's records had been destroyed on orders from Berlin, but that the main camp had about 40,000 people in it and there was enough food for three days.[5]

Then an incident took place which made a profound impression on the British officers: a number of inmates were shot dead by guards while raiding a potato patch. The British were shocked by the way the Germans did not seem to value prisoners' lives. They also began to see the camp and condition of the internees for the first time.

A great number of them were little more than living skeletons with haggard yellowish faces [Colonel Taylor reported soon afterwards]. Most of the men wore a striped pyjama type of clothing – others wore rags while the women wore striped flannel gowns or any garment that they had managed to acquire . . . there were men and women lying in heaps on either side of the track. Others were walking slowly and aimlessly about – a vacant expression on their starved faces.

Most of all, though, it was the discovery of large piles of unburied corpses in the camp which finally tipped the scales for the British. 'There were heaps of dead in every cage and it was quite obvious that unless food and water arrived soon the whole camp would starve to death,' Taylor wrote. Some 18,000 people had apparently died in the camp in March alone, and, unless something was done quickly, thousands more would die. Belsen was a humanitarian disaster.

The British were sickened and revolted. 'The things I saw completely defy description,' Colonel Taylor's deputy, Major Ben Barnett wrote. 'There are no words in the English language which can give a true impression of the ghastly horror of this camp.' Countless others would say the same thing over the next weeks – that Belsen defied language. But it wasn't just a matter of finding words: for Major Barnett the thing itself was beyond comprehension. 'I find it hard even now to get into focus all these horrors, my mind is really quite incapable of taking in everything I saw because it was all so completely foreign to everything I had previously believed or thought possible,' he added. The place immediately became known as the 'Horror Camp'.[6]

Kramer himself seemed to have no shame. He had done his best, he told Sington. The British simply couldn't understand how Kramer could have stayed at the camp and not fled like the other SS men; he had stayed because he had been ordered to, he told them. Gradually, the relationship between the British and Kramer changed, as Colonel Taylor tried to find a way to disarm the SS, while maintaining order in the camp and preventing disease from spreading. Over the next twenty-four hours, the British rewrote the truce with the Germans and began to redefine their task at Belsen. Much of their behaviour was irrational, fuelled by rage. For example, Kramer warned them repeatedly that if the inmates were allowed access to open spaces, rioting and disorder would follow. The British ignored him and there were indeed disturbances. When, however, these inmates were shot at by German and Hungarian guards, the British were revolted. By the second day, the Germans had been disarmed and Kramer arrested – which was not supposed to be part of the truce at all.

'The priority the first night was food, water, and more troops,' a British officer later recalled. 'We really thought at first that we should only be able to keep order and prevent the spread of infection by stopping people from breaking out.' On the evening of 15 April, the British grouped tanks around the food store in Camp 1 and tensed themselves to see what would happen. Much to their relief, there was no mass break-out by prisoners, nor was there a concerted attack on the SS guards. But the prisoners were busy that night. Hundreds broke into the food store, ignoring the

Sherman tank planted across its doorway and the warning rounds fired into the air by British sentries. The next morning, it was 'bare of everything but some black, hard loaves of Wehrmacht bread, and some sacks of flour'. Kramer's private sty of twenty-five pigs had vanished; a hut full of SS clothing and tents had been liberated by French women (only recently arrived from Ravensbrück) and a vast pit of turnips had been completely cleaned out, leaving only 'a gaping square pit where the turnips had been'.[7]

Over in Camp 2, in the Panzer Training School, where more than 15,000 newly arrived male prisoners were housed, there was more serious violence that night: 'the Russian and Polish inmates who had any strength left began to hunt down the capos, block captains and their lackeys'. Many of these men, who had tyrannised their own people on the Germans' behalf, were thrown from upper-floor windows. One survivor claimed that as many as 150 were killed.[8]

The next day, 16 April, backed up by more troops who had arrived overnight, the British became bolder. Derrick Sington drove around Belsen once more, announcing that the British were now taking possession of the camp and that food and medicine were being rushed in; Colonel Taylor disarmed the SS men and, in an attempt to contain the violence, began to divide the prisoners in Camp 2 by nationality.

By then, the British were getting a rough idea of who was in both camps. Sington reckoned that the inmates fell into three main categories – political prisoners, Jews (the bulk of the women) and criminals (a small minority). About 25,000 of the 40-45,000 inmates of Camp 1 were women and of these some 18,000 were Hungarian, Polish, Romanian, Czech and German Jewesses. 'They were a large part of the survivors of European Jewry, hastily piled into Belsen,' Sington wrote. 'The greater part of the Jewish women were sole survivors of families who had perished in the gas chambers of Birkenau and Treblinka.' But there were also about 2000 Russian women and 5000-odd Yugoslav, Polish, French and

Belgian women who had been arrested by the Gestapo for resistance to German occupation. A large proportion of the 15,000-plus men in Camp 1 were Poles and Russians.

Sington found people incarcerated for almost every conceivable kind of offence – including a Russian prisoner of war who had attempted to escape from POW camps, Russian women who had attempted to escape from forced labour or had assaulted their German employers, numerous Frenchmen and women who had assisted the Maquis, French and Belgians who had helped British pilots, German anti-Nazis, Polish partisans who had taken part in the Warsaw rising and professional German thieves and prostitutes.

'In the accounts I have read of the camp the impression is given that practically all the inmates were Jews,' a British officer who was in Belsen in the early days wrote later. 'This was certainly not the case when we were there.' Captain William Roach was briefly in charge of the large men's section in Camp 1: 'there were 15,287 in all. The largest group was the Russians, followed by the Poles. Together they made up about 60% of the inmates. There were some 500 Greeks and about the same number of French and Belgians and Czechs and 120 Dutch, plus a good number of Yugoslavs. The Germans together numbered between 1600 and 1800 and there were several hundred gypsies.'[9]

What could the British do to help all these people? The first need of all, it seemed, was for food and water. On the first evening, a desperate appeal had gone back to 8 Corps Headquarters and most of the following day was spent trying to procure and then issue food and water to Belsen's population. Finally, at 4 p.m. on 16 April, a convoy of water tankers and three-ton lorries carrying cooking equipment arrived. The British then decided that the only way to avoid a riot was to 'order all the inmates of the camps into their blocks and then get volunteer helpers to take the food to each block'. There were some problems in making an announcement in all the necessary languages and it took Sington and his colleagues with loudspeakers two hours to 'order, cajole, or persuade the inmates to return to their blocks'. When the food was ready, each block senior with his helpers was given a quantity appropriate for the numbers in his block, the British telling them that they relied 'upon their honour and humanity to see that the sick get their share of the food'. All this took time; it was late in the evening when food reached the last huts in the women's camp. But after all their labours, the British felt moderately satisfied. 'I am sure that most of those walking received something to eat,' Colonel Taylor wrote.[10]

The original idea had been to give the inmates hot stew prepared in copper cauldrons in two of the camp's five kitchens but problems in one kitchen caused a rapid change of plan. According to Sington, 'packing-cases of American stew in tins and biscuits were hurriedly unloaded from the lorries, and distribution of cold food was planned.' Another British soldier remembered that 'the food consisted of British 12-man "compo" rations and some USA army compo packs'. 'Compo rations', the British soldier's main source of food when in the field, consisted of packs containing enough to feed one man for fourteen days. The food was 'all tinned and included such things as bacon, sausages, Irish stew (made in Argentina), steak and kidney pudding, meat and vegetable, fruit, puddings, butter, cheese, and jam'.[11]

Belsen survivors have vivid memories of this moment. 'They started to give us pork tins. I never forget that,' Edith Fuchs, a Czech Jewess, later recalled. 'It was like corned beef but it was pork with a lot of fat in it.' Hedi Szmuk, the young woman from Transylvania, remembered 'tins of ham, baked beans, thick soups – rich, heavy food, good for soldiers'; Sarah Bick, another survivor, had memories of 'cans of beans, honey, syrup, evaporated milk'.[12]

Those who got the food wolfed it down. 'The people ate greedily and to excess,' Viktor Mamontov, from Leningrad, remembered. 'All this was consumed with tremendous appetites.' Some inmates were able to take such a rich diet – Sarah Bick, for example, was 'very fortunate to consume the canned food without any ill effects and accepted it gladly whenever it was offered to me' – but for most it was disastrous. Their weak and shrunken intestines were much too sensitive to digest that kind of nourishment. 'You would take this and eat it and it would come right out because you couldn't hold any food,' Hans Fink, a German Jewish prisoner, remembered. 'I also ate, but I vomited afterwards. I couldn't keep it in,' Freddy Knoller, an Austrian Jew, told an interviewer.[13]

Fairly soon, prisoners 'were just falling over like flies', mainly from diarrhoea. The arrival of food also created new divisions among the survivors. No one in Edith Hoffman's hut could speak English, but one girl somehow got herself an English boyfriend, who 'gave her things like corned beef and bags of sugar. Up till then, right through, we'd shared everything, but for some reason she wouldn't share with us anymore, and she died of the food.'[14]

It was later estimated that some 2000 people perished as a result of being given the wrong food. The British had made their first mistake.[15]

4

The Plan

BRITISH SOLDIERS REACTED with outrage and disbelief to what they saw at Belsen. 'This letter will read like fiction,' Gunner George Walker wrote home, 'but I swear that as sure as there is a God in heaven what I have told you is the Gospel truth.' Often their disgust expressed itself in brutality towards the Germans left in the camp – visiting Belsen a week after its liberation, a journalist found most of the SS men 'spattered with blood' and British soldiers seized by 'genuine and permanent anger'.[1]

But there was also recognition that this was a good chance for propaganda. General Dempsey, commander of British Second Army, visited the camp himself and 'from the first was very keen' that journalists 'should see Belsen and write about it'. The cameras were sent there almost at once, and army cameramen captured images of human degradation which redefined forever the moral landscape – a scene that one British officer described as a 'barren wilderness, as bare and devoid of vegetation as a chicken run', with piles of corpses 'naked and obscene' lying everywhere, 'some in huge piles where they had been dumped by other inmates, sometimes [lying] singly or in pairs where they had fallen as they shuffled along the dirt tracks'; and, amidst the dead and dying, the living going incongruously about the business of life: 'a woman too weak to stand propping herself against a pile of corpses, as she cooked the food we had given her over an open fire; men and women crouching just anywhere in the open relieving themselves of the dysentery which was scouring their bowels, a woman standing stark naked washing herself with some issue soap in water from a tank in which the remains of a child floated'.[2]

Himmler had not only handed the Allies their greatest propaganda coup; he had allowed the British, in a single step, to seize the moral initiative and turn their war into a righteous crusade. Belsen justified everything – the bombing of German cities, the economic blockade, unconditional surrender. But would the British match their words with deeds, by sending to Belsen the resources needed there? That would depend, to a large extent, on Second Army's medical chief.

Brigadier Hugh Llewellyn Glyn Hughes looked like an army doctor. A huge man, built like an ox, with a coal-black moustache, he had been a rugby player and war hero in his youth. But appearances were deceptive, for Glyn Hughes was not a regular army officer – he was a London GP before the war – and the rough exterior hid a warm Welsh heart and sensitivity to the needs of others.

The son of a British doctor, Hughes was born in 1892 in the tiny, remote South African town of Ventersburg. When he was two his father died of septicaemia, contracted while carrying out surgery. On the family's eventual return to England, Hughes was sent to Epsom College, a minor public school which took the sons of impoverished doctors, where he excelled at rugby and won a scholarship to University College Hospital in London. When the war interrupted his medical studies, he volunteered immediately to go to France but returned home the following year to take his finals. He then went back to France and served in a field ambulance for the next three years. He was twice decorated for bravery; the first time for going out in daylight and under fire to retrieve wounded men; the second, for calmly disposing of a Mills bomb. At the end of the war he was severely wounded.

Like most of his generation, Hughes was marked by his years on the Western Front; but he did not remain in the army. Instead, he became a doctor in rural Devon, enjoying the simple life and sometimes riding long distances on horseback to visit patients. He was sorry to give it all up for a smarter practice in Kensington in London, so that his children could have a decent education and his wife a social life. Rejoining the reserves in the late 1930s, Hughes was sent to France to command 5th Division's Field Ambulances and was among the last to be evacuated from Dunkirk in 1940, in an old china barge. By the time he landed in France on D-Day plus 2 he was a Colonel and early in 1945, after showing outstanding leadership during the Arnhem operation, he was made chief doctor to British Second Army, with the rank of Brigadier.[3]

Glyn Hughes was no intellectual, more a simple, practical man of action, well suited to wartime medicine. The doctor's task, as his generation saw it, was 'to amuse the patient and then leave the rest to nature'. His particular qualities were an intense physical energy, an old-fashioned delight in competitive sport, a strong sense of duty and a warm-hearted nature that enabled him to get on with almost anyone.[4]

Hughes had arrived at Belsen on the afternoon of 15 April and was present at the interrogation of Kramer. That same evening he sent for the camp's medical chief, Dr Klein, and ordered him to produce by the next morning answers to a questionnaire on the medical facilities and the medical state of the inmates. The following day he made a detailed examination of the conditions in the camp.

Camp 1, Hughes estimated, contained approximately 41,000 people, made up of 28,185 women and roughly 12,000 men, housed in three compounds for men and one small and one very large compound for women. There were five cookhouses. Everywhere he found overcrowding.

Some of the huts had bunks, but not many, and they were filled absolutely to overflowing with prisoners in every state of emaciation and disease. There was not room for them to lie down at full length in each hut. In the most crowded there were anything from 600 to 1000 people in accommodation which should only have taken 100.

There were no bunks in a hut in the women's compound which was containing the typhus patients. They were lying on the floor and were so weak they could hardly move. There was practically no bedding. In some cases there was a thin mattress, but some had none. Some had blankets and some had none. Some had no clothing at all and just draped themselves in blankets, and some had German hospital type of clothing . . .

There was no sanitation: 'the compounds were absolutely one mass of human excreta. In the huts themselves the floors were covered and the people in the top bunks who could not get out just poured it on to the bunks below'; everywhere there was 'extreme emaciation and complete malnutrition of all those who had been there for any length of time at all. Only those admitted within the last week were in a reasonable state of health.'[5]

One of the men's compounds, No. 3, had only just begun to fill up and conditions there were not too bad. But it was an exception; everywhere else conditions were terrible. In No. 1 compound in the men's quarters 'conditions were exactly as described'. No. 2 was 'the worst of the men's compounds . . . there were about 8000 there and conditions were very bad . . . typhus was rife'. The smaller of the women's compounds, on the left, had only about 6000 inmates, but 'conditions here were infinitely worse. They were absolutely frightful.' The main women's compound, No. 1, on the right of the road, 'was very large and contained between 22 and 23,000 women. The huts were set amongst trees and conditions here were frightful, but perhaps not quite as bad as No. 2 Women's Compound. In this compound there was a very large pile of corpses.' In Hut 208, which was close to the corpses, 'there were dead women lying in the passage, which was so full that no woman could lie down straight. The main room on the left of the passage was one mass of bodies and you could not get another into it.' Hughes estimated that, of the 23,000 inmates in No. 1 women's compound, '17,000 required to be in hospital immediately if they were to be saved, and of these a large number were so ill they had no chance of recovery'.

Apart from a small store of drugs and medicines, Hughes could see no evidence of any attempt by the camp staff to do anything for the sick. He also found a large number of Red Cross boxes sent by Jewish relief organisations, containing meat extracts and foods of all kinds, biscuits, milk but 'no issue of the contents had been made, except an occasional issue of sweets to the children'. To treat the 17,000 patients, there were 474 bunks in the huts which were supposedly set aside as a hospital, organised by the internees themselves. There was also 'a small compound of children who were in a fairly good condition, and obviously the woman internees had sacrificed themselves to look after them. The hospital compound in that area was very well run by the internee doctors – very well run.'

Hughes's overall conclusion was that 70 per cent of the inhabitants of Camp 1 required hospitalisation, and that 'of these at least 10,000 would die before they could be put in hospital. Every form of disease was prevalent, but the ones mainly responsible for the frightful conditions were typhus, starvation, and tuberculosis.'

Among the 15,133 men put into Camp 2, in the Panzer Training School, in early April, conditions were much better, 'although malnutrition was evident and there was death occurring'. Hughes noted that although the barracks were pretty foul 'as regards health, their general condition was not too bad and their clothing was quite reasonable. There was no typhus.'[6]

Hughes's anger at what he saw is barely contained in his report. As he toured Belsen, he wept. 'At the sight of the huts, with their dead and their half dead, the Brigadier, a medical man hardened to human suffering, cried unashamedly,' Dr Hadassah Bimko, the Polish dentist, recalled a decade later; she had been chosen to take him round. Hughes 'decided on the spot to save as many of the sick as possible in spite of the conflicting calls of military casualties'. That evening, he began to summon medical reserves.[7]

His problem was that there was 'very little in the "kitty" to deal with this situation'. The whole British Army was in action, and there was little spare capacity. 'If we had had a division in reserve we might have had a great deal more transport to bring up our medical units.' All that was immediately available was a Light Field Ambulance, a Casualty Clearing Station and two Field Hygiene Sections (one of which was already at Belsen).[8]

Eleventh Light Field Ambulance was a unit of some 200 men, trained to follow British tanks into battle and evacuate their wounded. It had had a busy year – taking part in the battles of the Bulge and the Reichswald – two of the bitterest engagements of the campaign. After crossing the Rhine at the end of March, the unit's commander, Lt. Colonel Mervyn Gonin, had finally gone on strike, demanding that his men and vehicles have a rest. But only four of the promised seven days had passed when he received the Brigadier's summons and, as special requests at Army level were not to be denied, the unit moved on, pulling its ambulances behind it. 'We went to Belsen on 17 April and we were a very tired unit when we got there,' Gonin recalled a year later.[9]

By contrast, 32 Casualty Clearing Station was fresh. It was a mobile surgical unit designed to carry out basic surgery on wounded soldiers, made up of two operating teams with ancillary staff, including eight nurses. After taking part in the D-Day landings and the liberation of France, 32 CCS had been in reserve for several months, running a small hospital near the German/Dutch frontier. It was now ordered to move towards Hamburg and, in the early hours of 17 April, the unit's commander, Lt. Colonel Johnston, was woken by a liaison officer from HQ Second Army and told to proceed to Bergen-Belsen where a concentration camp had been liberated on the 15th. Although Johnston had heard of German concentration camps, he 'had very little idea what I was likely to find when

I got there'. 'It was difficult to imagine,' he later wrote, 'how my two hundred bed unit could hope to achieve much with the sort of numbers I envisaged we might have to cope [with there].'[10]

Lt. Colonel Gonin, the officer commanding 11th Light Field Ambulance, was a general practitioner, and keen Territorial, from the Suffolk town of Ipswich. Lt. Colonel James Johnston, who commanded 32 Casualty Clearing Station, was a regular army officer – he was therefore made Senior Medical Officer at Belsen, while Glyn Hughes remained at Second Army. The relationship that emerged between Hughes and Johnston can perhaps best be explained by an analogy with the more frivolous world of the film industry. In the drama of Belsen, Hughes would be the producer, the man who conceived the project, assembled the talent, kept the front office happy and turned up at night to raise fallen spirits; whereas Johnston was the director, in charge on the floor, making the day-to-day decisions and trying to reconcile a hundred conflicting demands.[11]

Johnston would prove well suited to this role. Like many British military doctors, he was a Scot, born in 1911, a graduate of Glasgow Medical School, who had entered the army in 1934 and taken part, the following year, in one of the great triumphs of British Army medicine, the relief operation following the earthquake at Quetta (in modern-day Pakistan) in which 30,000 people were killed in the space of thirty seconds. Led by a dynamic commander, the army had performed 'miracles of rescue work' there. Johnston had a 'cheerful and unruffled' temperament and a good deal of charm; almost everyone liked him. 'Johnny, as all called him in the end,' a medical colleague at Belsen wrote, 'was Scottish, small, with a slight burr in his voice and brown, kind, clever eyes.' He was 'a human creature in an army world . . . Perhaps most of all it was his approachableness, his lack of army form and his simplicity that endeared him so, and yet he was a regular officer and could command with the utmost authority when it was needed.'[12]

On 17 April these officers assessed the task facing them at Belsen. Johnston reckoned they needed twelve 1200-bed General Hospitals. Instead, they had '8 nurses, about 300 RAMC chaps, a regiment of Light Anti Aircraft. 'What we had not got' Gonin wrote, 'was nurses, doctors, beds, bedding, clothes, drugs, dressings, thermometers, bedpans or any of the essentials of medical treatment, and worst of all no common language.' Johnston later admitted that, 'the task allotted to my small unit with its handful of doctors, sisters and orderlies seemed totally impossible.'

The British did have two assets – the Panzer Training School and the internee doctors. Fifteen thousand Belsen prisoners were already housed in the Panzer Training School, only a mile away from the 'Horror Camp'. This symbol of Germany's will to rearm had been laid out on a grand scale as a training ground fit for Hitler's new Wehrmacht in the mid-1930s, when the Führer still needed to keep his generals' support and reward them for their loyalty. It consisted of twenty-seven large squares, each made up of four four-storey buildings and a large canteen with modern kitchens clustered round a parade ground; a lavish officers' mess; numerous married quarters buildings; a cinema; and, half a mile further away, a modern, well-equipped military hospital, filled with German wounded and nurses. Going round it, British officers marvelled at the gracious formality of its design and the amplitude of its facilities.

Johnston made a quick tour of the Panzer Training School on the afternoon of his first day, accompanied by the Senior Military Government Officer from HQ Second Army, who would be responsible for the administration of those Belsen inmates designated as 'fit'; he then earmarked an area of eleven squares in the central barrack area for the hospitalisation of the sick. He also asked for the German Military Hospital, which Brigadier Hughes agreed to clear of its 650 German military patients, and for the officers' mess. That would be sufficient for 10,000 patients – good enough, he thought, for a start.[13]

The other asset was human. Touring the 'Horror Camp' on
16 April, Glyn Hughes had become aware that its huts contained
a considerable number of doctors and nurses. He spoke to many
of them that day and established an immediate rapport with Dr
Bimko, who spoke fluent French. She made an equally
favourable impression on his colleagues. 'I was fortunate in
meeting [Dr Bimko and her assistant Dr Ruth Gutman] on that
first day,' Johnston later recalled. 'These two remarkable women
controlled the so-called hospital area in one section of the female
laager.'

> They had managed, without any assistance from the
> authorities and without any medical or other equipment, to
> maintain some sort of order out of the chaos that prevailed
> around them. The hut in which they lived was the only clean
> hut in the entire camp. I will never forget my first encounter
> with them. In the midst of this mass of human squalor and
> degradation these two women, physically clean, mentally
> whole, calm, serene, and dignified, stood out as a shining
> example to their fellow internees, a personification of the
> triumph of good over evil.

Colonel Gonin considered Dr Bimko 'the bravest woman I have
ever known, who worked miracles of care, kindness and healing
with the help of no medicines but the voice and discipline of a
Regimental Sergeant Major of the Guards'.[14]

Given the meagre resources available, it was obvious that little
medical attention could be given to individual patients. All the
British could realistically hope to do in the short term was to try
to prevent further loss of life from starvation and disease by
carrying out several obvious priority tasks – providing suitable
food for the internees; stopping the further spread of typhus and
other infectious or contagious diseases; removing all internees
from the 'Horror Camp' into clean areas; and burying the dead
before the hot summer started cholera. When those objectives had

been met, it might then be possible to 'help those who lived to regain their humanity'.

The solution, to these military doctors, was obvious: triage. 'It was first decided to give the best chance of survival to the greatest number, and therefore to move out at once into the Barrack area the supposedly fit and well, thereby making room in the huts and supervision of feeding easier,' Glyn Hughes told a conference a month later. Gradually, as the 'Horror Camp' was cleared, its huts would be burnt, until all the survivors had been moved to new facilities at the Panzer Training School.[15]

Military triage divides battlefield casualties into three categories – those who will inevitably die, those who can be returned to the front and those who will live but will not fight again – and concentrates resources on the lightly wounded while ignoring the dying. Similarly, at Belsen, 'One had to get used early to the idea that the individual just did not count,' Gonin recalled. 'One knew that five hundred a day were dying and that five hundred a day were going on dying for weeks before anything we could do would have the slightest effect. It was, however, not easy to watch a child choking to death from diphtheria when you knew that a tracheotomy and nursing would save it.'[16]

The division of labour was equally simple. Gonin's Field Ambulance would evacuate and feed the sick in the 'Horror Camp', while Johnston's Casualty Clearing Station created a hospital in the Panzer Training Barracks. Military Government would move the 'healthy' inmates and the Field Hygiene Section would bury the dead and control typhus by spraying with DDT. Now the men had to be told of their jobs.

After 'idling for months in Holland', a private with 32 CCS wrote, 'we were happy, thrilled at last at the prospect of going into active service again'. Then they were told that plans had been altered: 'We weren't going into action after all. Our job was to be a unique task for any medical unit – to treat the sick of a large concentration camp. That was all we were told.' After pitching camp near Belsen, they were addressed by Colonel Johnston, just back from the 'Horror Camp':

> It is unbelievable. There is no organisation, no food, nothing. Half-starved, emaciated, spiritless, demented, these people roaming the camp have been reduced to animal level . . . I have seen some sights, I thought I could take anything – but this 'shook' me, made me want to vomit.

'We'd no idea whatever what Belsen was and not a clue what it was like,' Fred Simpson, an orderly with 32 CCS later recalled. 'We were told that it was horrific and full of typhus and t.b. and anybody who didn't want to volunteer could drop out.' Only one man did fall out – he had been a prisoner of war in Germany, been evacuated to Britain because he was ill and then recovered and rejoined the forces. He couldn't face any more; but he was the only man who didn't volunteer out of the whole 250 or so.[17]

Cecil Warren, a stretcher-bearer with 11th Light Field Ambulance, remembered that Colonel Gonin had them on parade and said, 'Well, lads. You'll be going to a place that will be front page news all over the world tomorrow.' Frederick Riches recalled that when they drove past Belsen in a small ambulance, his orderly turned to him and said, 'Coo, Fred, what a blooming smell'. Their officer told them they had passed a concentration camp. That evening, 'we were told by the officers and the head boy that our job was to go in and evacuate anybody we could out of Belsen. We said, "Belsen?" He said, "Yes, that concentration camp down the road".'[18]

The next morning they were all given inoculations against typhus and typhoid and set off.

5

Frustrations: 18–23 April 1945

ON 18 APRIL, the British set to work on Hughes's plan – burying the dead and evacuating the living to the Panzer Training School.

The burial of the dead had already begun. On 16 April, squads of SS men were put to work, under British supervision, lifting corpses from the heaps in Camp 1 onto carts and lorries and then unloading them into vast mass graves – first those left by the Germans; and, when they had been filled, new ones dug by Hungarian guards and army bulldozers. The thirty SS women were also made to do this work, and so were German civilians and soldiers.

There was a strong theatrical element in the process, with the emphasis as much on retributive ritual as on efficient disease prevention. The SS men – mainly technicians and clerks, because nearly all the guards had fled before the British arrived – worked in hot sunshine in full uniform, goaded by Tommies with bayonets, struggling to retain their dignity and health as they held the corpses at arm's length like wheelbarrows. The burial parties, Sington thought, provided 'a tremendous emotional release for the inmates of Bergen-Belsen. Each morning a crowd would form near the mass grave in the sandy clearing, in the south-west corner of the camp, to howl and yell execrations at their former tormentors.' But they also provided a similar outlet for British soldiers' feelings. 'The one thing I saw that pleased me was the SS men being bullied into work,' a member of the British medical team wrote on 22 April. 'They collect dead and infected clothing – push their carts by hand and throw the mixed loads into enormous mass-graves (5000 each). All the time our armed troops shout at them, kick them, threaten them, never letting them stop for a moment. What horrible types they were – these SS! – with their Hollywood criminal features. They are being shown no quarter – they know what end is in store for them when their work is finished.'[1]

The SS men were given starvation rations and forced to handle bodies without gloves, the general expectation among British troops being that they would be worked to death – and ultimately twenty of the fifty SS men did die of typhus. But, after a few days, higher authority intervened. The SS were removed and thereafter most of the work was done by German prisoners of war.

At an early stage, the British also brought in bulldozers to try to speed up the process. They were used mainly to dig pits – which was difficult in the sandy Belsen soil – but also to move bodies; some of the most stomach-turning film images showing tumbling cadavers being compelled towards the grave by the bulldozer's plough. The machines tended to split the bodies open and made the smell even worse, so that drivers could not stand the work for long and had frequently to be replaced. The Hungarians were at first very slow gravediggers but 'speeded up remarkably', the British noted, 'when burials commenced at one end of the pit in which they were still working'.[2]

Progress was slow. On 20 April, a visitor noted that 'there were still bodies all around. I saw about a thousand. In one place, hundreds had been shovelled into a mass grave by bulldozers.' Three days later, Colonel Johnston admitted that the burial of the dead was proceeding more slowly than had been hoped – partly because his original figure of 3000 corpses was 'proving to be a gross underestimate as large numbers of dead had been retained within the living huts'; but also because people were continuing to die faster than they could be buried. Nothing the British had done so far had had much effect on the death rate. Indeed, by giving the inmates inappropriate food and letting them circulate around the camp, they had raised it. About 500 people a day were dying at the time of liberation, on 15 April 1945, but, according to British figures, the death rate then climbed to 825 on 19 April, fell briefly to 400 on 21 April and then soared to over 1000 people a day on 22 April 1945.

Furthermore, Glyn Hughes's plan had scarcely begun to be implemented – a week after the British arrival at Belsen the evacuation of the sick from Camp 1 had only just got under way, and the evacuation of the 'fit' had not started at all. This long delay was undermining the plan's whole rationale – of concentrating resources and staff, not in the 'Horror Camp' but at Camp 2, at the Panzer Training School.

It was chicken and egg. No one could be evacuated from the 'Horror Camp' until a 'hospital' to receive them had been created in Camp 2, and that took longer than anyone had expected. While some of the staff of 32 Casualty Clearing Station supervised the clearing and cleaning out of barrack rooms by 400 Hungarian soldiers – who threw the furniture out of the windows – others scoured the countryside for equipment. 'We simply went into local towns and villages and demanded equipment,' said Colonel Johnston. 'Within a few days we had cleared and equipped two canteens and eight buildings.' The unit anaesthetist, Captain 'Frosty' Winterbotham, equipped 7000 beds at the rate of 1000 each day by scouring the district and 'freezing all he could lay hands upon' and Gonin's lorries got over 250 tons of medical equipment into the hospital area in the first week. But this was only a start. Johnston estimated that 14,000 blankets, 5000 stretchers,

7000 straw paliasses, 700 bedpans, 700 urinals and 7000 cooking utensils were needed.[3]

The barracks also had to be emptied of German troops. The 800 Wehrmacht soldiers left behind under the truce were supposed to leave on 19 April, but British transport for them failed to arrive in time, delaying their departure by a day – by which time the Germans had learned that instead of being allowed to become prisoners of war (as 8 Corps had originally permitted) they were to be returned to their own lines (as Second Army was now insisting). The German soldiers marched out in good order, in their peaked ski caps and camouflage jackets, with their MG 34s and Schmeissers, having left behind a little surprise – they had sabotaged the water supply in the barracks.[4]

'Zero day' for evacuating the sick patients from the 'Horror Camp' had, after 'many maddening delays', been fixed for that day, 20 April. When it was learned that a further delay was necessary because the water had failed, the 'ghastly disappointment sent inmates' morale to new depths', Gonin wrote. 'At this stage it was morale that was keeping people alive and nothing else; if they saw we did not keep our word they just lost again the will to live.' He 'went to the poor expedient' of sending his ambulances into the camp: 'We did not lift a patient, but the word went round the camp that the ambulances had come. No one knew that they left, as they arrived, empty.'

The evacuation of the sick from Camp 1 finally started on 21 April, in the small women's camp. Problems arose at once. The original intention was to 'evacuate patients by disease categories'; that is, to remove severely ill cases of typhus as a priority and leave behind the less seriously ill and 'those who were already beyond help'. The typhus cases could then be brought together in wards and given simple specialist care. The British duly handed out skin pencils to the doctors earmarked for the job – most of whom were themselves Belsen internees – and instructed them in a marking code they had devised. 'T' for typhus, 'PT' for post-typhus (a case recovering from typhus) and so on was to be marked on each patient's forehead for easy recognition by the stretcher-bearer collecting them. [5]

This idea made sense, medically, but it broke down on the very first day. 'It was the human element that failed us,' Gonin said later. For one thing, internee medical staff proved to have other priorities: 'If the doctor or nurse in a particular laager was Polish then all the Poles were suffering from typhus and could be saved; if the nurse was Czech then all the Czechs were suffering from typhus and so on.' Also, it soon became clear that survivors were determined to stick together: 'cold-blooded selection' produced 'pitiable distress in those left behind', while evacuating typhus cases first 'only served to make those who had not the disease complain of it'. And so the British quickly abandoned 'tidy diagnosis and the careful selection of cases to be moved in order of priority' and 'it eventually came to a question of evacuating hut by hut'.[6]

Even with this compromise, there still had to be selection. A squad of one British medical officer and several stretcher-bearers was assigned to each hut; the doctor then went in and marked on the forehead of each patient a cross to indicate to the bearers that this patient should be moved. He 'made no attempt to fix a diagnosis', Gonin recalled. 'All he did was to decide whether a patient had any chance of living if he or she was moved or what the chance of survival might be if the patient was left in the Camp for another week. It was a heartrending job and amounted to telling hundreds of poor wretches that they were being left to die. But, as I have said, the individual did not count.' Once the doctors had indicated those who had been chosen for hospitalisation, stretcher-bearers 'just went down, pointed out three people, out they came', Corporal Frederick Riches later recalled. 'There was no names, no nothing at all, just – we was sorry we couldn't get 'em all out at once. They were all putting their hands up, "I'm next, I'm next". They were shouting out, "Take me, take me". You went to the front and said, "Right, you come out, you come out and you come out". And that was it.'

Many of the bearers were youngsters who had 'experienced nothing except the clean deaths of battle'; Gonin was proud of them. 'They were magnificent,' he wrote after the war. 'They spent from 8 a.m. to 5 p.m. with an hour for lunch in those huts in the worst stench in the world, the stink of the unwashed living with every disease on God's earth mixed with that of the long unburied dead. They had to strip those living corpses of their rags, wrap them in blankets and carry them to the ambulance cars. They had to use brute force to prevent the more or less well from fighting their way into the vehicles and to argue with excitable and half crazy central European doctors as to why their own particular friends should not be moved.' Despite being vaccinated, twenty-one of the bearers caught typhus.

The hut inmates selected for evacuation were taken by ambulance to a converted stable building in Camp 2, chosen because it had a well-drained central passage way with stalls on either side. Into each of its twenty stalls a table, towels, scrubbing brushes and soap were put and a mobile bath unit obtained from Second Army provided a constant supply of hot water.

In this 'human laundry', each patient was carried by a German medical orderly to one of the tables and then washed, shaved and dusted with DDT by two nurses from the German Military Hospital, supervised by two German doctors under a British officer. Hair that was long and thick or heavily infested with lice was clipped off, although the British relented somewhat when they saw 'the deleterious psychological effect this had on women who were well enough to realise what was going on'. Johnston admitted that most of the inmates were 'not really in a fit state to withstand such treatment' – it was 'not funny having soap rubbed into a painful ulcer' and 'very painful to those with severe conditions such as bed-sores'. But there was no alternative. Of the 14,000 people who eventually passed through the 'laundry', only two died. Some of the fitter female inmates objected to the immodesty of the procedure but most were too apathetic to care.[7]

'Going into that place, who could forget it?' wrote Molly Silva Jones of the Red Cross.

Living corpses, skeletons covered with parchment like skin, discoloured by filth and neglected sores lay on the bath tables. Mostly they lay inert, occasionally they moaned as they were touched by the nurses. They lay with open eyes sunk deep into hollow sockets, eyes which registered little, save fear and apprehension, mainly they were expressionless.[8]

The German nurses brought in to work in the Human Laundry were initially hostile. They 'laughed, joked, were definitely truculent, made no effort to get things ready for the job in hand, damned if they were going to work for the something British.' But when the first patients started to arrive, 'those nurses stood with their mouths open and gazed horror struck as those bodies were brought in, first one then another started to sob until almost the whole sixty were weeping. There was no more truculence after that.' The 'humanity and professionalism' of these Germans soon wore down British hostility. 'Those girls worked like slaves,' Gonin wrote. 'They grew thin and they grew pale but they worked and they toiled from eight in the till six at night. They earned our respect, in the end we gave them tea in the mid morning, and cigarettes.' The German nurses were of course at high risk of contracting typhus themselves. According to Allied accounts, they were offered immunisation but the German officer in charge of them refused it 'on the basis that they had received it recently'. A month later, 'when 32 of the 48 nurses were in bed with typhus', he 'admitted that they had not had typhus vaccine and gave several lame excuses for his refusal'.[9]

Once cleaned and DDT-dusted, the patients were wrapped in clean blankets and sent in a clean ambulance to the hospital in Camp 2. On the first day, 21 April, 320 sick women were evacuated from the 'Horror Camp', the following day the figure rose to 520, and on 23 April it was 344 – well over 1000 people removed from the squalor. It was a start, though there was still a long way to go.[10]

Getting the sick out was, however, only half of the programme; the British plan also called for the '*immediate* removal of those fit to walk to more sanitary conditions'. Yet on 23 April, a week after the arrival of medical teams, Johnston wrote that 'the evacuation of fit personnel from Camp I to Camp II has not yet commenced'.[11]

What had gone wrong? It was partly a failure of command. Although Glyn Hughes was in charge overall, with the rank of Brigadier, he was still doing his day job as Second Army's Chief Doctor, while at Belsen there was no single officer of sufficient authority and seniority in charge of the camp. There were three kinds of troops there – medical, military government and garrison – and authority was divided between Colonel Johnston, the medical head, Major Miles, in charge of Military Government, and Colonel Montagu, the Military Garrison commander (who had replaced Colonel Taylor on 20 April). Moving 'fit' prisoners out of Camp 1 was not a medical matter at all; it fell to Military Government and the Garrison troops. The result was a log jam. According to the journalist and don Patrick Gordon Walker (who arrived at Belsen on 20 April), 'no major decisions were taken at all. At the end of a whole week no single step had been taken to evacuate [the fit from] the camp'. The married quarters in the Panzer Training School provided obvious housing for healthy internees from the 'Horror Camp'; yet, Gordon Walker noted with amazement, 'not until the eighth day was any step taken to evacuate the Germans who are in the houses in the training school . . . apparently it was the Garrison Commander who held up the decision' – in other words, dragged his feet about kicking them out. The evacuation of the Germans, which could have been done by the fourth or fifth day, was not completed until the twelfth or fourteenth day, and so eight days were lost. 'In the meantime,' Gordon Walker wrote in his diary, 'thousands died, of whom hundreds could have been saved. People who risked their lives for us have fallen ill and sickened and some will die, who could have been saved.' It was 'not so much a question of manpower,' he thought. 'There were enough men here. It is a question of decision and authority.' For want of a brigadier, he believed, thousands of lives were lost.[12]

This was a serious failure by the British. It remains unclear where the blame lay. Derrick Sington was full of praise for the officers of No. 224 Military Government detachment, who arrived at Belsen on 17 April. 'Major Miles had been in a London finance house; Capt. Farmer had been a Yorkshire police official, Captain Gibbons a Lancashire businessman and Capt Balston a university student,' he wrote. 'What work, tenacity, good will and shrewd improvisation could achieve they achieved. They pressed forward feverishly the preparations to evacuate the relatively healthy. They started to organise and watch the feeding. They began to clear up the pestiferous compounds.' Major Miles himself blamed the 'considerable delay in clearing the accommodation in the Wehrmacht barracks on the lack of appreciation of Mil Gov methods by the Military Commander'; meaning, presumably, that the latter had not been tough enough with the Germans left there. He also complained that the whole Belsen relief operation had 'in fact been one of individual effort' and his work 'an attempt to coordinate without authority', not helped by the frequent changes of command or by wartime conditions. He argued that in future Military Government should have the decisive voice in any such situation.[13]

The Garrison Commander's report gives no explanation for the delay, but simply prints a list of twenty-five tasks which had to be carried out (with water supply and food provision at the top), adding tartly that 'the solutions varied from day to day according to the relative urgency of the different points and the availability of means to cope with them'. Clearly the handful of Military Government officers who were supposed to be in charge of strategy were too thin on the ground – strung between both camps – and too junior in rank to achieve much with the Garrison troops.

Things only improved when a more senior officer, Colonel Spottiswoode, was sent to Belsen, on 21 April.[14]

British junior officers who saw around them the consequences of delay were driven to despair by 'the lack of higher decision and initiative'. Derrick Sington was approached by Mona Georges, a French nightclub singer jailed by the Gestapo for Resistance work. 'Monsieur, seven more women died here today,' she said. 'If we stay in this place we shall die of the pestilence. In a few days, unless something is done, there will be no women left here.'

> There amid scattered turnips and excrement, the smell of burning leather and the noises of women defecating, her logic seemed unanswerable and inexorable. One felt powerless, desperately powerless. One knew that the organisation and equipment of the reception camp and the reception hospital were being pressed forward with all possible speed. But in the meantime were these women to be left in this death-trap to contract infection and die?

Sington and a colleague were able to get this group of some fifteen French women out of their hut into a new dormitory they had made in the former SS clothing store and several well-known and well-connected individuals (one of them the niece of a British aristocrat) were quietly removed.[15]

Others were less fortunate. When Bertha Ferderber, the Cracow housewife who had arrived from Auschwitz at the same time as Anne Frank, tried to get medicine for her sick sister-in-law, she was turned away empty-handed. Her relative's death left her understandably bitter. The British, she noted, 'excelled at one thing, collecting the dead'.

> It has been two weeks since we were liberated, [she wrote in May 1945] and even more wagonloads are being wheeled from the camp than before. There they lie on the wagons,

the liberated people, the shaven heads lolling, shaking slowly with the steps of the person pushing them . . .

The spectacle gives me no rest . . . I see neither the rays of the spring sun nor the green of the trees . . .

It is true that there is a difference between the funerals of today and those of yesterday. Now it is Germans who are pushing the wagonloads of corpses. Formerly we did that. But how great is the difference, the dead are laid in mass graves whether they died as prisoners or as free men.

She later described how a British soldier, thinking she too was dead, grabbed her leg and called to his companion to help him move her:

'Have patience, not yet,' I answered him from above, in English.[16]

The delay in evacuating inmates from the 'Horror Camp' made it all the more important that decisive steps be taken to bring food, water and medical treatment to the thousands of people stuck there. Steps were indeed taken, but not decisive ones; the 'broad policy' was to concentrate on 'the preparation of Camp No. 2 as a large reception and Hospital area' while providing 'minimal necessary services' in Camp 1. The 'Horror Camp' was not neglected altogether, but the measures taken were half-hearted. For example, by 30 April only 200 latrines had been constructed there, while 530 had been built in the grounds of the Panzer Training School, which already had functioning sanitation. And the water-supply problem was addressed, but only in the most basic way. Mobile baths reached the 'Horror Camp' by 19 April – army cameramen filmed French girls soaping themselves in the showers on 22 April – and a Captain in the Engineers managed, by 'energetically "acquiring"' twenty men from the Celle Fire Brigade, to get water pumped from the local stream to static water tanks in the camp and thence to the kitchens. But it was of poor quality – 'dead bodies were found in the tanks' – and not fit to drink.[17]

Similarly, the first attempt by the Field Hygiene Section to dust all huts and inmates with DDT – and thus to try to contain the typhus – was 'unsatisfactory'. 'In view of the appalling conditions under which the men were required to work,' Johnston reported, 'few were able to stand the sight and smell for more than very short intervals at a time and it was impossible to more than super- ficially dust the majority of patients.' Perhaps most importantly, the logic of the plan meant that the inhabitants of Camp 1 received no medical attention. 'Emergency medical measures were totally lacking. No medical post of any sort was set up in the camp,' Gordon Walker noted.[18]

Given this background, it is hardly surprising that only slight progress was initially made with the most intractable problem of all – feeding the inmates in Camp 1. On the supply front, the British had considerable success in organising provisions locally. On 16 April, a German supply depot had been found near the Panzer Training School which contained 600 tons of potatoes, 120 tons of tinned meat, 30 tons of sugar, 20 tons of dried milk; cocoa, grain, wheat and other foodstuffs 'which had they been distributed earlier might have saved countless lives'. The Panzer Training School also turned out to have its own vast bakery and staff, capable of producing 60,000 loaves a day, while, not far away, dairies and slaughterhouses existed which were willing to provide milk, butter, vegetables and meat for the camp.[19]

Supply, though, was only part of the equation. After their disastrous early experiences with overfeeding, the British now realised that the food needed to be more appropriate to the inmates' conditions and that something had to be done to ensure it was fairly distributed. A rudimentary attempt at different diets began, with the German food such as potatoes cooked up in the 'Horror Camp's' rudimentary kitchens while milk was made available for the more delicate. With the distribution of food still being done through the hut 'representatives', however, it soon became clear that the stronger were getting the bulk of the food and the bedridden little or nothing. A 'milk bar' was created to supplement the main meals but opinions varied as to its success.

The inmates of course did their best to divert any food. The cookhouses in Camp 1 were staffed by 'women internees who were reasonably fit. They soon became fitter as they had access to as much food as they could get' and, in the end, to prevent the rifling of food, provisions had to be distributed to the cookhouses just before a meal. At the same time, inmates began asking for the sorts of food they were used to or 'which they feel will quickly restore them back to healthy life' – a Polish woman asked for sauerkraut so that she could make herself a little 'Kacha'. This provoked some impatience among British catering staff who had themselves endured army rations for years. The fitter, or more resourceful of the inmates, particularly the Russians, simply disappeared into the surrounding countryside to 'organise' food for themselves. 'You have to say: a Russian is a Russian. The English gave them [food] to eat, but they stole all the same,' a Russian prisoner recalled. Military Government reported that it was quite impossible to prevent very large numbers [it estimated 5000] from going in and out of the camps as they pleased without very severe measures such as shooting, which was not considered to be justified.'

An almost continuous cloud of the immates spread over the country. Many of these merely went out for freedom and returned after a walk. Others did not return at all or only after days and weeks. Many returned laden with loot, food, clothes, and valuables taken off the Germans who were on the whole too cowed to make incidents.[20]

It was now eleven days since the British, had first heard of Belsen and a week since the relief effort had begun. In that time, 7000 people had died in the camp, and on 23 April alone no fewer than 1700 had perished. The task seemed utterly hopeless.

Every evening at about nine the medical team reviewed

progress. 'The problems peculiar to the ladies would be discussed first, about eleven o'clock they would be dismissed, gin, brandy, and champagne would appear and we would finish our business by twelve or one in the morning – it was not a party but damned hard work which those meetings produced,' Colonel Gonin recalled. 'I am very certain it was the very considerable quantities of liquor that we got through at those meetings that kept those of us who were responsible for the administration of the place from going as mad as most of the internees in the Horror Camp.' A Jewish chaplain saw it rather differently. The Revd Isaac Levy found the medical staff of 32 CCS 'relaxing after a long and gruelling day'. They were 'drinking heavily, sinking into a state of complete intoxication. "If we were not to drink," they said, "we would go stark, staring mad. We are doctors and are supposed to heal, but this task is hopeless. They die on us as soon as we touch them."' Another visitor reported that Colonel Johnston, 'with wholly inadequate resources, is wrestling with an appalling medical problem . . . which can have few parallels'. A relief worker agreed. 'All of us are doing an impossible task – saving, perhaps, a handful of people (might be 4 or 5, might be 6 or 7 thousand) out of 40,000.'[21]

6

The Chaplain's Tale

ON 16 APRIL 1945, the Jewish chaplain to British 8 Corps returned from Holland to the regimental headquarters at Celle. The Colonel wished to see him, Leslie Hardman was told. This officer then informed him that a concentration camp had been uncovered nearby and he ought to go there the next day. 'It's horrible,' the Colonel said. 'But you have to go there. You'll find a lot of your people there.' And, as Hardman was leaving he added, 'Keep a stiff upper lip, padre.'[1]

The following day, forty-eight hours after the first British troops, Hardman drove to the camp. Confronted by the mounds of corpses, he felt helpless and inadequate and never got further than the huts near the entrance, formerly occupied by the SS. He spent most of the day there talking in Yiddish to a group of inmate nursing sisters, Jewish girls from Poland and Lithuania, encouraging them to reminisce about their lives before the war. 'I felt that I could help most if I could slacken a little the almost intolerable tension of their sorely afflicted minds; if I could kindle some warmth in their frozen hearts; if I could inject some emotion into their withered bodies.' At one point, one of the girls broke quaveringly into a few lines of a Hebrew song. 'The pathos of this attempt was so poignant that I put my head on the table and wept; and then they comforted me.'

When Hardman went off to collect some Matzos biscuits from his truck, he saw two British soldiers carrying sacks of potatoes into the camp.

And then, almost as though they had emerged from the ground itself . . . a number of wraithlike creatures came tottering towards us. As they drew closer they made frantic efforts to quicken their feeble pace. Their skeleton arms and legs made jerky, grotesque movements as they forced themselves forward. Their bodies, from their heads to their feet, looked like matchsticks. The two Tommies, entering the camp for the first time, must have thought they had walked into a supernatural world . . . They dropped their heavy sacks and fled.

Immediately the prisoners pounced on the sacks like locusts. Hardman watched as they fought for the potatoes, and plunged in to rescue a tiny skeletal figure, a young girl in danger of being crushed. She showed no awareness of him, and tottered off back to a hut. Considerably shaken, the chaplain returned to the nurses' hut and was gratified by their response to his gift. He reached his room in Celle late that night, 'almost prostrate with physical, mental and spiritual shock and exhaustion'.

The son of an Austrian Jewish draper interned as an 'enemy alien' by the British in the First World War, Leslie Hardman was born in Neath, South Wales, in 1913, and grew up in Manchester and Liverpool in a strictly orthodox kosher home. 'I seemed to catch religion much more than my sisters,' he later recalled. After attending local Jewish schools, he qualified as a *shocator* (or ritual slaughterer) and took an English degree at Leeds before becoming rabbi to a Sheffield synagogue. But the young man's interests lay more in Zionism and the fate of European Jewry than with the mundane concerns of his congregation and, from the first rumblings, he wanted to be part of the war. It took persistence but finally, in 1942, he was taken on as an army chaplain.[2]

Back in Belsen the following morning, Hardman found a bull-dozer at work, pushing a mound of dead bodies towards a vast pit it had already excavated. Was it not possible to show more respect for the dead? he asked the officer in charge. Sadly not, he was told, but if he returned when the pit was full, he could say prayers over the bodies. The chaplain went off to distribute cigarettes to the women inmates, noting with sadness how they stole more whenever his back was turned.[3]

Leslie Hardman's version of Belsen, written in 1957 in collaboration with a journalist, is quite different from other British accounts. As a Jew, a rabbi, a Yiddish speaker, he understood what he was witnessing and realised that a large part of the survivors of European Jewry were piled into Belsen. Almost from the start, the women asked him about family members last seen at Birkenau and Treblinka. He could not distance himself or take refuge in euphemism, and the magnitude of what he confronted overwhelmed him. Far from keeping a stiff upper lip, Hardman is constantly overcome by emotion and reproaching himself for his 'inability to remain steadfast in the face of the human suffering it was my daily lot to see, hear and share'. During a late-night chat with Patrick Gordon Walker on 21 April, he 'broke down completely and sobbed out loud'. Distributing wedding rings to Jewish women who have lost their husbands, he suddenly finds the 'unspeakable anguish' of one of them more than he can bear. 'My distress touched a chord and broke her. She fell across the table in an agony of weeping. It was more than I could stand. I handed the box of rings to the Hungarian woman who was acting as my assistant, and instructing her to share out the rest, I fled from the hut.'[4]

On Friday 20 April, Leslie Hardman conducted the first Jewish service heard at Belsen, observing *Kiddush*, the sanctification of the entry of the Sabbath, in the open air in the midst of Camp 1. A few hundred people were gathered together and sobbed openly. Afterwards, Hardman was pressed to stay for an 'evening meal' which 'consisted of a concoction made to resemble *gefilte fisch*, a traditional Jewish dish' and, not wishing to offend his hosts, ate some of it and drank some 'beverage' they had made. The next day he suffered 'excruciating pains' and was very ill; it was forty-eight hours before he was functioning again. But he was soon once more 'working like a maniac'.[5]

Identifying so strongly with his fellow Jews, Hardman was driven nearly mad by the army's dithering and delay. 'They were too slow,' he said later. He appealed to the Senior Medical Officer for more to be done. Johnston listened 'gravely and sympathetically' and allowed the chaplain to set up a 'first-aid centre' in Camp 1. Hardman chose the hut that had previously served as the SS dispensary and got hold of two SS women to clean it up for him (until he was told he could not use SS women in this way). There was room for about a dozen beds, which held about twenty to thirty patients; not much, but better than nothing. Here a Polish doctor gave emergency treatment to sick and dying people, using German drugs from the pharmacy, in an attempt to tide them over till they could be evacuated. Some 200 people passed through the improvised hospital.[6]

The food situation, too, tormented Hardman. Why were the British not doing more? One day he climbed into his truck and drove into the surrounding countryside and, after calling at several houses and encountering 'a mixture of wariness, docility, a feigned eagerness to please, and complete ignorance of the horrors of the camp', returned with 'a truckload of preserved fruit and pickled herrings'. When told that a famous Polish historian was dying in a hut that British soldiers refused to enter, he went in himself and fed the man with fruits from the jar. 'Hold on, hold on,' Hardman told him. Then he was ordered to stop; no food was to come into the camp, he was told, except that provided by the authorities.[7]

Hardman also recognised another problem. Whenever he spoke to inmates at Belsen, he urged them to write to all their relatives and promised to post the letters, but he then discovered that, officially, only short prisoner-of-war cards – on which preset phrases such as 'I have been captured by the enemy' and 'I am well' could be highlighted – were permitted to be sent. Hardman told the Colonel that was not right and urged the inmates to write at length. When letters of reply started to come back, he created a postal service within the camp.

Hardman describes his efforts to plead with his brother officers to show patience towards the prisoners, to understand that they had been subjected 'not only to a deliberate extermination of themselves as a people, but to a disintegration of their souls'. His criticism of the British was not so much that they were anti-Semitic – though he did meet one officer who said loudly, 'Bloody Jews! Serves them right'; more that they were indifferent and fatalistic, their stock of humanity exhausted by the war. Some officers said frankly that it would be more merciful if everyone at Belsen died.[8]

Eventually, Hardman became an irritant to the British. It is not clear whether this was because he had identified what was going wrong and tried to do something about it, sabotaging the army's plan and undermining the discipline of triage by answering the calls of his own heart; because he annoyed the British by nakedly expressing emotion and not conducting himself with the restraint and self-control they regarded as appropriate; or because he disobeyed military orders. But Colonel Johnston asked Hardman's superior, Rabbi Isaac Levy, the senior Jewish chaplain stationed at army headquarters at Celle, to 'find him and remove him as he was becoming hysterical'. Levy went over to Belsen and walked through the main path that divided the camp in two. Like everyone who came there for the first time, he recoiled from the half-clothed 'animals' and began talking to 'two young girls from good families in Prague' who had arrived in Belsen shortly before the British and were 'still normal and human'. Then Hardman appeared. 'I stretched out my hand to greet him and he fell on my neck and wept like a babe,' Levy wrote to his wife. 'The people round me saw it and joined in the weeping and I had to take him aside and make him pull himself together. He is not hysterical, he is tired, and should go away for a while'.[9]

Hardman adamantly refused. 'My response was to take him into one of the worst huts. He came out with a face as white as a sheet. "Now repeat your statement," I said. But he could only mutter, "It's terrible, terrible." I saw him off at the gate, and he took my hand. "You must stay here until more help arrives. I shall do all I can."' Levy did, though, manage to persuade him to get rid of the pistol with which he was armed.

The contrast between Hardman's rapport with some prisoners and the inertia of the army has led some historians to argue that had Jewish doctors been present at Belsen from the start all would have been different. Maybe; but Hardman himself had difficulty in changing things overnight. 'The huts remained filthy for some time,' he wrote, 'as their inmates had little inclination to clean them. Death was still too frequent a visitor for them to be concerned about cleanliness. I tried hard to persuade, even to goad them into doing more for themselves; but people whose will to live was at an ebb, and who saw more of death than life, had no reserves upon which they could call . . . It seemed that the death rate would never be checked.'[10]

Nor was this a uniquely British problem. A visitor to Dachau concentration camp, liberated by the Americans on 29 April, noticed that 'the incoming troops, after the first inrush of indignation, seemed to slump back into accepting Dachau, not as 32,000 fellow human beings like themselves, but as a strange monstrosity to be treated on its own standards'. 'How else,' he wrote, 'can one explain the fact that ten days after the liberation no one thinks it strange that there are no trucks to carry the dying to hospital and no proper diet in the hospital? If a town of 32,000 people had been struck by a cyclone, an immense rescue apparatus would be organized. But these 32,000 outcasts are so remote from civilization as we know it that we are content to leave them as they are, improving slightly their living conditions.'[11]

7

Reinforcements: Camp 1, 24–30 April 1945

ON 23 APRIL, British Movietone News arrived to shoot the first sound newsreel of the camp. Whereas army cameramen had hitherto been content to record (on silent film) what they saw at Belsen, Movietone's Paul Wyand was an experienced provider of material to match the strident commentaries of the newsreels. A vast, corpulent man – the rigours of reporting the Italian Campaign had reduced his weight to a mere 300 lb – he had also received instructions from the Ministry of Information on how to provide the government with evidence of Belsen, which could not be dismissed as 'atrocity propaganda'.

To that end, Wyand placed a series of witnesses in front of Belsen settings and got them to make statements on camera. Some were British – a vicar who complained that the place was 'indescribably ghastly'; a genial artillery Major who described his men's work supervising the burials; and a soldier who gave an eloquent statement of the common man's view:

> Today is the 24th of April of 1945. My name is Gunner Illingworth and I live in Cheshire. I'm at present in Belsen Camp doing guard duty over the SS men. The things in this camp are beyond describing. When you actually see them

for yourself you know what you're fighting for here. Pictures in the paper can't describe it at all. The things that they've committed, well, nobody would think they were human at all. We actually know now what has been going on in these camps and I know personally what I am fighting for.

Several inmates also gave statements, among them Dr Hadassah Bimko. She fluffed at first, then pulled herself together and spoke in German at some length, with firm authority and no trace of emotion, about what had happened at Belsen. Finally, Wyand put several of the German staff in front of the camera, standing them in front of heaps of bodies; and, by humiliating them, succeeded in making them seem pitiable. Dr Fritz Klein, who had carried out selections at Auschwitz, had by this time been burying bodies for a week and had become known as 'the mad-doctor of Belsen'; he was given the full treatment.

I posed Klein on the edge of the pit into which he had been dumping corpses, and the background showed other bodies being disposed of in like manner. Two soldiers had been detailed to assist me, and one stood on each side of the doctor. Klein was trembling with fear and was half crazy after the work he had been doing for the past few days. The [Polish] girl [interpreter] explained what was wanted, and as he started to talk I filmed him. He had only spoken a few words when the girl cried 'Stop!' and explained that although Klein had told me his name and where he was, he had given the wrong year. On hearing this the Tommies clouted the German with their rifle butts, and the Polish girl screamed at him. Klein began again and this time he kept to the truth.

Soon after this, Klein was photographed in a pit filled with corpses.[1]

The Ministry of Information also wanted to make sure that German civilians were implicated in what was found in the camp.

On the afternoon of the 24 April, the Burgomasters of Celle and other neighbouring towns were brought to Belsen and taken round. Then they were 'brought first to the burial-pit which was already half-full of bodies and skeletons. The SS men and women paraded on one side of the yawning grave, and the German mayors had to stand upon the brink.' Derrick Sington's loudspeaker car was then brought up and Colonel Spottiswoode, the Military Government Commander, read a long denunciation in German, 'while the crowd stood silent'.

After reminding the burgomasters that the British had been cleaning up Belsen for a week, so that things had improved considerably, and that it was far from being the worst camp, the Colonel launched into his peroration:

> What you will see here is the final and utter condemnation of the Nazi Party. It justifies every measure which the United Nations will take to exterminate that Party. What you will see here is such a disgrace to the German people that their name must be erased from the list of civilised nations.

Seen now, there is a particular English amateurism about the whole bizarre tableau. The setting – the white sand of the grave; the small birch tree which has somehow managed to survive beside it; the burgomasters placed against the skyline in their long bourgeois coats, felt hats held in their hands – suggests university dramatics. Colonel Spottiswoode's speech reads adequately on the page, but, as delivered in his Oxford-accented German, has the quality of underproduced theatre – of undergraduates taking on Greek tragedy and straining for an eloquence they never find. The language is at once clumsy and oversophisticated for its purpose:

> You who represent the fathers and brothers of German youth see before your eyes a few of the sons and daughters who bear a small part of the direct responsibility for this crime. Only a small part, yet too heavy a burden for the human

soul to bear. But who bears the final responsibility? You who have allowed your Führer to carry out his terrible whims.

Spottiswoode paused repeatedly to emphasise the German word '*Sie*':

> You who have proved incapable of doing anything to check his perverted triumphs. You who had heard about these camps, or had at least a slight conception of what happened in them. You who did not rise up spontaneously to cleanse the name of Germany, not fearing the personal consequences. You stand here judged through what you will see in the camp. You must expect to atone with toil and sweat for what your children have committed and for what you have failed to prevent.

According to Sington, 'during the speech one of the German mayors covered his face with his hands and wept'. A journalist who later asked, 'How did they take it?' was told that 'one of them was sick and another wouldn't look. They all said they had never dreamed this was going on'. It was a common refrain in Germany at that time.[2]

In fact, Movietone's cameras had got to Belsen just in time; a day or two later, and Wyand would have found the story changing. 'There's quite a different air about the place the last two days,' a doctor told a journalist on 24 April. 'They seem much more cheerful now.' Things had started getting slightly better in the camp. For a start, the British had finally begun to get on top of the problem of burying the dead. 'The burial rate has gone down considerably,' a British Army Captain said that day. 'I'm handling just under three hundred a day now. It was five hundred to begin with. And we are evacuating five hundred every day to the Panzer training school.' The backlog of corpses was finally cleared on 28 April and after that the dead were promptly buried, though still in mass graves. Piles of unburied corpses were no longer to be seen. That made a huge difference to the atmosphere[3]

Another reason for the lifting of spirits was that the SOS which Glyn Hughes had sent out on the evening of 15 April was beginning to be answered and medical reinforcements and expertise starting to come to Belsen. The most important new arrival was 21 Army Group's expert on typhus, Captain W. A. Davis.

For centuries, typhus had been a spectre hanging over military medicine, ready to strike whenever soldiers were gathered together. The Thirty Years War, Napoleon's invasion of Russia and the Bolshevik Revolution had all produced epidemics of the disease. However, in 1909, a French doctor established that the body louse was the vector of typhus and so paved the way to the delousing procedures which enabled the vast armies of the First World War to keep the disease largely at bay. Building on that experience, the British had managed to keep the typhus rate quite low during the desert campaigns of 1940–3 by a combination of public education, frequent inspections of the troops and routine disinfection of all 'native' labourers and prisoners of war with chemical disinfectants and mobile steam baths. But the Americans had made the real breakthrough in treating typhus by coming up with two new weapons – the 'Cox' vaccine, developed at the Rockefeller Institute in New York in 1940, and the insecticide DDT. Dichlorodiphenyltrichloroethane, first synthesised by a German chemist in 1874, had only recently been revealed as an efficient pesticide, when used on Colorado beetles threatening the potato crop in Switzerland in 1939. President Roosevelt, by creating the USA Typhus Commission, had given the campaign against the disease real muscle.[4]

The effectiveness of DDT against insect-borne typhus was dramatically shown after the Allies occupied Naples in 1943. When it became clear that a potentially serious outbreak was threatened, which the local health authorities were incapable of dealing with, a team from the Rockefeller Institute 'whose experiments in mechanical dusting with insecticide powder had revolutionized anti-typhus measures' was drafted in and, in early 1944, some 1,750,000 delousing operations and 50,000 inoculations were carried out in Naples and its environs. As a result, there were almost no deaths from typhus.[5]

The handling of the Naples epidemic was hailed as one the great medical feats of the day. 'The scientists of the Rockefeller Foundation must be credited with the miracle performed in Naples,' the *New York Times* wrote in 1944. 'Typhus, more dreaded than bullets in any Army, is now simply unknown among our soldiers and sailors . . . DDT seems almost too good to be true.'[6]

Captain Davis's experience at Naples proved invaluable in Germany. He soon showed himself energetic, resourceful and flexible. 'He was cracking', a British doctor later recalled, 'the only doctor who really understood typhus' – 'one of the first rate type of Americans – full of enthusiasm, beauty of drive, dark and keen-looking: he is full of preventive medicine and the value of vaccination,' another wrote. On 22 April Davis ventured into the huts at Camp 1 to confirm that typhus was indeed present. It wasn't easy – 'the internees were so covered with dirt, sores, scabies, and vermin that it was almost impossible to distinguish a typhus rash even in good light' – but twenty patients from ten huts were examined and found to be 'heavily infested, probably averaging a hundred lice per person'. The greater ease of movement around the camp after the arrival of the British had probably helped to spread the disease.[7]

The delousing programme began at once, using five dust guns on 40-foot leads, which enabled the dusters to get to the back of the huts. 'The work went well but slowly,' Davis later wrote. There was no problem with the internees, 'whose gratitude and meek cooperation were pitiful', but it took time to get at everything in the overcrowded huts, and it was seldom possible to do more than thirty persons per hour per man. The real difficulty, though, was the reluctance of the delousers – 'the smell was so overwhelming that several officers refused to enter'. In the end Davis solved this problem by promoting all British soldiers to 'supervisory positions' and getting Hungarians – the ubiquitous Hungarians – and Polish girls to do the actual dusting. The preliminary delousing programme was completed within nine days. 'By 30 April, approximately 30,000 living persons and their beds had been powdered in Camp 1 . . . Although this was not expected to eliminate all lice from the camp, it was expected that it would so reduce both the incidence and degree of louse infestation that it would stop the epidemic. Accordingly, May 21st was set as the day on which the surveillance of the internees for typhus would end.'[8]

At the same time, Davis and his team worked vigilantly to prevent typhus developing in Camp 2 and made sure that inmates leaving Belsen were thoroughly deloused before they went – 'the large powder duster with a team of Hungarian soldiers was located at the loading point and evacuees deloused before boarding the vehicles'. In the part of Camp 2 which housed the inmates in better health, 'the cumbersome old German apparatus for delousing by hot air was abandoned, and a station for delousing by DDT powder was installed. This was staffed by Polish girls who had worked in the bath houses under the Nazis.'[9]

Other medical specialists were also now arriving. 'A dietician is here – if not several – and they give conflicting advice,' a relief worker wrote. Although Johnston remained in charge, Lt. Colonel Martin Lipscomb took over as British consultant on 23 April. A 'humble, quiet, courteous man' in his late fifties, Lipscomb had spent most of his career in India, acquiring 'a vast fund of knowledge and experience' of geriatrics and tropical medicine, but was not a nutritional expert, although his primary task at Belsen was to sort out a diet to suit the stomachs of its starving inmates. The rough jottings in his notebook show him rapidly educating himself in the subject, conferring with nutritional experts such as the great Sir Jack Drummond (the arbiter of British diet during the war) and Dr Arnold Meiklejohn, a nutritionist sent to Belsen by UNRRA.[10]

The British were still learning the limits of what a starved body can take, and trying to impose some uniformity on the regimes offered: the records suggest that they varied a good deal. Thus, at about the same time as they were discovering 'that many of the internees were incapable of assimilating the fat in the tinned milk we were issuing and we were forced to dilute the milk with equal quantities of water until the arrival of dried skimmed milk flown out from home', they were also devising two diets – 'normal' and 'hospital' – broadly similar, except that the normal got 16 oz of potatoes and some tinned meat and veg, whereas the 'hospital' had much less of tinned meat and vegetables.[11]

Lipscomb organised a more sophisticated three-tier diet which was approved by Sir Jack Drummond when he visited Belsen on 29 April. Extreme starvation cases were to be given milk, sugar and vitamin tablets; cases requiring a light diet got separated milk and sugar, plus small amounts of bread, tinned meat and vegetables, potatoes, butter, soup and (when available) egg; while those able to eat ordinary meals got a daily intake of 2300 calories and a liberal allowance of animal protein and lots of bread and potatoes, which was intended to fatten them up.[12]

British efforts to apply these diet scales ran into huge problems, the Russians proving especially difficult. In addition to the Russian civilian internees in Camp 1, in Camp 2 there was the 'major part of a Russian battalion which had been captured more or less intact'. Soon after the British arrival in Belsen, a young Russian liaison officer appeared, demanding that, under inter-Allied agreement, the Russian prisoners should get British field rations. When Johnston tried to explain the dangers of feeding such food to starving people, the liaison officer replied that 'the Russian stomach was different' and that the Russian POW battalion must be given the full British field service scale of rations forthwith. His demand was 'accompanied by unpleasant threats'. As a result, the Russians got a daily caloric allowance of about 3020, which the British officers hoped would satisfy them as they were 'in a truculent and rather dangerous frame of mind'. 'In the end,' Johnston wrote, 'we were forced to segregate all Russian internees and hand over responsibility to their own internee doctors.'[13]

Glyn Hughes's appeal for help also produced a response from another quarter. Six Red Cross aid teams and eight Irish nurses already working in Europe were rushed to Belsen, after being given fourteen hours' notice to move from Holland to a 'job of great urgency in Northern Germany. The army had uncovered a concentration camp in which conditions were frightful and typhus raging.' After a long drive, which involved crossing the Rhine by a shaky pontoon bridge, the Red Cross teams arrived on 21 April.[14]

Some of the twenty-four Red Cross men were immediately drafted in as auxiliary ambulance drivers, ferrying patients from the 'Horror Camp' to the 'human laundry' and the hospital; others were sent to help in the kitchens at Camp 1. While doing so, Bill Rankin and Bill Broughton, two Quakers working under the Red Cross umbrella, discovered that the main concern was the dreadful quality of the water supplied there. No one from the army seemed to be doing anything about it, so they tackled it themselves, with a team of Hungarians as labourers. First, the two huge open tanks were scrubbed and cleaned – 'the stench was appalling, but with hard labour it was emptied, cleansed and water running by the time we left for supper – then chlorination was introduced, with one tank being allowed to sediment while the other was used.

By now, both Rankin and Broughton were in great demand: 'Field Hygiene were still anxious to keep us both with them.' This unit of thirty soldiers had, it turned out, been too busy burying bodies and dusting with DDT to do much about water and drainage. They now asked Bill Broughton to tackle the sewers, which were 'in a shocking condition'. With the help of Hungarian labour and German civilians recruited locally, using a combination of fire hoses and digging, he laboriously traced the sewage system from the sewage farm past numerous blocked manholes which had created a 'filthy and noxious marsh' over most of the lower end of the camp. One particularly stubborn manhole took three days to clear and yielded 'two overcoats and two blankets, a good sackful of sodden rags and two good feet of sludge'. Broughton's report conveys something of his brand of heroism.

With constant flushing we kept the sand moving and now attempted the next stretch, which again had to be divided into two lengths by digging. Here the ground was high, and we had to dig some eight feet deep, rivetting the sides of the trench to prevent the shifting sand from falling in. We got our water jets within a few yards of the next manhole by pushing up-sewer from this digging, but here we stuck.

They eventually discovered that the nearby stream, the camp's source of drinking water, was also the outlet for its sewage. It is impossible to say how many people had died as a result.[15]

Most of the Red Cross team were female, however. The prospect of being joined by women had caused some dread in army medical circles. 'There was a moan of disgust and at least two more bottles than usual were drunk that night,' Colonel Gonin later recalled. The fear was that they would be 'just more people to show round, just more helpless folk that would have to be looked after'; the women would 'want everything there isn't and write letters home complaining'. But his attitude changed when he met an English Quaker soon after her arrival and was briskly told that the accommodation was fine and would he come and have a gin.[16]

Nonetheless the women's role was clearly defined, as a Red Cross sister discovered when she went, on arrival, to a meeting of Army doctors from 32 CCS, chaired by Colonel Johnston. Myrtle Beardwell found the atmosphere tense and the doctors 'worn and tired', their faces 'white and strained'. Johnston 'started by saying that he did not think that women ought to be there – however we soon prevailed upon him to let us remain. "But," he said, "only on condition that you do not go into the horror camp."' The following evening, however, he did offer to take Beardwell and another sister – 'As we were trained nurses he thought we could stand seeing the horrors better than those people who had had no hospital experience.' 'After some discussion and considerable persuasion', the personable Jean

McFarlane got Colonel Gonin to take her in. 'It was from no morbid desire that I wanted to see the worst that Belsen had to show, but it seemed that the picture would be incomplete without.'[17]

Keeping women out of Camp 1 was very much in keeping with British Army tradition. Was it a mistake? One of the team didn't think so. 'A lot of people said later, nowadays, with equal opportunities, that it was ridiculous to keep the women out,' Jane Leverson told an interviewer in 1995, 'and it would have been if the women hadn't had a lot to do where we were. And as it is, I think it was quite a good division of labour and I personally am *ever so pleased* that I didn't go in in the early days.'[18]

The arrival of these women undoubtedly lifted the atmosphere and removed some of the gloom at Belsen. Although only four members of the Red Cross team were trained nurses, many had considerable experience of wartime social work; some were middle-class, well-educated, self-confident and independent-minded; a few were attractive. Socially, they raised the tone. They were also inexhaustibly cheerful, full of admiration for the men and of the same sex as most of the patients. Their arrival, Johnston wrote after the war, 'made all the difference to us and changed what appeared to be an almost impossible task into a quite possible one'. The women were sent into the newly created hospital area in Camp 2 to take care of the first 600 sick patients who had just been admitted there.[19]

However, probably the most important reason the atmosphere in Belsen lifted somewhat on 24 April was that the 'evacuation of the 'fit' from the 'Horror Camp' finally began that day. 'This was the announcement we had been waiting for day after day,' Derrick Sington wrote. 'For it was obvious that the concentration camp was a death-trap for the healthy as well as the sick. Only by getting the still healthy out of the pestilence quickly could we save thousands of lives.'[20]

The plan was to evacuate the people in nationality groups following a certain order. 'The first to go out would be the French,

Belgians, Dutch and Luxemburgers, the reason being that these West-bound people were sure to return home sooner than the Eastern Europeans and would thus vacate the new quarters in a comparatively short space of time. It was decided to evacuate the women before the men.' Four processes were involved at the departure end. The people had to be called out of their blocks; registered; bathed and disinfected; and, finally, embussed on to lorries. At nine o'clock on the morning of 24 April one of Sington's sergeants drove his loudspeaker car to the smaller women's camp and invited all the French, Belgian, Dutch and Luxembourg women to assemble with a few possessions: 'They stood outside the compound in two ranks in their striped peignoirs or dusty overcoats, many with scarves round their heads, and with their little bundles of crockery, clothing or food.'

A lorry then brought them to the registration point, the former SS canteen, 'a big hut, with a small musicians' platform, and a side door leading out to a bar, still plentifully stocked with cut-glass beer tankards'. The women were registered by volunteer clerks sitting at tables as they passed through. 'The evacuation proceeded steadily all day, with the waiting women sitting on their bundles in the square or lying down and dozing in the sun.'

Inevitably, there were attempts to jump the queue. Sington came across a Hungarian woman trying to find her French husband and a Romanian Jewish girl trying to find her French lover.

Towards evening I went into the bathhouse with loaves of brown bread for the women who were still passing through. The steam was rising from the baths, and in one room two British soldiers were blowing anti-louse powder on to the women as they came out. The lorries were standing outside, and I waited to see off this last batch of women.

They came out of the bathhouse, and as soon as the flap of the first lorry was lowered they rushed for it and pushed and scrambled their way inside. Some of the stronger women elbowed the others aside. Others dropped their bundles or got them twisted up in the throng. There was a continuous babel of cries, appeals, remonstrances. I tried to make each woman show her identity card, but after a minute or two was myself pressed against the back of the lorry and pinned there, while women climbed up round me and levered themselves up by pressing on my shoulders. This was one of the legacies of the Germans: the stampede behaviour of the concentration camps. These people had become so conditioned to the terrible struggle for survival that they still reacted to a situation as in the days of the SS . . . only by fighting one's way to a transport could one stay with one's sister or friend.

Eventually Sington intervened and extracted from the throng an obviously sick woman who was 'swaying helplessly backwards and forwards as the crowd milled around her', and drove her and her children to the new camp in his jeep. She was the wife of a Belgian Jewish shopkeeper who had been 'sent to Poland'. He last saw her lying on a heap of straw-filled paliasses, 'waiting her turn to go with her children to one of the rooms'.

Six hundred 'healthy' women were evacuated from Camp 1 on 24 April, and a further 600 the following day. Thereafter the daily tally rose to a thousand and by 28 April all 'West-bound and Czech women' were out of Camp 1. To make room for them, the first healthy personnel also began to leave Camp 2 – as they had not been exposed to typhus, they were allowed to go home. On 25 April, a joyful group of Frenchmen clambered on to trucks, playing an accordion and trumpet picked up from somewhere and singing the 'Marseillaise', to which British soldiers danced.[21]

Given what was at stake, it was asking a lot of those who were not in the favoured categories patiently to wait their turn. Eventually what the British had feared happened: there was a stampede to try to get on to the ongoing lorries. 'Curiously enough,' Sington wrote, 'it took the form of a surging throng trying to force a way into the registration hut. They uprooted the posts supporting the wire fence surrounding the canteen, and formed a solid mass inside the hut before any British officer could reach the spot. On the following days twenty soldiers had to stand guard round the registration point. One could not blame these people for this panic attempt to force a way out of the pestilence-ridden camp.'[22]

As always in Belsen there were exceptions and people who made themselves exceptional. Zdenka Fantlova was such a person. She had one great advantage, having learned English in 1939. After being expelled from her school following the German takeover of Czechoslovakia, she had insisted on going to Prague specially to learn the language. Zdenka was twenty-three in 1945, the daughter of a Czech-speaking industrialist from Rokcany, near Plzen. Her family was 'of Jewish origin' but did not strictly observe the Jewish religion and spoke Czech at home. Her father – 'a real Czech-minded patriot' – was arrested for listening to BBC broadcasts in October 1940, and carted off to Buchenwald. Zdenka, her mother and sister were then sent in January 1942 to Theresienstadt, where she worked in the kitchens and took a minor part in the theatrical activities of the camp. In October 1944 the three of them, along with the Theresienstadt artists, were drafted for a transport bound for Auschwitz – though she didn't know of it at the time; and, on arrival there, she was separated from her mother by Dr Mengele. She was marched off to be shaved, given an odd set of clothes, and, soon afterwards, was one of a group of women sent east-wards to 'build fortifications against the Russians – trenches'. Later they worked in a forest, carrying huge tree trunks to a sawmill.

On 21 January 1945, these women started to march westwards. 'We learned that you could walk and sleep at the same time,' Zdenka said later. After crossing the River Oder on a raft, some of them were allowed to stay – and were liberated by the Russians a day later. The rest, Zdenka included, reached Gross-Rosen camp, south-east of Berlin, where they were put on coal trucks. After a long journey, via Weimar, Mauthausen in Austria, and a brief glimpse of her home town in Czechoslovakia from a train, Zdenka arrived at Belsen in February 1945.

Zdenka caught typhus in Belsen and her sister died there. Interviewed in 1985, aged sixty-three, she was very critical of the British. 'There was really no immediate evidence that the English army has arrived, at least for us,' she said. 'When they came they had to take it systematically . . . everybody needed help then, on the spot, but it was impossible. If they had to do a work of rescue they had to have some system, I can imagine. From the beginning: this line, that line, the one after. It just couldn't be done all at once. So a fortnight passed till the end of April where I don't remember any big improvement'.

She recalled that along the way she had acquired a 'survival kit' – 'some inner force tells you exactly what to do and what not to do'. Acting on this instinct, she decided one day in Belsen that, although still unwell, she had to get out. She crawled into a 'hut with the red cross in it' and was found there the next day by an English officer who demanded to know what she was doing there and sternly told her she must go back and wait her turn. But she managed to recall enough English to appeal to him. 'How would you feel if a member of your family was involved?' she remembers asking him. In the end he softened and allowed her to stay in the hut overnight. The next day he came back with an ambulance car and a stretcher and blanket. He ripped off her 'memorable costume' – the motley collection of garments she had worn for the last two years – wrapped her in the sheet, strapped her in the stretcher and put her in the car.

> I remember when the car started to move I looked back, sort of found enough strength to turn back and through the slit of the back door I saw Belsen retreating and changing to the past, and I thought, 'After this, nothing but nothing can ever happen to me.'[23]

Zdenka got out, but thousands of others remained stuck in Camp 1, waiting to be evacuated. On the evening of 25 April, a British Army cameraman recorded the scene there. Outside the

Bergen-Belsen.
Part of the main camp from one of the watchtowers ten days after the British arrival.
On the right, the road through the camp; on the left, the cookhouses and blocks of
the large women's camp.

Two blindfolded German officers are led through British lines after negotiating a truce around the area of Belsen camp. 12 April 1945.

Josef Kramer, the commandant of Belsen, paraded in irons before being removed to the POW cage at Celle. 17 April 1945.

Lt. Col. James Johnston (left), the British Army doctor in charge at Belsen, with the inmate doctors Hadassah Bimko and Ruth Gutman and Captain 'Frosty' Winterbottom, on the day of his arrival, 17 April 1945.
(*Below left*) Luba Tryszynska, the 'Angel of Belsen', and some of the Dutch children she helped, pose for Army cameramen after being evacuated to Camp 2. 26 April 1945.(*Below right*) Brigadier H.L. Glyn Hughes, who masterminded the Belsen relief effort.

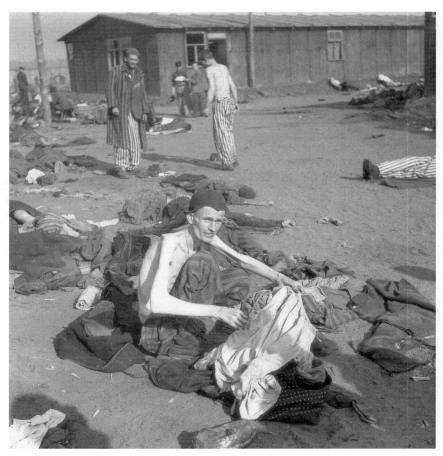

A survivor picking over clothing, Camp 1. 17 April 1945.

'They were so slow': the squalor in the 'typhus hospital' at Belsen, eleven days after the arrival of the British. 26 April 1945.

Inmates prepare a meal, oblivious of the corpses behind them. 17 April 1945.

The overcrowded interior of one of the women's huts, 17 April 1945. Cameramen did not record the worst conditions.

British soldiers supervise the distribution of food outside a cookhouse, Camp 1. 21 April 1945.

The clear-up begins. A bulldozer pushes bodies into a mass grave, 19 April 1945.

British Tommies force German soldiers to remove bodies of the dead in Camp 1.

The evacuation of the sick from Camp 1 finally begins. A woman, wrapped in a blanket, is carried out of one of the huts. 22 April 1945.

24 April 1945. Recently arrived women prisoners collect freshly baked bread from a cookhouse. Despite their cheerfulness, there were many complaints about the bread.

huts, there was still a scum of filth and dirt and the air was thick with smoke from cooking fires. 'Most of the inmates just wander about aimlessly,' he noted. 'Others settle down to the job of lice picking while others prefer to sleep.'

Wandering over to the wire, he found a group of inmates picking through swill bins full of potato peelings brought out of the main cookhouse for 'likely morsels to serve as a later meal'.

This is an absolutely incredible sight. But though feeding is Priority One on the list, care has been exercised not to over-feed. At the same time most of these Zombies (as they are called by the camp staff) have not eaten for such a long time that no matter how much they get they still want more. They have sunk to such a state of degradation that anything does for food. There they are, men and women, acting like pigs – the result of years of merciless treatment, mental and physical, for the MASTER RACE.[24]

By 2 May, after some two weeks, the British had started to make a real difference at Belsen, but much still remained to be done. 'The death rate in this camp is still extremely high and starvation is the main cause,' Colonel Johnston wrote that day. 'The failure lies in the distribution of food. Fit internees are interested only in their own feeding and will make no attempt to feed the thousands who are prostrated from weakness or disease. The result therefore is that the fit get the rations of the unfit, in addition to their own, and diarrhoea ensues; the unfit die of starvation.' Then he noted that 100 British medical students had arrived and were to be 'employed in the feeding of the unfit'.[25]

8

'Would We Mind?'

AT THE BEGINNING of April a notice had gone up at the London medical schools asking for volunteers to go and work with starved children in Holland, using a new and experimental technique – 'it would be our job to go into a town and give them protein hydrolysate-glucose-vitamin fluid by stomach tube'. Many of the students felt guilty at not having fought and saw this as a last chance to do something in the war. There was a rush to volunteer and soon ninety-six candidates had been accepted, vaccinated against typhus and other diseases and issued with battledress uniforms – which they were told to wear at all times. As the weeks passed and no summons came, the students became rather disgruntled.[1]

On 28 April, they were suddenly told to report to Red Cross headquarters. 'We were in a hall in London, waiting to go to Holland,' Roger Dixey later recalled. 'Lady Falmouth, the Queen Bee of the Red Cross, came in and said that a concentration camp had been disclosed by the Army and would we mind being diverted from Dutch children to a concentration camp. And we said, "No of course, we don't mind" – and went to Belsen instead.' The camp had been liberated for ten days, Michael Hargrave recorded, and 'all that they had succeeded in doing was to separate the living from the dead . . . We were all so excited about going, after a month of waiting, that we did not think much about the change of destination.'[2]

The same day they caught a train from Paddington to Cirencester, and then spent three frustrating days in a transit camp waiting for the bleak late spring weather to ease enough to permit flying; although several aircraft took off, none crossed the Channel before being turned back. Several of the students hitchhiked into the local towns, to drink beer and dance with the girls; one visited friends; others sat morosely in the camp. Finally, on 2 May, the six Dakotas took off and dropped them at Celle in north Germany. Most had never flown before. After more delays and drama they finally arrived at their base – the Panzer Barracks at Belsen. The next morning they saw the camp proper for the first time.[3]

Most of the students had some advance idea of what a concentration camp was. Belsen had been all over the papers; they had been warned that they were going to somewhere foul and horrible. But nothing could prepare them for the reality of what they saw – more than two weeks after the liberation there were still dying people everywhere, still women defecating in the open. The overpowering impression, Roger Dixey later recalled, was of 'powdery dust, an all-pervading smell, total desolation and a very large number of dead bodies just lying about, being bulldozed'. But 'it wasn't as totally horrifying as you might reasonably expect it to be. It was on such a huge scale it was rather like trying to count the stars. There were thousands and thousands of dead people and you couldn't really relate to them as people.'[4]

Besides, there wasn't time to take it all in. The students were each given a hut to work in (some singly and some in pairs) and told to get on with it. 'We had a great deal of work to do and there is nothing like hard work to take your mind off the appallingness of what you are doing . . . if you've got to do it,' said Peter Horsey. 'So it was no good sitting back and saying "This is awful". One had to roll up one's sleeves and get on with it.'[5]

No one forgot the moment of first entering 'their' hut. 'We walked in, held our nose, walked round, walked out again, looked at each other and said "Where do we start?"' Ian Proctor remembered. 'It was full of the most emaciated people I have ever seen in my life. There was supposed to be a loo at the far end but they couldn't get up to go to it. It was almost up to the top of one's boots in excreta. One just stumped about in it. People by now were too weak to use the lavatory and were just lying there in their own faeces and urine which dripped down from one bunk to the next – quite appalling.' Writing in 1945, Alan MacAuslan caught more precise details:

> We took a look round – there was faeces all over the floor – the majority of people having diarrhoea. I was standing aghast in the midst of all this filth trying to get used to the smell which was a mixture of post-mortem room, a sewer, sweat, and foul pus, when I heard a scrabbling on the floor. I looked down in the half light and saw a woman crouching at my feet. She had black matted hair, well populated and her ribs stood out as though there were nothing between them, her arms were so thin that they were horrible. She was defecating, but she was so weak that she could not lift her buttocks from the floor and, as she had diarrhoea, the liquid yellow stools bubbled over her thighs.

Just as distressing was the mental state of the patients. 'In the beginning they all used to cry "Herr Doktor, bitte schön. Herr Doktor, Herr Doktor" and they would clutch at our sleeves as we went by,' MacAuslan wrote. 'Even after we had passed, they would cry for us to come back again, so that they could tell us their pitiful tale over and over again! "My mother and father were burnt alive in Auschwitz." "Will I ever be beautiful again, Herr Doktor"? "My husband was flogged to death by the SS".' It probably helped to have David Bradford's stolid temperament. 'The first day was spent having a look round the hut, teaching the fit people to look after the sick people, and seeing that the food reached everybody', his diary for 3 May records.[6]

The huts varied enormously in the number of inmates they housed: one had 200 women, another had 1045. Some contained Polish and Russian women; some Western European men. The Jewishness of most of their women patients seems to have escaped the students. Typical products of their education system, few spoke their patients' language; but some sort of communication was usually possible, via a hut inmate who spoke English or French, often an educated Polish Jew. For the more lumpen English students 'the language barrier was complete' and the suspicion of foreigners unbroken; whereas the better travelled and more adventurous tried to see beyond present squalors to the world their patients had once inhabited. One of the few Jewish students was almost unique in trying to compile 'some sort of record of the individual'.[7]

The students went about their work in very different ways, depending on their temperaments. Some found a hut and stuck with it; others moved around constantly. One group of ten quickly decided that it was hopeless trying to work in the existing huts and volunteered to work on a plan devised by Captain Gluck, the British Army doctor who had finally been sent into Camp 1 on 30 April. His idea (similar to Rabbi Hardman's) was to convert some of the now empty huts in Camp 1 into a special hospital area where the 'most seriously sick could be cared for under hospital conditions pending removal'. Gluck – who was Czech-born and Jewish, and described by students as 'a veritable firebrand who . . . worked miracles', 'he gets everything done and doesn't mind cursing people to make them do it' – supervised the disinfection, scrubbing and creosoting of three huts. Meanwhile, patients were extracted from the dirty huts, processed through local versions of the 'human laundry', and put to bed in the 'hospitals'. Within two weeks 1200 patients had been 'washed, disinfected, reclothed and returned to the renovated huts'.[8]

By contrast, Peter Horsey stayed where he was. He found himself in a hut run by four remarkable Polish women, all medical graduates of Warsaw University, who 'in spite of years of living in the most appalling filth, discomfort and brutality had lost none of their self-respect'. When the British arrived they were still making sure that the dead from their hut were properly buried. Horsey was humbled by them – 'morally they were of a tougher fibre than I had ever met before' – and happy to let them do most of the medicine in the hut. He spent hours talking to them, a subject which caused them a great deal of amusement being the educational system in England. Horsey found that 'to explain the status of "Public Schools" and to point out that in spite of their name they catered for a fraction of 1% of the population was beyond me'. The Polish girls were also 'amused to hear that women students were not admitted to St Thomas's Hospital'.[9]

The students practised the most rudimentary medicine. After a solid breakfast at the Panzer Barracks, they got to the camp at about 8.30 and collected their Hungarian labour. 'The Hungarians were, to say the least, a curious bunch,' two medical students wrote.

They would appear every morning at about eight, some in ragged uniforms, others with no distinguishing marks save an inability to speak any language but their own. On one's arrival one would advance towards them, hold up two fingers and shout 'Hungarische' or 'Hungar' or just 'George', at which two would run up, relieve one of any burden, even if it was only a note-book, and then follow one around for the rest of the day . . . the business of explaining the day's work to them took quite a while as it had to be done through the medium of signs, assisted by half-a-dozen interpreters who spoke everything except English. Often they could not understand or were wilfully dull, but an appropriate threatening sign was usually enough to start them off.

In fact the Hungarians were indispensable. 'Without their help to do all the slave work, we could have done practically nothing,' Roger Dixey recalled. They 'really are very efficient . . . and don't complain at all as far as I can tell,' Alex Paton wrote in his diary.[10]

Then they went into the hut. The first job was to remove the overnight dead – no easy matter when the living and the dead were intertwined and often interchangeable. 'One of the greatest problems was having to decide who was dead and who was not,' one student recalled. Sometimes, too, there were terrible wrenching scenes when the living refused to be parted from the corpse of a relative or friend. But it had to be done, and once the dead had been removed by Hungarian orderlies and put outside the hut, ready to be collected and taken away by German orderlies, the next stage was reached. 'Having got rid of the dead, you then, so to speak, made a ward round,' said Roger Dixey

The students could diagnose the inmates' illnesses – starvation, diarrhoea, famine odema, tuberculosis – but not really treat them. 'Medically, there was little we could do during the first fortnight because the few drugs available were limited in supply and nursing help was non-existent. To explain to a Pole who speaks a little French how to give a course of sulphonamides to a Russian with erysipelas [fever] is no easy matter,' a student wrote in 1945. 'Medical treatment is pretty well impossible,' David Bradford noted in his diary. 'What could you do? You gave out a pill here and there,' said Roger Dixey, 'either one aspirin or one opium tablet to each. We did no good medically. Let's hope we did something about showing them somebody *minded*.' The complete absence of proper medical equipment forced them into desperate measures. Michael Hargrave 'opened a breast abscess with a razor blade heated in a flame and then cooled in alcohol', but he had no anaesthetic or painkiller to give his patient, not even morphine.[11]

The students' primary task, however, was to feed the patients; starvation was still the biggest killer and Johnston wanted them to make sure everyone in the huts of Camp 1 got something to eat. It wasn't easy. 'Trying to get food' was a 'superhuman task', Alex Paton's diary records. The inmates of Camp 1 were still being catered for by the original five cookhouses, each containing some six to twelve steam cookers capable of holding 300 litres.

There Royal Artillery officers tried to supervise an 'assortment of Poles, Russians, Dutch, French, etc who had been co-opted as assistants'.

While British records for this period talk about the nutritional seminars and 'diet scales' being devised in Camp 2, the students' diaries show that the meals actually served up in Camp 1 mostly consisted of greasy soup containing meat and vegetables and black bread, which was 'almost universally rejected by the sick as being too rich and causing vomiting' and felt to be inadequate by those in better health. The difficulty, one student saw, was that many of the internees needed a square meal and building up on a high, full diet, and many others needed salvation treatment with small, bland and frequent feeds. The simplest answer would have been to segregate the two types and cook for each accordingly, but, that being administratively impossible, an attempt was being made to strike a balance. And minor improvements did slowly come. The soup was 'reconsidered and made far less rich', biscuits became available to replace the black bread and luxury goods such as jam began to appear.

Improving the food was one thing; making sure it reached everyone was quite another. So far, the British had simply brought meals to the door of the hut and left their distribution to the block leaders, with consequences that were plain to see. When student Ian Proctor first entered his hut, his eyes travelled across the skeletal bodies of the inmates and finally came to rest on the 'extremely well covered' frame of the block leader, sitting at a table 'eating the rations provided by the British Army'. A couple of days later, when Proctor had begun to undermine this man's authority, he simply disappeared. After that, distributing food was easier. Two other students 'endeavoured to provide a fair distribution first by polite request, which got us nowhere'. So they stood over each container as it arrived and made the healthy drag it right round the hut under supervision. 'We were unable to turn our backs on any food distribution for nearly a fortnight, after which time we were rewarded by a little response.'[12]

It was a rude awakening. 'One quickly learned about human nature,' student Mark Raymond later recalled. 'When the fit discovered that the bunk-ridden had food brought to them, they all became bunk-ridden . . . After all, they were survivors.' Such understanding of what the inmates had been through and how their time in the camps had conditioned their behaviour was rare. Probably more typical was Eric Trimmer's response. 'Almost overnight we had to move from the schoolboy values of what was right and what was proper that one had at that time to this new position, realizing for the first time that there is evil in mankind' – in the inmates, that is. 'From carefree, humorous, rather cavalier medical students, we changed within a few days to people who were mature and . . . profoundly overwhelmed and upset by what we were involved in.' Trimmer was put in charge of 'an enormous store of goodies donated by the British Army and by people locally . . . chocolates and tins of food and eggs', which was locked in a shed with a door made of bars. One night 'one poor inmate squeezed his way into this store of goodies' and ate so much that he swelled up and couldn't get out again. Trimmer discovered him there the following morning, 'looking very sick and sorry for himself'. To his astonishment, the army insisted on court-martialling the man.[13]

Many of the people in the huts were, however, much too far gone to take ordinary food; but there were now hopes that they could be helped by new experimental nutritional techniques being sent from Britain.

Inevitably, the British were influenced by their own experience and research. The effects of starvation had long been one of the concerns of British colonial medicine and official policy had evolved from the supine *laissez-faire* detachment which allowed millions to die in the Irish Famine of 1845 to 1848 to the elaborate preventive public-health measures which became the norm in late-Victorian India. By the turn of the century, it seemed that famine had been conquered. Then things went wrong: in

1943, some three million people died in the Indian province of Bengal.[14]

Whether it was simply caused by the failure of the 1943 rice crop and wartime disruption of imports from Japanese-controlled Burma; or (as Nobel Laureate Amartya Sen has argued) by failures in distribution and market distortions, the Bengal Famine was one of the darkest chapters of British rule in India. The only people who came well out of this episode were the Army, which dealt efficiently with the problem of bringing relief to the stricken countryside, and a group of medical researchers in Calcutta who came up with simple recipes for feeding the emaciated people dying in the city's streets. Those who could still swallow were given a cheap dietary supplement known as the Bengal Famine Mixture; those too moribund to take fluid were injected with predigested protein hydrolysates, more familiarly known as amino acids.[15]

The doctors in Calcutta were drawing on two decades of medical research into the effects of prolonged starvation and illness on the body's systems. Experiments in the 1920s had shown that fasting slowed the metabolic functions of the body and gradually destroyed the cells of the small intestine, reducing its capacity to absorb nutrients until food 'acted merely as an irritant, causing diarrhoea and dehydration'. Some alternative way of restoring the body's systems was therefore needed, and by the 1940s the idea of giving proteins by injection or nasal drip was being tried. The injecting technique seemed to have a miraculous effect on the Bengal Famine victims and, in a paper published in April 1944, three Indian researchers claimed 'results were very encouraging' and produced 'marked and rapid improvement' in most cases.[16]

Although this work was later played down, it undoubtedly raised high hopes; immediate steps were taken to apply it in north-western Europe. The Consultant Physician to General Montgomery's 21 Army Group announced, in a circular to military doctors in early April 1945, that 'the Bengal Famine, in conjunction with much experimental work on proteins ha[d] opened up a new field of treatment, and the results [we]re sufficiently encouraging to warrant wide application'. Meanwhile, in London, the Medical Research Council also took the lead. When the Dutch government appealed in March for help for the starving population of northern Holland, the Council persuaded British drug manufacturers hastily to produce enough protein hydrolysate for 60,000 people and recruited the 100 London medical students to test the technique in Holland. Then, at very short notice, the War Office sent a small team of medical researchers, led by two formidable and well-connected women, Dr Janet Vaughan and Dr Rosalind Pitt-Rivers, to Brussels to test out hydrolysates on returning British prisoners of war. When they were unable to find many POWs, this team was sent instead to Belsen – to join the medical students who had already been diverted there.[17]

The students brought with them on the plane large amounts of a glucose-vitamin mixture. Mixed with lemon juice, it proved popular with the patients. A couple of days later, the experimental foods arrived and trials began in the huts. On 4 May, Peter Horsey spent 'a solid hour' doling out 80 litres of the Bengal Famine Mixture – a thick gruel made of sugar, dried milk, flour, salt and water' a litre of which was supposed to provide enough nutrition for a man for a day. 'Everybody who was too weak to walk got some,' he recorded proudly.

But the verdict was negative: 'After one or two days,' wrote Roger Dixey, 'it . . . was rejected on the grounds that it was far too sweet and caused diarrhoea.' 'I can't understand it, Padre,' the UNRRA nutritionist, Dr Meiklejohn, complained to Leslie Hardman. 'This preparation has saved thousands of lives, but people here simply reject it.' Hardman explained that, coming from Eastern Europe, the Belsen inmates were used to highly seasoned food and found the Mixture – designed for sugary Bengali taste buds – revoltingly sweet. Peter Horsey had a heated argument with a Red Cross officer in charge of one of the cook-houses 'who said that the internees "are too bloody particular" and takes the view that if they don't like the Bengal Mixture tasting like saccharine, they can't be hungry'. Efforts were then made to adapt it to the Belsen palate, with partial success; some of the students persevered with it, most did not. Milk puddings were found to work better.[18]

Next it was the turn of the protein hydrolysates. 'Started a few people today on experimental protein,' Humphrey Kidd wrote on 6 May. 'Flavoured it with Bovril and forced it down their throats.' If the Mixture was only a partial success, the hydrolysates were a complete failure. For one thing, it was soon clear that any technique involving injection or nasal tubes was out of the question with these patients because the Germans had injected dying Belsen inmates with petrol in order to make them burn better in the crematorium. The moment a British doctor produced a needle there would be a 'piteous wail' of 'nix crematorium' and violent physical resistance: 'They thought they were going to be done to death.' For similar reasons, the use of nasal tubes for feeding was equally unwelcome. And patients refused to take it by mouth. 'It smelt like vomit and undoubtedly tasted unpleasant.' 'It really is foul,' was Peter Horsey's verdict, after sampling some himself. Even when the doctors did manage to administer hydrolysates, they frequently had no effect at all, or killed the patient off.[19]

The failure of the new technique was a particular blow to the leader of the Medical Research Council team. Although Janet Vaughan belonged, both as a socialist and as a doctor, to a medical generation much concerned with the relationship between disease and malnutrition, her primary expertise was in blood disorders rather than nutrition. But she was a grand and rather formidable person – the daughter of the Headmaster of Rugby School; the pupil at Oxford of the famous physicist J. B. S. Haldane and the celebrated physiologist Charles Sherrington; a woman working in a male-dominated field. For all these reasons, she did not like to fail. But the evidence was clear. 'On the few patients we got to take them by mouth the results were bad,' Janet Vaughan wrote to an American friend. 'Things can be planned in London, but reality is something very very different,' she continued. 'Practising science in hell itself is a queer experience.' In a talk at Belsen, Janet Vaughan frankly conceded that the hydrolysates had not worked. Frequent small amounts of food by mouth was the best treatment.[20]

That was it – as far as the medical students were concerned. Several poured their supply of hydrolysates away; others refused to make more. Yet the authorities persisted. 'They are doing yet another trial of protein-hydrolysate,' Alex Paton wrote on 23 May. 'I watched the horror and loathing of the patients who had to drink two cup-fulls of the stuff – triple strength. We also had to put one or two nasal tubes down – another thing they don't like.' The following day, 'we did another round of tortures. This I think is the last day – and left as soon as possible.'[21]

There are three possible reasons why the British persisted with the hydrolysates long after it had become obvious that they did not work. Army doctors are not in the habit of changing procedures for themselves and there may have been a reluctance quickly to reject the Indian evidence. The Medical Research Council, having invested much credit in persuading industry hastily to manufacture the materials, may have been unwilling to give up on them too soon. And, finally, elements in the British military may have felt that even though hydrolysates would do nothing to help Belsen patients, their experimental use there might yield evidence which could help to save the life of British prisoners of war also suffering from the effects of starvation, in Japanese camps.[22]

Everyone working at Belsen had to find a way of coping. For some, it involved switching off, detaching yourself; in medical language, dissociating. 'Everyone builds up a sort of mental wall against the gruesome sights,' Eugene Cole, an American Quaker wrote.

There are things here which would sound cruel and inhuman under other circumstances. For instance, when you can't take everyone to the hospital that ought to go you have to take the ones that have a chance of living and leave the ones that are going to die anyway. And you can't be kind and sweet and gentle to every patient you handle because you wouldn't get much done. All standards of privacy and informality are, of course, gone, in the interest of saving lives.

For the army cameramen, it helped to concentrate on the technical problems of filming. 'It was OK as long as you were looking through the lens,' one said later – though this technique didn't work with the great photographer George Rodger who was overcome by shame while taking a picture of a man dying at Belsen (for *Life* magazine). Rodger put his camera away and tried to help. He never photographed war again.[23]

The effect of Belsen on the medical students varied enormously. Interviewed in 1985, Alan MacAuslan doubted whether it affected them much, emotionally. 'It was fascinating from a medical point of view. All doctors are much more interested in disease than people. It's their only method of survival, I suppose . . . It was a great challenge. It's like any struggle . . . the struggle becomes important and the incidental pieces are incidental.' Michael Davys's letters home in 1945 tell a different story. The 'scenes of indescribable horror, filth, squalor and disease' he witnessed would, he felt, 'be vivid memories for the rest of my life'.[24]

Compared to their fellow relief workers, the students were quite pampered: the authorities worked hard to keep them sane, with the UNRRA nutritionist Arnold Meiklejohn, a mild, diplomatic man, acting as their moral tutor. Every evening they returned to the 'quite astonishingly luxurious' Panzer Training School, where the comforts included baths, a bar which grew well stocked, a special nightly rum ration and numerous pep talks and films shown in the lavish cinema. David Bradford managed to see six films in a month and his diary juxtaposes heart-rending details about his patients with banal comments on films seen. (*Greenwich*

Village, with Carmen Miranda, was a 'typical Yank Musical Technicolor Film'.) There were also occasional dances and social events.[25]

The other main defences were tobacco, humour and alcohol. Everyone smoked continuously, trying to suppress the smell, and bad English humour flourished. The journalist Alan Moorehead noticed that a young officer supervising the counting and burial of bodies 'appeared to be in particularly jovial spirits', 'possibly as a form of immunization from the grisly work'. Among themselves, the army cameramen – even Michael Lewis, who was Jewish and profoundly moved by what he saw – made jokes about the corpses. 'Here's a good one,' they would say, pointing to a particularly horrible cadaver. And the British soldiers called the dying inmates – the 'Musselmen' who had ceased almost to be human and had retreated into a private world of starvation – 'zombies'.[26]

Alcohol played a vital role at Belsen, though the only photograph showing visibly drunk people is of a group of American Friends drivers. This is unfair: the men in the small AFS group, which arrived at about the same time as the British medical students, quickly made themselves popular by their cheerfulness, adaptability and level-headedness. They had driven ambulances through the war in France and Italy and, though Belsen shocked them deeply, they took it in their stride.[27]

Social life in Belsen moved up a gear on 8 May 1945 when news came that Germany had surrendered and the war in Europe was over. The British responded with jubilation and celebrations, the medical students celebrated by 'drinking all they could lay their hands on and letting off any firearms or explosives available', but most inmates greeted the news with profound apathy. Their war was far from over.[28]

Survivors' accounts seldom refer to the phase immediately after the liberation; it is forgotten or ignored. But the students' diaries all describe a narrative arc. At first, early in May, their work seems quite fruitless; the death rate continues to run at about

500–600 a day. Then there comes a moment, roughly ten days after their arrival – about the middle of May 1945 – when things suddenly improve. The death rate starts to fall and then, in some huts, no one dies at all. 'Nobody died today!' David Bradford's diary for 12 May 1945 reads. A note of optimism enters; students and patients have a new rapport. 'The hut was cleaner and the patients sang to us,' wrote Alan MacAuslan, adding, 'The only grim thing was an old woman, who sat about a hundred yards away and howled her head off, because all her lower jaw and the floor of her mouth was gangrenous and falling to pieces – we had no morphia.'[29]

By now, many of the huts had been turned into hospitals. MacAuslan was 'very conceited' about his, and 'very happy because we no longer had faeces all over our boots when we got back to the mess at night, and we could get near our patients without having to do acrobatics amongst the bunks'. The improved conditions also seemed to raise inmates' morale. Alex Paton brought a radio into the hut and 'caught one of the young girls who has tuberculosis trying to dance in her bed to the music'.

The more reflective students detected another change. 'Perhaps the most striking and worthwhile result that we achieved,' Gerald Raperport believed, 'was the change in the people's outlook. Apathy had gone from them. They no longer stared and grimaced in terror when approached by a man in uniform. They thanked us now for what we did for them and were anxious to talk to us and hear news of the outside world. Their sense of shame and decency had come back. Hope was rekindled within them.' He was exaggerating, but for understandable reasons.[30]

By the middle of May, the medical students were beginning to be redeployed, away from the remaining huts of the 'Horror Camp' to the hospital established a mile up the road in the Panzer Training School.

We now need to go back in chronology by three weeks and see what had been happening there.

9

The Hospital: Camp 2, 21 April–21 May 1945

ON 21 APRIL, after days of frustrating delays, the process of evacuating the sick to the Panzer Training School had finally begun. 'Today our Casualty Clearing Station began to receive some of these patients – all women,' Private Emmanuel (Manny) Fisher wrote that day. Over the previous days, his unit had hastily created the first hospital unit in the army barracks at the Panzer Training School, clearing a number of houses in the middle squares and placing army beds or straw mattresses in every available space.

The patients arrived, after passing through the 'human laundry' borne on stretchers by Hungarian soldiers, and 'were literally bundled into bed, for most of them were, or at least appeared to be, just nondescript bundles wrapped in three blankets'.

I helped to carry some of them in. They weighed three to five stone – less than my brother aged nine. Acting as interpreter – I had to talk to some of them. One Jewish woman, aged about 45, as far as I could guess by her conversation (it was otherwise difficult), said, as soon as she was put in bed, 'Please, I want to go to America. How long I have waited for this moment. They shot my husband and two sons in front of me.' Another said 'Must I die? I am only seventeen.' Another spoke to me in English. She was quite insane.[1]

Manny gave each of them a warm drink – one woman took a full minute to bring her arm out of the blanket and grip the cup.

I simply could not look at these human wrecks for more than a few seconds. I found my eyes filling with tears, and had to turn away from my soldier-comrades. These women were not easily distinguishable – the same formula applied to them all, from the neck downwards – just human skeletons. I hope none of them look at a mirror for the next month, at least. To see themselves would certainly treble their grief. Some of them are beyond human aid and will soon die. But they are happy and look forward to living again even though they might know it is only for a short while.[2]

Manny Fisher was twenty-five, an East End boy, one of eight sons of a Russian-born cabinet maker who had helped to found London's first Jewish Male Voice Choir; Manny had been a soloist in the synagogue and a boy actor in the Yiddish Theatre. When the war interrupted his training as a teacher, he volunteered for the cavalry – he was a keen filmgoer; but to his disgust, was posted instead to the Medical Corps. He learned later that the authorities had identified a particular shortage of radiographers and were looking for intelligent recruits capable of absorbing complex information quickly; they had seen from his records that he was bright. Manny was given a crash course, collapsing two years' worth of anatomy, photography, electricity and chemistry into four weeks, and landed in Normandy with 32 Casualty Clearing Station on D-Day + 2. He began assisting in the operating theatre immediately.[3]

But that experience hardly equipped him for what he was now

required to do at Belsen. By 22 April, Manny was in charge of a hospital holding 150 patients, in one of the many blocks of the barracks. Every day, roughly 500 more sick inmates (all women) were brought out of the 'Horror Camp' via the delousing centre and installed in another square, Colonel Johnston's plan being for British doctors and nurses to supervise the new facility and then move on, leaving it to be run by one internee doctor and eight internee nurses.[4]

It wasn't quite that easy, however. For all its ritualistic properties, the 'human laundry' did not transform the patients; even after being washed, cleansed and reclothed, 80 per cent of them still had diarrhoea, to say nothing of typhus or TB. Coping with them in an ill-equipped, hastily improvised 'ward' with no laundry service and only intermittent hot water was not easy. 'These people had because of starvation, illness, weakness, apathy, and the lack of sanitation in Camp 1 become used to defecating and urinating where they lay, possibly a few yards off if they could get so far,' one Red Cross sister observed. 'They could not grasp that some one would come if they called.' There was a chronic shortage of bedpans, perhaps twelve per block – and they had to double as feeding tins. Internee nurses often preferred arranging flowers on tables to emptying bedpans.[5]

The diaries of the British nurses and orderlies record their struggles to keep some sort of order. Coming in one morning, Manny Fisher found that one of the two night nurses had slept all night.

Dirty, smelly buckets, blankets and bed-pans were littered all over the building. Even parts of the floor were covered with faeces. There had been no electricity throughout the night, no coffee had been forthcoming from the canteen at 6 am. None of the patients had been washed. Nothing but chaos reigned . . . After my lunch, always a hurried affair, I came back to find my only efficient nurse weeping. She couldn't carry on, she said. The men had rioted during my

absence – had run about, naked, searching for food. They
had entered the doctor's room and stolen some biscuits I
had given him. They had even snatched a large, quite meat-
less bone . . . In the neighbouring house, four men had lain
stark naked since midday, on the concrete floor, under the
table used for serving meals, waiting for the next meal to
appear.[6]

There were the usual problems with food. Manny Fisher's
efforts to explain to a male ward that a 'plateful of hot, thin soup
and half a slice of sour, brown German bread' was an essential
part of their medical treatment got him nowhere.

Those men began first to murmur then beg, then complain,
then become hysterical and even cry. 'Let us go back to the
camp. We were getting food there!! Do you call this food?
Give us some clothes – We will make our own way.' How
could they be expected to understand . . . The tea meal (tea
plus a slice of bread and butter) and supper (6 pm) – more
thin soup and bread, satisfied them no more than had the
midday meal. They began to rave. Unfortunately – these
patients had not been sorted (there was no time for that, I
presume) – thus quite a number who were relatively fit had
been included. In the evening I gladdened 100 hearts by
giving out some cigarettes.[7]

With 500 new patients arriving from Camp 1 every day, the
eight doctors and eight nurses of 32 Casualty Clearing Station
who were supervising the 'hospital' were soon overwhelmed; it
became necessary to press into service the forty-eight Red Cross
volunteers who had recently arrived at Belsen. Jean McFarlane's
turn came on 26 April. 'An excellent driver, a good linguist, a
capable secretary, and a sweet soprano, . . . who simply hated
nursing', she donned the dungarees, army boots, gaiters and trian-
gular headsquare, which was the nursing outfit improvised to give

the maximum protection from the virulent attacks of lice and set
off to run a block.

This was certainly a shock to me as I hadn't the vaguest
idea what to do in a Hospital . . . On coming to slightly
it seemed I'd better locate the Staff, the Orderly and the
Oberschwester in particular – that was moderately easy
and I discovered that she spoke French, and that one girl
spoke English which simplified matters a little. Next I
decided I'd better have a look at the Wards and patients
and see what needed doing as I was there merely in a
supervisory capacity. The state of the Wards was dreadful,
very dirty and literally stinking – easy to understand with
overflowing BPs, insufficient in number and closed
windows. The patients themselves were pathetic, some just
lying there so still that they appeared to be dead except
for a very slight movement as they breathed. Others
behaved like animals and clamoured for food, and that
was almost worse than anything. On opening the door of
the second Ward, I only just avoided falling over a body
on the floor – there was no doubt that it was lifeless –
there was certainly no MO to call on, so I went quickly
for the Orderly who produced a stretcher and removed it
to the basement. Presumably I looked odd since he said
'Don't worry, sister.' I wasn't exactly worrying, but it
wasn't very nice. Anyway there was too much to do to
think for long – laundry to cope with – the dirty to be
removed, the clean indented for, other indents for various
essentials to be attended to and above all some kind of
routine to be established. One hundred and forty-two
patients had to eat or be fed if they were too weak to
manage for themselves, and the astonishing thing there
was to see how some of the sickest of them were able to
stretch out a skinny arm and get a heavy beaker to their
lips. Food was not plentiful, and they could not take

much, but the clamour and the waving arms when food arrived was horrible – they were so afraid of being left out, or of not getting as much as the one in the next bed. A very natural reaction after their Camp treatment no doubt.[8]

She then had to sort out an industrial dispute when the Hungarian soldiers, fearful of getting typhus against which they had not been immunised, refused to wash the floor. 'Eventually the Wards were cleaned (after a fashion) by the Hungarians, but their ideas on scrubbing correspond with those of other continentals, i.e. a bucket of water swished down the room, soaking everything, followed by a broom passed lightly over the surface which is left to dry if it will.'

By the following day, though, Jean had more or less got the measure of it – 'more brutal driving of half-fit Staff to empty over-flowing BPs, and to induce them to stop cleaning windows and attend to patients. It astonished me that they always did what I asked, seemingly taking it for granted that I knew what was what – that must have been the result of Nazi rule and just having to do what they were told.'[9]

But having to use half-trained British volunteers was not the real problem. Colonel Johnston's plan envisaged that the actual medical care of the sick would be done by the 150-odd doctors or nurses among their fellow prisoners from Camp 1, under the leadership of Dr Bimko. It quickly became obvious, however, that the internee medical staff were not up to this job. 'These people were weak from starvation and practically all had only one interest in life and that was food, and food they got at the expense of the patients,' Johnston reported. 'Consequently they had to be watched over, cajoled and bullied, and I had to get rid of a large number of them.'[10]

Was that judgement fair? Certainly, some of the internee staff – especially the male nurses – spent most of their time looking for food, so that steps had eventually to be taken to prevent them visiting one canteen after another and simply eating one meal after another. Equally, many of the doctors were too frail – 80 per cent were recovering from typhus – or had been too long away from the practice of medicine to be able to be much good. Manny Fisher complained that the Czech doctor in his block was 'so weak and dispirited he could only manage to "visit" fifty patients throughout the morning', while Red Cross nurse Molly Sylva Jones noticed that 'patients would often have to wait three or four days before being seen by a doctor'. Both were accustomed to the briskness of British military medicine. Allegations that 'many gave most of the time to their own country women' were also frequent, while on 27 April a Polish nurse who 'refused food to a Hungarian patient, and when [a] complaint [was] made, slapped patient's face', had to be removed.[11]

Against that, a British Jewish social worker working in the hospital was 'particularly impressed by the large majority of internee doctors'. 'Their pains-taking examination of patients, particularly of those who are frightened for themselves, or of death, and the confidence of the patients in the doctors', was 'quite incredible' to Jane Leverson. 'There are so many patients that I find it difficult to remember that each of them is sick, both physically and mentally, and that each is a person with very real feelings,' she wrote on 6 May. 'There is hardly a doctor who does not treat each patient as though she is of the utmost importance.' Others noticed that, as internee doctors recovered, they became better at the job: Molly Silva Jones was astonished by 'their quick return to more normal standards'; 'to fit them out with decent clothing, to provide the Doctors and Nurses with white coats and overalls and good shoes' helped them to regain their self-respect.[12]

Dr Bimko's memoirs are silent on this issue and most of the internee doctors remain shadowy figures; but a French physician did produce a kind of riposte many years later. Odette Rosenstock was the daughter of a Parisian jeweller – a strong and courageous woman who had organised a support network for the children of Jews deported from the South of France. Betrayed to the Gestapo, she was tortured in Drancy prison and sent to Auschwitz, where she worked as a doctor. She reached Belsen in poor health and was lucky to come through typhus, thanks partly to the bullying of Dr Bimko. Now Odette gradually learned, through friends working for the British as typists and interpreters, that 'we had disappointed our liberators'. The British had expected to find grateful victims, not 'beings come from another world'; when they had to intervene in wild brawls between the inmates, and discovered that no one could be relied on to distribute food and everyone was purely interested in their own personal profit, they had completely lost faith in the prisoners:

> They understood nothing about it; it seemed to them that they were looking after a zoo inhabited by savage beasts, with dominant species and the mass of the dying, an antediluvian zoo where it was as natural to dominate as to die.

She found it impossible, except in a few cases, to talk to the British; the common medical task created no bond. At a birthday party for a British doctor, 'they were all very kind, very welcoming, but I had the impression that they considered themselves representatives of a higher civilisation, come to train and feed the locals, loaded with all the evils of a backward country still unexplored at the end of the world'. For her part, she found their stories 'military drivel' and fled back to her own kind as soon as possible.[13]

It fell to Colonel Johnston to resolve this issue. Considering most internee doctors to be 'useless', he asked for qualified medical personnel to be sent from England, and received instead – Germans: doctors released from prisoner-of-war cages and nurses from the surrounding area. This was not a popular move. A British nurse witnessed the arrival of twelve German nurses from

Hamburg, 'each carrying a small suitcase, they all looked the acme of efficiency in their clean uniforms'.

> As they came in, the patients glanced at them indifferently – then a wave of passionate resentment swept the ward. In a moment, a shrieking mass of internees, among them even the dying, had hurled themselves at the nurses, scratching and tearing at them with knives and forks, or with instruments snatched up from the dressing trolleys. Within second[s] the nurses' clothing had been torn from their backs, and they were bleeding and crying for help. Troops had to be called in to restore order. The nurses were dismissed with instructions to clean themselves up, mend their uniforms (the Red Cross provided needle and thread), and report back for duty immediately they had finished their repairs. For a few hours there was a menacing atmosphere in that ward, but by the next day everything was quiet and the nurses were able to get on with their work unmolested.

'We learned to understand why we are the best hated nation in the world,' a German nurse wrote later that year.[14]

The English nurses too disliked the German women. To Evelyn Bark of the Red Cross, they 'had been picked for their brawn. Every one of them was a typical Brunhilde; with their massive bosoms and broad hips they formed an appalling contrast to the near skeletons they were handling. They showed very little sign of what they were thinking – but they can have had no doubts about the feelings of everyone else.' British men, however, soon came to admire the German nurses. 'All here agree that the hardest working and most energetic body in the whole of Belsen are – the German nurses,' a British soldier wrote in June. 'These girls have done remarkable things and the medical orderlies declare that they put the English sisters to shame.'[15]

The German doctors arrived in Wehrmacht not SS, uniforms, but the psychological effect 'was bad enough on me,' Dr Bimko felt; 'imagine what it was like on the severely ill'. She remembered saying to Colonel Johnston, "'Johnny, I just can't take those people." It took me a whole week to bring myself to work with them; but I had to for the sake of my patients.' The German doctors at first defied British authority by ignoring an order to parade at 7 a.m. on the morning after their arrival, and so enraged the normally mild Johnston that he threatened to hang their senior officer from a nearby tree. They proved more amenable thereafter – arrogant and unrepentant, but professionally competent. 'They strut about the place in a most alarming fashion terrifying all the inhabitants,' a Red Cross nurse wrote. 'However the British Tommy is marvelous in taking them down a peg or two.'[16]

The Germans were drafted into the three hospital squares with male patients, where conditions were worst. 'The internee staffs were cleared out. The result was an improvement,' Johnston wrote on 10 May. 'The policy now is to completely staff the new hospital area with Germans and to replace at least 50% of internees in the original hospital era with Germans as they become available.' [17]

By then the war was over and extra British units were also reaching Belsen. The 163rd Field Ambulance took over the staffing and supervision of the original hospital area and 'considerably lightened our task,' Johnston found. It was now apparent that Field Ambulances were the ideal units for employment in this type of role where 'initiative, drive and improvisation are the essential ingredients.' On 16 May another Casualty Clearing Station occupied the German Military Hospital near to the Panzer Training School, its 650 German patients having been moved to other hospitals to make way for 1600 Belsen inmates; in two days the new hospital was full. Meanwhile, that mighty behemoth for which Glyn Hughes and James Johnston had prayed back in April – a British General Hospital – finally appeared. A 'fully equipped hospital with complete facilities for the diagnosis and treatment of every kind of disease and injury' and 1200 beds, it took thirty lorries three days to transport it; soon another General Hospital was on its way. And, in addition, a team of six Swiss doctors and twelve Swiss sisters arrived on 3 May and, at the end of the month, a group of twenty-nine Vatican sisters from France. By the middle of May, Belsen had become the largest hospital in Europe, housing over 13,000 patients.[18]

This massive injection of resources brought a dramatic change. 'With more staff and sadly fewer patients because of deaths,' a British orderly later recalled, 'proper feeding routines were established enabling increasing nursing care to be given. Filthy bedding was regularly removed and replaced, screens and loo seats provided (but the smell persisted) and after some time some clothing.' The invention of the 'Belsen nightie' and oval aluminium feeding tins with double handles – to be used instead of bedpans – were important breakthroughs.[19]

A crude medical regimen had by now been established. 'The patients fell into two main groups, those whose health had been completely destroyed by the privations through which they had passed, or those who had contracted tuberculosis, and those who had merely been starved and degraded but who immediately responded to treatment, diet and mental liberation.' For those working in the hospital:

> The sight of those who recovered rapidly was one of the most exciting and comforting things that it is possible to imagine. People who had been skeletons, reduced to the last stages of starvation, who had lain half naked in such filth that all feelings of decency had had to be abandoned, now began to come back to life with amazing rapidity. Once the corner was rounded, they put on weight almost hourly, it seemed.[20]

Some survivors recall 'waking up' in the hospital. Anka Fischer was lying stark naked on 'a large 2-storey mountain of dead bodies' when the British entered Belsen. 'I was unconscious at the time,' she wrote in November 1945, 'and cannot remember the event.' Soldiers tried to resuscitate people from the pile – or simply tried to move it – and, when she showed signs of life, she was taken to hospital, and eventually emerged from the coma, still weak and sick with typhus, weighing only 32 kg. She was kept in hospital for nine weeks. Rena Salt remembered coming into the hospital in a bed 'with white linen. That was just heaven. You could stretch out for the first time in months.' Her first meal 'consisted of a quarter of a slice of white bread, topped with a teaspoonful of stewed apples. And the taste is still in my mouth today.'[21]

Even very simple steps helped the patients. 'A lot of the mental suffering was caused by separation of relatives when clearing Camp 1, which of course was inevitable,' a Red Cross nurse noticed, 'and if by devious searching of Blocks, two sisters or a mother and child could be re-united, the joy to the two concerned was worth all the hours spent.' In the early days there was no registration or records, so the nurses had to go to each room in each block and shout the name of the missing person, and 'if by good fortune she was found, get hold of two Hungarians with a stretcher, and carry the one to the other'. Once reunited, relations or friends would sit with the patients and get them what they needed.[22]

By mid-May, a hospital office had been established and efforts to register the patients had begun. The nurses started to make out personal history cards of the deportees which also gave particulars of missing members of their families. 'On one occasion a nurse asked a patient to state her name, nationality and place of origin,' Annig Pfirter of the Swiss Red Cross recalled.

The woman did not know what to say; at last she pulled up the sleeve of her nightgown and stammered:

'Me . . . no name – only number – no country, just a Jewess, do you understand? I am only a dog.'

The nurse tried all means of obtaining the required information but in vain. All of a sudden the patient looked at her, gave a deep sigh and said with fervour:

'How I wish I were like you – a human being.' Her words

shook the nurse – the unfortunate woman's eyes seemed to reflect the multitude of nameless people who could no longer believe that they were human beings.

She kissed the patient and tried to arouse memories of her childhood, spoke to her of games, of her doll, her little friends, and suddenly asked her:

'What name did your mother call when she was trying to find you?'

'Myriam,' said the patient and, surprised at her own answer, she started to tell her story.[23]

In this early process of recovery, some nurses were able, simply by kindness and patience, to help their patients. The letters which one of the Red Cross volunteers, Muriel Blackman, received from patients later in the year eloquently express their gratitude to her. 'I thank you very, very much for your kindness and all your help during the first difficult time,' a Dutch girl wrote. 'I owe you a great deal, I was depending on you during my illness, do you know that? Always waiting for you to pop in and say good-day to us.' Another patient's brother wrote to her from Tel Aviv,

I herewith beg to express you my deepest thanks for your most appreciate kindness consisting in helping my sister in the tragical time when a human being is not considered.

I am very pleased to have the opportunity to know that there are still people with human feelings like you possessing understanding and willing to help those who are in need.

I hope to have once the occasion to meet you and to express also personally my appreciation and thanks for all you have done for my sister . . .

'My English is to poor, to let me thank you so, as I feel, I want to,' wrote Guta Wickens. 'Be certain, Dear Miss Blackman, that we . . . will never forget you, and how hard you was trying to help us.'[24]

When the patients had recovered sufficiently, they were sent to re-equip themselves at the clothing store in Camp 2, known inevitably as 'Harrods', which housed the huge quantity of second-hand clothes and shoes which had by now been commandeered by the army from civilians in the surrounding districts of Germany – it was said that people had to give up 20 per cent of their wardrobes. The clothes varied enormously in quality and required a great deal of sorting. 'Unfortunately, the Army apparently never thought of compelling the civilians to tie their shoes together and the result,' Beth Clarkson of Friends Relief noted, was 'an enormous pile of odd shoes of the most depressing variety'. She was also 'amused to meet the same voluminous early Victorian drawers' – similar to those which British women had donated in response to an appeal for Greece. 'The Russian peasants appreciate them – in fact one can usually tell a Russian by the sort of knickers she chooses,' she noted. 'Otherwise these garments are useful as "comic turns" and as material for handkerchiefs.'[25]

In the clothing store, another ritual of transformation was enacted. The inmates would arrive in pyjamas or draped in blankets, utterly bewildered at first. Then, slowly, as they were offered clothes, their social personalities would return. A British doctor found it 'moving beyond words to watch the transformation'. 'Their excitement and happiness was a real tonic,' a soldier wrote. 'No woman coming from a sale with a hard-won bargain could have looked so triumphant; no child wearing its mother's high-heeled shoes could have looked prouder.' Beth Clarkson had a shrewder, feminine, take on it: 'Some of our customers, though practically naked, are extremely fussy,' she wrote. 'Though this is trying when one is very busy, we feel it is a sign of returning self-respect, for many of these people would once have been most particular about their personal appearance.' It was noticed, though, that many of the inmates 'behaved badly, obtaining more than one dress and stealing anything from ribbons to handbags'. One young girl was found 'with seventeen frocks'.[26]

Clad in their new finery, the inmates were finally driven over to 'Camp 3', the transit camp for 'fit' internees on the outskirts of the Panzer Training School, where they were housed in blocks according to nationality.

It was there, in the second week of May, that a terrible setback occurred: 'fit' survivors began to get seriously ill. This bitter disappointment derived from the harsh triage the British had had to apply when they first entered Camp 1 – dividing the inhabitants into three categories, the dying, the sick and the fit. In reality, about 80 per cent of the internees needed hospitalisation, but that was impossible; so a 'Belsen Standard of Fitness' was laid down, by which anyone capable of collecting his own food and maintaining himself was considered 'fit'. By 10 May, between 7000 and 8000 of these 'fit' people had been evacuated by Military Government from Camp 1 to the outer blocks of the Panzer Training School, known as Camp 3, and it was becoming clear that at least 2500 of them were in fact seriously sick and would have to be hospitalised.[27]

Johnston decided to give the 'fit' priority of admission to the new hospital area over sick from Camp 1. They began to be admitted on 9 May and evacuation of the sick was suspended. This had to be done, he argued, because 'unless the sick of Camp II were accepted at once into hospital, they would undoubtedly die [and] the effect on morale in this camp would be disastrous'. Besides, the 5000 sick still in Camp 1 were, he acknowledged, now being adequately cared for by the medical students. Indeed, Johnston added, the new hospital created in Camp 1 provided 'a higher standard of care and treatment' than any other hospital area, 'the reason being, of course, the adequacy in numbers of staff employed here'.[28]

Critics might see this as the ultimate irony in the medical drama of Belsen: the British, who had originally based their policy on concentrating resources in the Panzer Training School, in Camp 2, were now conceding that inmates stood more chance of living if they stayed in Camp 1. Johnston would, I think, have argued that by early May he had learned that flexibility and improvisation, not consistency, were what mattered at

Belsen. His willingness to adapt quickly was one of his best qualities.[29]

By recognising this new problem quickly, the British undoubtedly saved many lives; but they could not save everyone.

Edith Fuchs and her mother Käthe had arrived at Belsen at the end of March, when the Germans began evacuating camps in the north of Germany. Edith was eighteen years old, from Prostejov in Moravia, and a survivor of Theresienstadt and Auschwitz. She and her mother had been working in the Hamburg area for the past year, mostly at the Neuengamme concentration camp, and were very weak. When they were told that 'they would be sent to a camp prepared for the exchange of prisoners and given a meal first', they 'were all terribly happy,' she later recalled. 'We thought it can't get worse than it is now.'[30]

Many people escaped from the train on the way to Belsen, but she and her mother were too weak. After three days without food, they arrived at the station to begin the march to the camp. There Edith had a lucky break: there was a large pile of rhubarb on the platform and she was able to scoop several stalks up as she went by. 'We lived on those rhubarbs a whole week. Those rhubarbs saved my life. It came out red. It still gave the body something.' For three days they were locked in a filthy overcrowded hut, without water or access to a toilet. When they were let out, she and her mother lay in the pleasant spring sun, picking lice off each others' bodies, 'like . . . monkeys in the zoo'.

Edith and her mother starved but they did not catch typhus. Quite soon after the liberation, they were evacuated from the 'Horror Camp'. As she was getting out of the lorry in the Panzer Training School, her mother said, 'Look, who is here'; and she recognised the tall frame of her uncle Kurt, her father's half-brother, only three years older than herself. He was working as a cook and was already well established.

He then helped us and took us to our new accommodation. They were nice buildings which had toilets and bathrooms,

where the Nazis have lived quite well there. We had rooms
where we were living six in one. Again there were three
beds on each side of the room and I lived with my friend
[who had] been with me in school and her mother, [who]
were saved from Mengele – just like my mother, and another
friend from my school with her mother. We six – three
mothers and three daughters – we were living in that room
together.

Edith got 'sailor cigarettes' from British soldiers and, soon after
her arrival, went foraging for provisions with Kurt; they took
some food and 'a very nice little pillow' from an abandoned house.
But when she got back to Belsen, she didn't feel well and was
running a temperature: she had typhus. For the next three weeks,
her mother looked after everyone else in the room, the only one
not to fall sick. Three weeks later, when Edith had recovered, she
and her mother went for a walk in the country nearby.

We walked on the main road into the forest. It was the first
time I felt a little bit better and we were sitting down with
my mother onto a meadow. And then we see all the nature.
There were a lot of marguerites, flowers, round us and my
mother took one and made the joss – 'I love you', 'I love
you not', you know? And suddenly in this moment we both
realized that we are free. Being on a meadow on our own,
seeing flowers and doing how it pleases us.

And suddenly, only then actually, it hit us that we have
survived and now we [hugged] each other and we said 'We
made it. We are here. We have survived. We are alive. And
soon we go home . . .

And that was the moment I felt I was actually free. On
that meadow, seeing green grass and flowers, it was suddenly,
that was normal life again. And then we came back.

Next day my mother suddenly did get a temperature and
she did get typhus. And she was one of the last cases.

Käthe was taken to hospital; her case was quite mild and she didn't have a high temperature, but she was very weak. Edith visited her every day in hospital. After a week, however, she suddenly changed completely. Her colour went all yellow and she couldn't swallow or breathe. The doctors were mystified at first, but then decided it was a post-typhus complication, a swelling in the throat. They wanted to operate but weren't sure if she would stand up to the strain. The next day, when Edith came to visit her, the bed was empty; she was told her mother had died in the night.

Afterwards Edith learned that her mother had had an infection which could have been cured with penicillin. The British had supplies of the drug at Belsen – but only for dental cases. She also learned, from the Revd Hardman, that her mother was buried in the British part of the new cemetery in Camp 2, in a mass grave. But at least her body was labelled.

10

Burning the Huts

A MONTH AFTER the British arrived in Belsen, the evacuation of the sick from Camp 1 had still not been completed. A recently arrived American Friends driver was shocked by the conditions there. 'All afternoon I worked at the camp where the women were kept,' Norman Kunkel wrote on 16 May.

> We would take clean stretchers and blankets in the building and make the women strip off their flea-infested clothes and lift them on to the stretchers and take them to the Human Laundry. Ninety-five percent of them had T.B. It was ghastly to see them huddled on the floor in their filthy clothes and blankets pleading in hysterical tones to be taken out of the filthy place. Most of them had diarrhoea and ulcers and God knows what . . . We would lift them on stretchers and they would cry out from pain they were so emaciated and the skin was pulled so tight over their bones.

Kunkel was harshly critical of the British. 'God! How terrible!' he wrote on 18 May, after evacuating a further 500 women to the Camp 2 hospital. 'We took them to a big building but

the British again were trying to get by on just enough.
Net result was that many of those starving and diseased
skeletons had to sleep on the floor on straw pallets. It makes
me feel so bad because not over 1000 feet away a British
hospital is camped and they have 600 new beds not being
used.'[1]

On 21 May the evacuation was finally completed. Of the
40–45,000 or so people in Camp 1 at the time of liberation,
more than 17,000 had been 'evacuated and put on the road to
repatriation' and more than 12,000 had been put into the new
hospital. But 13,000 had never managed to leave and now lay in
mass graves in the original camp.[2]

As the huts were emptied they were burnt, the mushrooms of
black smoke adding a new toxin to the atmosphere. It was
decided to hold a special ceremony to mark the destruction of
the last hut, and a half-holiday was proclaimed and all British
personnel given permission to attend. Cameras were then
summoned and a special platform and flagstaff erected in front
of the hut, which was bedecked with a large picture of Hitler
and swastika and Iron Cross flags. At 1800 hours on 21 May
1945, Glyn Hughes, Colonel Johnston and two other Colonels
mounted the rostrum and Colonel Bird, the new Garrison
Commander, made a speech about how the British flag had never
flown over Belsen because it would not be identified with evil
but, now that the last hut was gone, it would fly over the new
camp. The Union Jack was then duly raised, 'for the first and
last time', and a salute to the dead fired by men of 113th Light
Anti-Aircraft Regiment – 'to whom', one medical student
thought, 'most honour was due in the story of Belsen'. They had
been in charge of burials and then of cookhouses and 'magnificent in every way'. Finally the three colonels each climbed into
a Bren gun carrier and fired a flame-thrower at the hut. 'From
the first hit the hut was burning as even the barren ground
surrounding it,' Jean McFarlane wrote in her diary. 'A pall of
dense black smoke rose to the sky and there was no sound bar

the crackling of the burning wood. Finally "God Save the King" was played.'

> And then we cheered. The inferno before us grew brighter and hotter every moment. Although almost all of us were openly excited, even then some of the internees present wore that sadly apathetic countenance bred in them through years of bitter inhuman suffering. The remains of what had been dear to them lay smouldering with the ashes amongst where they stood.

With that the British left the 'Horror Camp' for the last time.[3]

This was another of the strange rituals that Belsen seemed to produce: a great moment but with very different meanings. Medical students cynically noticed that one of the flame-throwers was accidentally let off before the cameras were ready and the fire had hastily to be doused before proceedings could resume for the cameras. To the American driver Norman Kunkel it was simply 'bags of propaganda for the British'. But one British student, Dennis Forsdick, found it 'all simple and straightforward – yet sufficiently touching to produce in one those queer shivers down the back that some of us experience at the sight of a contingent of guards marching down the Mall, or the glimpse of bright uniforms at a military tattoo'. Michael Hargrave, another student, liked the speech but was 'almost sorry that Hut 217 was just ashes. I had rather looked on it as home and now it was no more.' Yet, for Dr Hadassah Bimko, it meant a great deal: it was 'a moving and unforgettable moment . . . that symbolised the end of Nazism'.[4]

'That night we really did celebrate': Jean McFarlane of the British Red Cross had been invited by Colonel Johnston, no less, to the 'Coco-nut Grove' nightclub which had been created above the 'Harrods' clothing store and, dressed in her 'other' battle blouse and skirt, she was called for at 1930 hours. She found that 'the whole of one big room had been transformed into a

Night Club complete with Bar, tables and seating accommodation, shaded lights, band, and during the evening a Cabaret, the artistes being four of the fit internees all gotten up in very smart evening dresses made in the Camp sewing rooms'.

> It was the best party I've ever attended, maybe because it was the first dancing one since arriving in Belsen, and certainly because it was such a surprise to find a place like that in Belsen at all. Anyway I ate, drank, and was merry – so was Johnny – very – and the evening ended at 4 a.m. with the Brig [Glyn Hughes] holding my hand tenderly, and Johnny saying many times 'Oh Mac, I'm drunk'. He was rather! Finally we removed ourselves – me with my arm round Johnny's waist and the Brig bringing up the rear. When we reached the stairs I gripped Johnny and the handrail firmly – foresight on my part because he slipped on the top step and sat down in spite of me. The Brig rose to the occasion, placed him on his feet again and we made the car all right. Next morning Johnny had the impudence to call up the Office and ask how my head was.[5]

Johnston may well have been feeling demob-happy; he already knew that his unit was to be posted elsewhere at the end of the month. He took 32 Casualty Clearing Station northwards, towards Kiel, but in June he was sent to a medical conference to London and while there went to see the newsreel film of Belsen then showing in the cinemas. 'One of the shots showed a large pile of dead,' he later recalled. 'A woman sitting just in front of me turned to her neighbour and said, "They must have been put like that for the picture." I had difficulty in restraining myself.'[6]

The medical students left at about the same time, having spent the last two weeks working in the hospital in Camp 2, which they found quite different from the huts in Camp 1. The hospital squares were now more or less running themselves, 'food arrived regularly, there were reasonably adequate medical supplies, and water no longer presented a problem', while the German nurses 'worked extremely well'. These cleaner, more settled conditions did offer an opportunity to take full advantage of the wealth of clinical material available, even perhaps to carry out some more organised research and to assist army pathologists at post-mortems.[7]

Important work was done; for one thing, diarrhoea, the commonest complaint amongst the patients, was mastered. For weeks doctors had been struggling to find the best alternative to the most effective British drug, Sulphaguanadine, which was not sent to Belsen. Now systematic trials of the available German drugs soon established that 'in 4 out of 5 cases' the most effective treatment was a combination of nicotinic acid and sulpha-thiazole daily, which brought about a cure 'in four days', whereas Tanalbin, another German drug, 'proved, more often than not, quite ineffective'. Thanks to this work, the diarrhoea, previously so common, was 'definitely on the wane' by the end of May, only ten days after the complete emptying of Camp 1.[8]

Other important discoveries were also made – for example, that famine oedema, the horrible swelling of the legs that was a common symptom of starvation, responded best to blood transfusions, not to protein hydrolysates. And post-mortems revealed some of the mistakes which the British had been making. The most striking findings were the smallness of the heart and the condition of the lower bowel, patients' hearts turning out to have lost 40 per cent of their weight and 'in many cases the large bowel [being] so distended and thin as to be transparent'. This helped to explain some of the deaths at Belsen after the liberation.

Treatment of dehydration by rapid fluid replacement caused many deaths before it was realized that the body was adapted to a dehydrated state and that fluids could only be increased slowly because what is normally a small volume of fluid may in these patients produce an unexpectedly large increase in the blood volume. This dilutes an already anaemic blood and throws a great strain on the small hearts of these patients, which rapidly fail. This excess fluid accumulates in the lungs and causes what amounts to death from drowning.

'The moral is,' one of the pathologists later wrote, 'that the circulation of a starved person is much less adaptable and of far less capacity than that of a normal.' British doctors, used to treating haemorrhage and shock in well-fed people under wartime conditions with massive blood transfusions, had to 'drastically modify their ideas when giving intravenous therapy to the starved'.[9]

There was, however, no treatment for the condition from which most of the patients now suffered. 'The majority of them were obviously and terribly smitten with TB,' Peter Horsey wrote. 'The treatment of TB . . . was nil,' Roger Dixey recalled, 'in fact it was impossible to keep the cases in bed, as even if they understood the orders given to them, they were not likely to obey an order limiting their new found liberty. One old woman clad in nothing but a blanket flowing from her shoulders was found at the hospital gates valiantly setting out for Poland, such was her urge to get home.'[10]

Fascinating as this research was, many of the students who had worked most intensely in the huts now found themselves underemployed. Some were now ill with 'd and v' or dizzy spells and ten would ultimately catch typhus, albeit mildly. Others found that, as 'nearly all the attention required by the ill was nursing care, our work began to fall off'. Peter Horsey 'very quickly realised that my period of usefulness came to an end when [Camp] 1 was evacuated . . . It was difficult to take the work seriously at this time because of the continual feeling of being superfluous.'

Some of the students were able to monitor their patients' progress in the new hospital – or even to form new relationships. Andrew Matthews worked in Camp 2 in a woman's ward with more than fifty beds, run by a Swiss Red Cross sister helped by 'a diminutive teenage Jew from Czechoslovakia' called Lisl who became his constant companion and changed his 'inbred suspicions of Jews to respect and affection which has endured ever since'. But many grew disenchanted. 'Most of the women in Camp 1 seem to be getting their self-respect back,' Michael Hargrave wrote. 'Now that they are in decent clothes . . . they are attempting to keep themselves clean and look nice.' But at the same time, 'somehow I cannot bring myself to like the internees as they are making such an infernal mess of this camp, and their destruction is so wanton as they destroy anything which is no use to them at the present moment, irrespective of the fact that they might want it later, and they still live by the "law of the clutching hand"'.[11]

Hargrave's feelings may have coloured his judgement. He had worked with great dedication in one of the worst huts in Camp 1 and established an intense relationship with the Polish girls in the hut, several of whom he had persuaded to stay behind to help nurse the sicker inmates. He had also given daily English lessons to the pretty deputy block leader Zosia Wisniowska who, he learned, had 'run a resistance movement' in Poland. She had been deported to Auschwitz and there separated from her husband and five year-old son. When, however, the inmates of Hut 217 were moved to Camp 2, the girls (including Zosia) announced that they no longer wished to be nurses. Hargrave was bitterly disappointed, but put on a brave face. 'I do not blame them at all,' he wrote, 'as no compensation is offered to them for nursing. All the other fit internees have quite a good time with no work to do and they just wander round all day looting and agitating to go back to their countries.' But, meeting Zosia in the Panzer barracks a few days later, he noted with satisfaction that 'she does not look so nice, now that she has tried to make-up, as she did in Camp 1. She is still trying to learn English, but has no one to teach her.'[12]

The last straw for many of the students was the arrival at the end of May of a British General Hospital run by 'QAs': Queen Alexandras, army nurses, with set ways of doing things and no understanding of Belsen's history. 'The QAs were very objectionable and started bossing around,' one student wrote, 'so we let them have it and turned them out.' 'They were told, none too politely, where they got off. Then the Matron went round and started to criticise our Hospital and another chap blew at her,' another remembered. 'These people are hopeless. They don't realize this is not a general Hospital and think they can introduce hospitals and routine . . . The old Belsen informality and comradeship has all gone with the arrival of this rotten [hospital],' Humphrey Kidd complained. 'We have had first class rows with them and are no longer on speaking terms with them. All the original Belsen units . . . are going in disgust and so are we too, soon, we hope. Thank God!' A year later, Peter Horsey thought it was probably just as well that they left when they did. 'We had been long enough at Belsen to regard things with too great tolerance: it needed a conscious effort to remonstrate with an internee nurse who changed bed-pans and gave out food while wearing the same pair of rubber gloves, or to worry very much if the floor wasn't clean.'[13]

Most of the students spent their last week loafing around, going on trips into the German countryside or trading watches and other loot with British soldiers. 'Everyone is talking of how they can get various items of loot and drink home,' David Bradford noted on 23 May. At the end of the month, as fresh consignments of British nurses and more than 100 Belgian medical students arrived, the London students were on their way home: 'Landed at Croydon just before 8 p.m. with feelings that are too complicated to analyse at the moment,' Alex Paton wrote on 29 May 1945.

What had the students achieved? They had restored the moral order, Dr Meiklejohn told a London press conference in July. Until they arrived, he said,

the small number of British troops garrisoning camp . . . could do no more than deliver food from the cookhouses to the doors of the huts, where it was taken over by internees.

The result of such a method was that, in the moral collapse which prevailed in the camp, those who were able to walk took all the food they could get and became desperately ill from over eating, while those who were too weak to leave their huts died because there was nobody to feed them . . . The students saw to it that the food was fairly distributed.

In other words, people stopped dying at Belsen when the medical students went into the huts, restored a sense of altruism and showed that authority could be benign as well as corrupt. Confident representatives of the British elite, they had unwittingly reasserted the moral values of civilisation. Glyn Hughes was equally fulsome. 'They were given the heaviest of responsibilities and their initial efforts depended entirely on their own initiative,' he wrote in the *British Medical Journal*. 'One and all threw themselves into the task with unbounded enthusiasm; they worked long hours in the worst possible conditions and they never spared themselves . . . the fall in the death-rate was I am sure due to their magnificent work.'[14] The *Lancet* doubted whether an equal number of doctors could have worked together in the same way. 'Students carry the sense of community gained in schooldays into the wards of their hospitals: they have not yet been chiselled by life into the rugged individualists who distinguish our profession. It was a fine stroke of imagination to send them where their team spirit was of such moment.'

The attention given to the students aroused resentment in some quarters. On 21 July two army women doctors complained in the *British Medical Journal* that 'so far no mention has been made of the work of the Army nursing units . . . who were in the hospital area from the earliest days', having in many cases 'come to Belsen immediately following a hectic and gruelling time dealing with the casualties of the Rhine crossing, and the end of nearly a year's service with the B[ritish] L[iberation] A[rmy]'.[15]

This was a fair point; the students were overpraised and the women nurses (and Red Cross volunteers) undervalued. In fact the death rate at Belsen had begun to fall before the students arrived and the measures taken to control typhus by spraying with DDT (completed by 30 April) may well have had as much effect on mortality in the camp as feeding in the huts. And it would take more than a few British public school boys to restore the moral order at Belsen. But they certainly made a big contribution. Firstly, as one of them wrote later, they 'had come "fresh from the playing fields" and their radiant health and energy and willing enthusiasm contrasted so greatly with the illness and apathy riddling the camp that they provided, unconsciously and unwittingly, an example of health for the future'. Secondly, by going uncomplainingly into the huts, they had helped to restore the honour of British medicine.

11

The 'Holiday Camp'

IN LATE APRIL, 'a very large quantity of lipstick' had – for no obvious reason – arrived at Belsen. Male doctors who were 'screaming for hundreds and thousands of other things' were initially annoyed, then astonished by its effect. 'It was the action of genius, of sheer unadulterated brilliance,' Colonel Gonin thought.

> I believe nothing did more for those internees than the lipstick. Women lay in bed with no sheets and no nightie but with scarlet lips, you saw them wandering about with nothing but a blanket over their shoulders, but with scarlet lips. I saw a woman dead on the post mortem table and clutched in her hand was a piece of lipstick . . . At last someone had done something to make them individuals again, they were someone, no longer merely the number tattooed on the arm. At last they could take an interest in their appearance. That lipstick started to give them back their humanity.[1]

Saving the lives of the Belsen inmates was only part of the story; their minds too had to be rescued. By the end of May 1945, the British, 'aided by the fine summer weather and the ready-made facilities of the Panzer Training School', had, in Derrick Sington's words, 'carried out the immediate task of feeding, re-clothing and re-housing the inmates of Belsen'. But there still remained 'the tasks of psychological restoration, of rebuilding confidence, of making up for years of education lost, of re-accustoming 15,000 people to enjoyment in work, of teaching many of them to trust and respect authority rather than defy and outwit it, of persuading them to regard regulations and rules as benevolent and not diabolical. Obviously nothing more than a beginning could be made with this difficult work.'[2]

On the surface, an extraordinary change had come about. 'It is a privilege to have seen a miracle and that is what Belsen now is. More like a Butlin Holiday Camp than a concentration one!' Effie Barker of the Red Cross wrote on 8 June 1945. An army cameraman described, in estate agent's prose, how 'the Barracks of Belsen, this fine cluster of barracks, recreation rooms, canteens, etc, set in the beautifully laid out grounds with its fine lake and acres of pleasant forest land . . . once a training school for vicious Nazi "fanatics",' had become 'an excellent and providential reception station to the thousands of people who we have evacuated from the horror camp'. His film showed British squaddies and officers chatting to female internees, crowds gathering outside the camp cinema and well-dressed former prisoners strolling along tree-lined boulevards, like students on an Ivy League campus. An American ambulance driver noticed how 'hundreds of girls who were skeletons a month ago with shaven heads are now promenading along the roads coquetting with British Tommies and happy with their new lipstick and summer dresses'.[3]

But appearances were deceptive. 'A stranger visiting the camp for the first time,' a French doctor wrote, 'might easily have the illusion that he was entering a thermal station, when he perceives a hastening, animate crowd passing along the broad roadways or coming out of the cinema – a crowd whose noticeable variety of language gives even more resemblance to the cosmopolitan clientele of a fashionable watering place.' But when you penetrated below the surface, he warned, you soon saw 'what a terrible stigma their stay in the Nazi gaols has imprinted upon them'. Almost all of the inmates were 'extremely irritable, quarrelsome'. Most of them could not bear to be contradicted, and regarded any opinion which differed from their own as a personal offence. 'They feel – and rightly – that they are very different from others who have not shared their frightful experience, and they regard them with instinctive suspicion.'[4]

No one working at Belsen doubted that the survivors had severe mental problems. 'The mental state of many of the prisoners was remarkable,' a British medical student wrote. 'Some did not know who they were, many had no idea whence they had come.' Isaac Levy, the Jewish chaplain to Second Army, was 'certain that 90% of those who survive will never be normal. They have suffered too much.'[5]

How could you even begin to help them? As Sington put it, 'Three thousand British troops were faced with a problem in mental and moral reconditioning which might have defeated an equal number of psychiatric experts.' This was uncharted territory in 1945. In theory, some of the techniques for treating shell-shocked soldiers and civilian casualties which the British had developed out of their experience in the world wars might have been used with Belsen survivors – for example, the group psychotherapy sessions which helped broken-down soldiers and returning prisoners of war to regain self-confidence and social trust. And some British psychiatrists did advocate an ambitious programme – a 1945 UNRRA report warned that most camp survivors would be 'in need of special attention and treatment of long duration' and recommended a 'psychiatric team consisting of fully qualified psychiatrists, educational psychologists and psychiatric social workers' as 'most essential for dealing with personal problems'.[6]

In practice, no such plan was implemented. None of the acknowledged psychiatric experts – Anna Freud, Melanie Klein, John Bowlby among them – ever went to Belsen; the British military psychiatrists were preoccupied with their own prisoners of war; and the language barrier limited what could be done. The camp's psychiatric programme was extremely basic – a mental ward for schizophrenics and cases of post-typhus psychosis (most of which recovered); and some attempts at psychotherapy, such as art classes run by a former Chelsea art student. Many of its successes were inadvertent, as when a Red Cross worker galvanised an apathetic ward by distributing sewing materials to the patients who, being 'Jewesses from Poland, Hungary and Rumania, . . . had been tailors, seamstresses and designers before the war'.[7]

The first psychiatric report on Belsen was made by Major Phillips, the psychiatrist to British Second Army, who paid three fleeting visits at Glyn Hughes's request. After the first, on 20 April, he felt that 'these unfortunates' had 'lost all sense of decency and pride and their existence became animal-like', and doubted whether it was possible 'for people so badly treated to ever recover'. By 10 May, however, when most inmates had been moved to clean wards and given some attention, he detected 'a general feeling of relief and happiness' though coupled with 'signs of terror' (for example when X-rays were used) and mass hysteria. Finally, on 30 May, as the medical students were leaving, 'signs of general improvement were obvious', even though 'on first entering a ward one was struck by its similarity in atmosphere to that of a sick ward of a mental hospital'. Talking to patients, Phillips realised 'that these people, although still physically weak and therefore apparently apathetic, were now of good morale and would in time make good recovery – but how perfect this would be depended on their own basic personalities, intellect and upbringing'. There was still some hysteria, but 'habits had improved to almost perfection. As one sister put it: "they now use the receptacles for the purposes provided".' They were house trained again. His conclusion after six weeks was that 'a large proportion would again become reasonable citizens – but how long for and how deep will remain their painful memories is impossible to say'.[8]

When the threat of psychosis had lifted, other doctors found continuing fear, social anxiety, apathy, irritability and a sort of emotional deadness. 'The common normal affects such as joy, happiness and gladness noticed since the liberation were seldom the true expression of the feelings of these people,' one wrote. 'They were only a pose – a means to express their gratefulness to their liberators.' Derrick Sington detected other underlying problems: 'a kind of famine psychosis – a refusal to believe that the days of famine were over' – which led to food riots and hoarding of provisions; and 'extreme sensitiveness combined with anti-social behaviour', which caused tensions between the British and the inmates.[9]

Given the shortage of personnel, most therapy at Belsen was done by the inmates themselves. It took three principal forms – a rediscovery of the body, a reconnection with families and a reassertion of Jewishness.

When the British proudly established a library at Belsen, they soon 'found that a craving for pleasure rather than for knowledge possessed a great part of the survivors'. Sington thought this was true particularly of the young women. 'They wanted to "live" rather than to think. We soon realised that to the mass of people in Belsen entertainment and sport would make a greater appeal than books.' Survivors agree. 'The times of crying were past,' Fela Bernstein recalled. 'Now was the time for the good life . . . I was young, I had no worries. I didn't think a great deal of anything.' 'I was a young girl again. One interest eclipsed all others: boys,' Hedi Szmuk wrote later. 'Life flowed easily . . . On the surface it seemed almost normal, a woman's world of gossip and intrigue, centred on men and food. Only today mattered: filling our bellies, and a little romance.' Forty years later, women remembered the joy they felt as their breasts returned and they began to menstruate again.[10]

This recovery of sexuality was, of course, taking place in the presence of men, most of them ordinary soldiers. Many survivors remember with gratitude the respect and restraint of the Tommies; at one of the first social events Bob Collis was astonished by the willingness of British soldiers to dance with 'skeletons'.

> One day we heard there was going to be a dance for the recovering internees. It took place in one of the squares between the blocks. Here green trees had been planted and flagpoles erected and coloured lights strung up. An orchestra from the Royal Air Force supplied the music and a great crowd gathered. The girls came dressed in their new finery. Some could hardly walk, others looked as if they'd break in two. The music started and the dance began. Each British soldier took a girl and swung her on his arm. The tanned faces of the soldiers showed up strangely against the pallor of many of those with whom they danced. One very tall Canadian Air Force sergeant danced with a tiny girl who came up only to his waist, holding her in his huge arms as he waltzed around with a great smile upon his boyish face. She looked so happy, it was hard for those who saw her not to smile or cry.

Some relationships remained on this plane. Sarah Bick was befriended by a British soldier, 'Tommy', who took pity on her when he heard her story and saw how terrible she looked. He brought her special food, which helped her to recover. 'The good nourishment that Tommy provided had a marvellous effect on me,' she wrote later. 'From day to day, I gained weight, and my face filled out and I began to look normal.' Tommy took her to the cinema, but behaved with perfect decorum throughout. She remembered him as a perfect gentleman, a middle-aged married man, whose 'companionship made me feel that there was someone who cared for my well-being and respected me. For all he had done for me I had a deep feeling of gratitude to Tommy.'[11]

Inevitably, though, when the women had recovered physically, things became more complicated. This was partly because the

Allied policy of 'non-fraternisation', prohibited contact between British soldiers and German women but laid down no such sanctions against relations with women 'DPs'. 'Meetings were organised during the day,' the French doctor Odette Rosenstock recalled. 'A soldier drove by in a jeep and persuaded one or two of the more presentable deportees to climb in beside him to go off on a drive outside the camp.'

> One knew what that was meant to say. Certain of us, who only wished to escape our barbed wire, hoped that the driver would be happy simply to show us from afar the world of free men, without demanding anything in exchange. Others, on the contrary, threw themselves, like frightened people, in the way of caresses or a rapid coupling. Be that as it may, his tour over, the soldier disappeared for ever.

'Some sought love because it made them feel like human beings again,' Dr Gisella Perl thought. 'Others because they wanted to prove that they were still men and women; others again because they wanted to enjoy their newly won freedom to the fullest. Then there were those who sold their bodies for cigarettes, chocolate and other small comforts.' Magda Herzberger, a young woman at the time, later recalled that 'after liberation there was sex going on in the camp – in the forest area. Sometimes people found their mates there, and they came home and got married. They were young people, men and women of all ages thrown together.' She herself was not interested – 'I grew up with certain values' – and because of that sometimes some of the women were really nasty: '"Oh, you act like an old maid. Here comes the old maid." It hurt me. I didn't like that, but they wanted me to conform.'[12]

At times, life at Belsen in 1945 seems to anticipate the freedoms of the 1960s; but, of course, there were no female contraceptives. Dr Gisella Perl was a celebrated gynaecologist from Budapest; in Auschwitz, she had performed abortions on young women to save them from the gas chambers. Now, in Belsen, she

faced a new dilemma – pregnant girls came to her begging her
to help them, but she was not permitted to; angrily, she debated
the issues with Rabbi Hardman, who insisted that these women
could only take their place in society 'when they have respect for
certain conventions and honour for themselves'.[13]

Sex may have preoccupied the young but older survivors had
a single thought – to find out the fate of relatives. Throughout
1945 the business of tracing went on, at first slowly and infor-
mally, then, increasingly through well-established channels. By
July it had become clear that a central search bureau, where news
and information could be pooled, and to which people could
apply, was needed in each zone in Germany.

Each survivor went through a variation of this story. Some had
a happy outcome: Leslie Hardman describes cases of couples who
were re-united, of men and women whom he helped to regain their
love for each other, of survivors put in touch with relatives in
America. Some Belsen survivors recall wonderful reunions: for
example, Freddy Knoller, an Austrian Jew who had fled to France
and worked for the Resistance before being sent to Auschwitz, Dora
and Belsen, was sent to recuperate in a French village; one day there
he ran into his brother, now in the American Army. Bertha Ferderber,
the housewife from Cracow, returned to her home town and found
her two teenage daughters selling cigarettes on a street corner. But
most stories, inevitably, ended unhappily. Anka Fischer, after being
rescued from the discard pile at Belsen and nursed back to life in
the hospital, began to make enquiries about her sister Vera. Soon
afterwards a private car arrived to take her to Prague for a reunion.
Vera was alive; but her 'beautiful, vivacious, and clever sister' was
now, she found, 'an old, wrinkled, shabby-looking widow'.[14]

Dr Gisella Perl had been sustained through Auschwitz and
Belsen by thoughts of being reunited with her husband and son.
When conditions stabilised, she set off to look for them:

to wander from one camp to another throughout Germany,
trying to find my husband, my son. After nineteen days of

wandering on foot, along destroyed highways, I learned that my husband had been beaten to death shortly before the liberation and my son had been cremated.

When I returned to Belsen, I did not want to live.

She took poison, but was found in time and saved. As she recovered, Leslie Hardman visited her and noticed that a British doctor was also an assiduous caller. Eventually, Dr Perl confided in the rabbi. Should she marry the British doctor, she asked. He advised against it; Dr Perl went to the United States.[15]

By this stage at Belsen it had become possible to focus medical attention on children. After the liberation, on 21 April, one of the first groups to be evacuated to Camp 2 had been the so-called 'Children's home' for Dutch Jewish orphans which Luba Tryszynska and Hermina Krantz, the nurses from Auschwitz, had established under the protection of Dr Bimko. These children were given a special block to themselves in the Panzer Training School and soon became favourites of the army cameramen. Misguided efforts to replace 'Sister Luba' with English welfare workers were dropped, after resistance by the children themselves.[16] But there were another 400 odd children at Belsen who were still with their parents and who had not been shielded from starvation in the terrible early months of 1945, as the Dutch children had been. It was estimated that over a hundred of these children died and two-thirds of them developed typhus or TB.

Early in May a paediatric specialist arrived. Bob Collis was forty-five, from a large and cultured Anglo-Irish family and, after a conventional English education, had done important work in medical research. In the 1930s he returned to Ireland to practise paediatrics and to pioneer 'social medicine' in the Dublin slums; he also wrote plays, played rugby for Ireland and rode horses fearlessly. Collis was a 'medical buccaneer with the traditional heart of gold' and inspired love and devotion wherever he went. He was one of the first people to record the extraordinary story of Luba and Hermina and played his part in creating the legend of 'the angel of Belsen', but his account of his work at Belsen also offers a gently comic portrait of the two women.[17]

Collis recognised at once the power of Luba's personality – 'she gave out an essence of vitality that seemed to blow against one like a stiff wind' – and saw that she had by now become an important Belsen personality. 'Luba's room in the children's hospital,' he wrote, 'became a boudoir with curtain, cushions, large dolls and trickets of all kinds. Here she and Hermina entertained like royalty. We often went to lunch, occasionally meeting Russian staff officers and other unlikely personages.' He took pains to establish an 'entente' with her, respected her role with the Dutch children, and created around her a children's hospital, in which he struggled to save some of the young patients with TB. Food was not a problem. Thanks to Red Cross parcels from Britain, the USA and Canada, there was now 'butter and jam and marvellous Canadian milk, lemon curd and orange juice, cheese of the finest type, soup, biscuits, creamed rice, and pineapple, and much else'. Dinnertime was like feeding time in the zoo. One child gained 10 lb in weight in a week.[18]

The children were felt to have 'premature development' – to have grown up too fast, learning to be 'expert at organising food and medicament for their sick parents'. Collis tried to help them to revert to childhood, but his indulgent approach to their crimes alarmed one English nurse who found the children 'unwieldy little things, quite undisciplined, unscrupulous and untruthful . . . I often wonder what has happened to them and if, with their fearful background, they will ever grow up to be decent normal citizens', she wrote in 1951.[19]

In July 1945 a little Dutchman appeared in the children's ward and announced that he had come to collect the Dutch children. Luba, he said, was welcome to come too. According to Collis, 'he promised Luba orders from the Queen of Holland and much besides' and eventually Luba agreed to go. But three days later she was back in Belsen and was tearfully reunited with Hermina.

She hadn't liked Holland, it seemed. There was 'Nix in de winkel' – nothing in the shops – and she thought the children's reception was terrible. No one had given a thought to the fact that Luba was not Dutch, but Polish, by nationality; at the border, officials were reluctant to let her in. And the welcome given to the children was not very friendly – a large room with straw mattresses and a toilet outside. Luba was so offended by the tepid reception in Holland that she insisted on going back to Belsen.

In the strange community that emerged in the early summer of 1945, the Hungarians had a special place. Some British officers fumed that they still enjoyed special status, carrying arms and working under their own officers, but they were forced to concede that the Hungarians' willingness to do jobs that no British soldiers would touch made them too indispensable to send to the prisoner-of-war cages. Perceptions also changed with familiarity. One Quaker volunteer commended the bravura singing of the Hungarian soldiers marching to work 'absolutely in tune and in time'. Their songs, she wrote, were 'marked by extraordinary sudden pauses and equally sudden starts' which they attacked in a fashion which would make her English musical friends weep for joy. Horsey people like Bob Collis quickly discovered that the Hungarian officers had brought horses to Belsen – 'chargers, beautiful thoroughbred creatures used to galloping across the open plains of their own country'. Soon Collis had arranged to have a horse brought round every morning at 7 a.m. and was having a morning gallop before going to the wards. '"Fraternization",' a British officer complained, 'is too mild a word for the relationship existing between [the Hungarians] and a considerable proportion of the British and DP personnel working in the Camp . . . any restrictions on their freedom are so mild as to make a formal invitation of all British personnel by the Hungarian Commander to a party a possible occurrence.'[20]

Almost from the start there were arguments at Belsen; that was inevitable with everyone working under such strain. Early

in May 1945 the British Red Cross sent out Miss Effie Barker
as Chief of Staff to 'do a bit of peacekeeping'. It is not clear
what the original problem was, but other issues soon took its
place. 'All I do is rush around in my Opel listening to worries
and try to make peace between the Swiss Mission, the Vatican,
and ourselves,' she wrote. 'Long and linguistically weary hours
are spent drinking coffee and going round and round the point.'
A Colonel's daughter and Master of the Garth Hounds, an accom-
plished angler, marksman and pig-sticker, Effie Barker knew how
to talk to the army and observed life in the camp with quiet
amusement.[21]

Like many of the British, Miss Barker was initially convinced
that only the very toughest of the prisoners could have survived
at Belsen. 'The highly cultured failed to exist as one had to be
almost criminally minded and tough to get food and remain sane,'
she wrote on 15 May. 'The exceptions of cultured people who
lived are fantastically interesting to talk to – although lack of
speaking German is a problem.'

I was asked to drink coffee with some Czech women last
night. They were Jews who had been through the horrors
of Auschwitz and Belsen and were carried out of Camp 1
too weak to lift their heads. They received us charmingly
dressed in clothes made from some coloured table cloths.
Their little room was like a miniature salon with large vases
of syringa. The conversation would have done justice to any
dinner party. One woman – a very distinguee person, obviously the owner of a beautiful house in Prague mit butler etc,
assured me she had no fears for the future. She had never
looked back but always forward – a philosophy which had
saved her life and reason. Seldom have I listened to so much
wisdom as expounded about future European peace . . .

Effie also discovered that all sorts of talents could be found among
the inmates. 'Just had my skirt altered by brilliant Rumanian

tailor, the Andersen and Shepherd of Bucharest and my hair washed by the Antoine of Prague – price 15 cigarettes and much talk,' she wrote. 'So amusing and incongruous. Then one gets powdered with delousing stuff and wanders through hordes of typhus stricken humanity. A queer life.'[22]

'Belsen' – the community now living in the Panzer Training School – even became something of a cultural centre. It wasn't just that Yehudi Menuhin and Benjamin Britten gave recitals and the Old Vic company came and performed Shaw's *Arms and the Man* there; the inmates themselves began to give entertainments. It started when two Red Cross welfare ladies, with Derrick Sington as interpreter, persuaded them to put on an international cabaret. 'We had to boot them to begin but in the end everyone wanted to perform,' Effie Barker wrote. The first efforts, modest affairs in one of the canteens of Camp 3, in which national songs and dances were performed, were so successful that it was decided to mount a much more ambitious production in the grand 800-seat Tented Theatre attached to the Officers' Mess of the Panzer Training School, which Major Berney, the new British camp commandant, had placed at their disposal. Eva Stojowska, a professional actress from Warsaw, and her colleagues flung themselves into the work, ingeniously conjuring costumes and decor from hospital gauze and bits of cardboard. The programme was a strange mixture of operatic arias, Hungarian gypsy violin music, Jewish traditional songs and a rousing rendering of 'Hokey Cokey', the British soldiers' song, that went 'You put your left leg in, you put your left leg out', sung by four pretty Jewish Polish girls. Sington reported that for weeks afterwards the 'Hokey Cokey was sung and whistled all over the camp'.[23]

'It was a new and joyful experience for us,' the Swiss nurse Annig Pfirter wrote, 'to see our former patients looking so relaxed and happy. It was hard to describe our feelings when those people, who a short time previously had behaved like animals, revealed, quite suddenly, their individual personality and artistic qualities.'

Joyce Parkinson, a Quaker relief worker, 'got very lumpy in the throat'.

> One reason I was so thrilled with the concert was for its effect on the soldiers there. They are good-hearted fellows, and they have taken a great interest in their patients. But I think they have got into the habit of thinking of them as poor benighted foreigners. I think this performance taught them that there are some pretty unusual people among the internees and inspired respect.[24]

'Belsen is very gay, parties and internee concerts every night,' Effie Barker wrote home. 'Far too much drinking but after all it must be remembered that it is the most highly populated spot in Germany as far as English women are concerned. Personally I haven't met anything I would cross the road with *mais tu sais comme je suis avec ces militaries très ordinaires*.'[25]

12

'Our Northern Hosts'

IN LATE MAY 1945 it became known at Belsen that Sweden had offered to take all the sick patients from the camp and to give them six months' treatment in its sanatoria. This news produced a frenzy of activity among the inmates – and intractable difficulties for the welfare workers.

The Swedes said that their general policy would be to 'keep families together'. This meant that if a sick child was being taken the mother could go as well and any other children in the same family who were not sick. If both parents were dead and if an aunt was actually acting as mother, she would be permitted to go, but uncles and other relations could not be considered. According to Bob Collis, 'this ruling resulted in the creation of thousands of aunts, genuine and imaginary, who came claiming the most profound affection for every orphan child we had. They protested in Polish; they wept in Hungarian; they howled in Roumanian and all spoke together in a sort of German.'[1]

The British had by now learned that it was hopeless to try to separate families and 'soon began accepting just about anybody who wanted to go', much to the annoyance of Dr Arnoldsson, the highly efficient head of the Swedish Red Cross. He 'had said that he would take sick persons and the authorities kept sending him well refugees'. It was generally reckoned that, of the 9273 camp survivors evacuated to Sweden between 23 June and 25 July, about 7000 came from Belsen and 'roughly one third . . . belonged to the stretcher or walking-skeleton category. Another third were in need of rest and recuperation with perhaps some medical attention, while the remaining third were in excellent physical condition.'[2]

Hedi Szmuk had recovered from typhus, but 'managed to fiddle permission' to go to Sweden so that her sister could be with her sick Polish boyfriend. She wasn't quite sure where Sweden was, but knew the king played tennis and the people were honest. She didn't intend to stay for long – 'six months and then back to Romania'.[3]

On 19 June 1945 the first Red Cross train, with 350 stretcher-borne and fifty sitting cases on board, left Belsen for the German port of Lübeck. There the patients had to be washed and fumigated all over again before they could be put on board ships. An American relief worker who had not worked at Belsen could not understand why 'it was difficult to get many of these people to take a steam bath voluntarily'. Many of the women especially, Marvin Klemme noted, 'would let out such screams as they were led into the place, or as the steam was turned on, that one would have thought that they were entering a slaughter house'. Eventually, 'a Jewish doctor explained that some of this fear resulted from a sub-conscious feeling that they were about to enter some kind of torture chamber'.[4]

It was also very difficult to segregate the patients on the ferry over to Sweden. 'Sisters absolutely insisted upon sleeping together, even though the bunks were really too narrow to accommodate two people. Several times we found as many as three fully grown girls sleeping in the same narrow bunk – two sleeping at the head and one at the foot.' In the end, the refusal of families to be separated forced the Swedes to change their plan to take stretcher cases on special hospital ships and convalescent cases on ordinary ferries. 'When families, regardless of health, absolutely refused to be separated, the idea was given up.'[5]

British accounts gently mock Swedish earnestness and efficiency and their strange Nordic bathing customs. On the boat going over, 'some of our Sisters had a shocking time,' wrote Bob Collis. 'They'd hardly got off all their clothes before seven men came in and began to undress beside them.' A British nurse thought that 'the Belsen mothers and children were very homesick. They found the rather severe manner of the Swedes very different to the British Tommies' easy humour and to the freedom allowed them by the British Red Cross.' Although Collis was very impressed by the Swedish TB sanataria, he wondered whether 'our northern hosts' really appreciated what the survivors had been through psychologically.

The Swedes' motives were mixed, of course. Before the war, Sweden's policy towards Jewish refugees was as unwelcoming as anyone's. The country was culturally and politically within the German sphere of influence, had many Nazi sympathisers and most Swedes 'maintained a distinct antipathy towards people and things Jewish'. In the early years of the war, the Swedes had allowed German troops to pass through their country and had practised 'ball-bearing neutrality' – continuing profitably to sell the means of making war to the Germans. None of this endeared them to the British.[6]

The Swedes had changed tack, however, as early as 1942, partly because they could see the way the war was going and feared that, with Germany defeated, they would end up in Stalin's post-war embrace. To avoid that fate, it was important for Sweden to endear itself to the Allies, especially to the Americans, 'whom the Swedes considered to be very concerned about the Jews'. But, alongside the element of diplomatic calculation, there was also genuine humanitarianism in the Swedish position, born especially out of solidarity with the sufferings of their Scandinavian neighbours under German occupation. Officials in Stockholm rapidly came to understand what the Germans were doing in Eastern Europe in a way that their counterparts in London and Washington did not.

The first manifestation of the new, bolder Swedish policy was the successful rescue of Denmark's Jews in December 1943; the second, the attempts of Swedish diplomats to rescue Jews in Budapest in the autumn of the following year. By the early months of 1945, the Swedes were looking to rescue Scandinavian prisoners held in German concentration camps and had initiated contacts with Himmler using Count Folke Bernadotte as their primary negotiator. As we have seen, at an early stage in these negotiations the fate of the Belsen camp was uncoupled from the package.

Bernadotte persevered, playing on Himmler's wish to open negotiations with the Western Allies and gradually secured further concessions. First, a Swedish team was allowed to enter Germany and gather Scandinavian prisoners together at Neuengamme Camp; then Himmler agreed that they could remove Scandinavian Jews from Theresienstadt; finally, he allowed 7000 women to be taken from Ravensbrück. 'In total, nearly 21,000 internees from a variety of camps were transported from Germany through Denmark to Southern Sweden before the end of the war.'[7]

The story of how the 'White Buses' of the Swedish Red Cross drove around the country, boldly removing prisoners even as the Allied air forces bombed Germany, is an extraordinary epic of heroism and devotion which, had those involved been American, would have been re-enacted on movie screens many times. But the British have always been grudging in giving credit where it is due. The historian Hugh Trevor-Roper, for example, questioned how many Jews the Swedes actually rescued – the answer was about 6500 – and suggested that Count Bernadotte was in fact anti-Semitic.[8]

Similarly, Sweden's part in the Belsen story has always been strangely ignored; this may be because Anglo-Saxon historians have found it difficult to forget her pro-German neutrality earlier in the war, but the Swedes are among the real heroes of the tale. Their country 'took in thousands of survivors and did everything possible to rehabilitate them'.

Many survivors have fond memories of Sweden. This is partly because they recovered, were born again and returned to life there. 'It was like coming to heaven,' Benny Grunberg recalled of his arrival at Helsingborg, 'a clean city untouched by the war, with friendly and helpful people.' The beauty of the Swedish country-side is the setting, too, for many narratives of regeneration. Rena Quint, a nine-year-old Polish girl who had spent two years working in a glass factory disguised as a boy before being sent to Belsen, always remembered the church steeples, apple orchards, and the lakes amidst which she reclaimed herself.[9]

Most survivors have profound gratitude, too, for the efficiency of the arrangements and excellence of the medical treatment they received. 'There was nothing the Swedish Red Cross wouldn't do for us,' Kurt Schmidt said later. The proficiency of the medical arrangements was faultless. 'We were given complete outfits of clothing, all new; and during the time that we were in quaran-tine we were excellently looked after; we wanted for nothing. I remember that the Swedish military catering was excellent.'[10]

There is also in many survivors' testimony a real affection for the Swedish people and genuine appreciation for what they did. Charlotte R. was a nineteen-year-old girl who arrived in Sweden, having lost her mother in Belsen; she 'weighed maybe like a 5 year old child' and 'had no desire to live and no desire of any kind'. She spent three months in a makeshift hospital in a converted school building in a small town near Uppsala – bedridden, unable to walk, while her body slowly regained its ability to function. A nurse befriended her and invited her back to her home, and the family then paid for clothing, train fares and even for psychotherapy. 'These people treated me unbeliev-ably good,' Charlotte recalled. 'Anything I wanted they gave me. They restored my belief in human beings. Beside, they restored my health to a degree.'[11]

She was unusually fortunate in finding such understanding. Kurt Schmidt's experience was probably more typical. 'What was lacking was psychological help,' he told an interviewer, 'but that was under-

standable; people really had no idea of what we had been through.'
'Why did they send you to a concentration camp?' one Swedish
couple asked Hedi Szmuk. 'You must have done something.'[12]

Once survivors had recovered, they faced a choice – to stay in
Sweden or to move on somewhere else. Many different factors
determined the outcome. Hedi Szmuk and her friends, who were
mostly quite well when they reached Sweden, spent six weeks in
quarantine, and in August 1945 were moved to a camp on an
island near Stockholm, a barracks behind a barbed-wire fence.
'There we awoke to reality. Summer was approaching its end,
and with it the end of our holiday. It was made clear to us that
we were no longer guests. We were refugees. This word was new
to us and it did not feel nice.' Hedi and her friends discussed
whether to return to Romania but, as they no longer had any
family there, eventually opted to remain in Sweden. Hedi managed
to get out of the camp by finding a job teaching English to a
family and, four years later, having learned Swedish, worked in
a factory and got herself a well-paid secretarial job, she married
another survivor of the camps, from her part of Romania and
some years older than her.[13]

By the late 1950s about half of the Jewish refugees had been
integrated into the Swedish Jewish community. Interviewed today,
they speak initially of their gratitude to the Swedish people; but,
as they warm to the topic, they begin to express dissatisfaction
that they had to work so hard for comparatively little money and
that nobody really asked them what they had been through or
made much effort to understand their experience. There is talk
of the 'opaqueness' of the Swedes.[14]

Others chose to leave Sweden. 'I never wanted to stay there,'
Hadasah Modlinger told an interviewer. 'They were very kind to
us but they never really made us feel that we belonged. I was
there for five years, and I learnt the language and I absorbed the
culture; but I never felt at home there.' She went to Israel. Others
ended up in the United States.[15]

*   *   *

Renée and Hertha G. were the young daughters of a jeweller in Bratislava, in Slovakia; Hertha was completely deaf. In the summer of 1943 their parents sent them to stay with a Christian family in the countryside, where they remained undetected and passed themselves off as gentile, a task made easier by Hertha's condition. But in the spring of 1944 they were told that, as their parents had failed to pay their keep for the last five months, they would be sent back to Bratislava. Renée recalled later that the prospect of returning to their home town was in fact something of a relief. But their parents were no longer there. For three weeks the two little girls tried to survive, walking the streets by day and hiding out in shops at night, before they eventually decided they might as well turn themselves in and went to the police. Renée told them her parents' name and that she wanted to join them. At first the police laughed; then they wondered what to do with the girls. Eventually they were sent to Sered, a gathering point for the last remaining transports, where Renée learned that her parents had been put on a train to Auschwitz two weeks before. It was the first time she had heard the name.

A fortnight later the sisters were themselves on a train, and looking forward to rejoining their parents in Auschwitz, but constant bombing during the journey caused the train to be rerouted – to Belsen. Thirty years later Renée remembered thinking to herself, as she fell asleep on her first night at Belsen, that life had played a terrible trick on her by not sending her to Auschwitz to join her parents.

Although only eleven years old, Renée quickly developed the skills necessary to survive at Belsen. She made sure that she and her sister had the top bunk near the door of the hut, and, to keep her hopes alive, questioned each new transport to see if it contained anyone from Bratislava with news of her parents. She also learned Polish, so as to be able to communicate with the other children and to tell her deaf sister what was happening. 'My sister tried so hard to please me,' Hertha later recalled. 'And she would tell me what they said. I kept asking her what certain people said.

She would come and explain to me. I was so very, very lonely. I was the only deaf person in the camp.'

Renée was badly ill with typhus when the British arrived. 'I have no recollection of what happened when the English came to Bergen-Belsen, none of the things that people told me afterwards about the joy and the sense of being moved from where I was to what was converted into a hospital which was outside.' Her sister miraculously escaped the disease. They were put into the children's wing of the hospital, while the operation to try to locate their family began.

In July 1945, my relatives in Brooklyn, who were listening assiduously to the radio, heard my name. They immediately got in touch with the Red Cross, but it was still too chaotic for them to do anything about it. And I was finally sent to Sweden, where I was for three years.

In Sweden a doctor immediately decided to fatten Renée up – 'at the age of eleven I weighed as much as a three year old child' – and she slowly began to recover. Her sister Hertha who had curiously survived the camp without illness, had turned into a very

quiet silent child whose sense of the world was totally cut off . . . The only person she had to communicate [with] was me and during the time that I was sick, she had grown completely mute because there was nobody to communicate with except these women who had taken care of children.

Both girls still thought their parents might be alive. Hertha remembered that, one day, while they were staying in the temporary home provided by the Red Cross, Renée was summoned to the office. When she came out, she looked very angry and walked out of the room. Eventually she said that she had learned that their parents were dead. 'My sister was crying so hard and I tried to comfort her . . . I knew then that I would never go back to Bratislava.'

In Sweden, they went to live near Malmö. Hertha was the only deaf child in the area and found it hard to keep up at school, so she was sent to a school for the deaf in Stockholm, 1500 miles away. It was very hard to be separated from her sister for the first time in her life, but 'seeing so many kids who were just like me' and – when she had mastered the new technique – being able to communicate with them, was 'thrilling, a new life'.

In 1948 an American cousin of the girls came to Sweden and was able to cut through the red tape. They went off to the United States, though it took some persuasion to get US Immigration to admit a deaf person.[16]

13

Divisions

ONCE THE IMMEDIATE medical crisis was over, Belsen survivors became, from the British perspective, one small element in the wider problem of displaced persons. The 30,000 people in the Panzer Training School were just a few of the ten million or so foreign slave workers and prisoners of war stranded on German soil when hostilities ceased. British policy towards these people was straightforward: to sort them out by nationality and then send them home. More or less from the start, they had been dividing the population of Camp 2 into different nationalities, not just to stop the Poles killing the Russians but to make it easier to repatriate the groups. Once the typhus was under control, the different nationalities began to leave – the French, Belgians and Dutch at the end of May, the Czechs in July, the Yugoslavs in August and most of the Hungarians and Romanians in September.[1]

Many of the inmates did not, however, wish to go home. Poles did not want to return to a Russian-dominated Poland, while Polish Jews, a British Red Cross worker noted on 6 May, 'view with despair, the idea of returning home, and ask me anxiously what will be done with them. Many of them have relatives or friends in England, America and/or Palestine, and are anxious to join them.' It gradually became apparent from talking to inmates that the camp experience had changed them in a fundamental way. By targeting the Jews of Europe, the Germans had forged a new Jewish identity and spirit of self-help and proved to many the Zionist case that Jews had no future in Europe. Going home, for these people, would mean returning to a virulently anti-Semitic society in which they had no prospects. The departure of the other nationalities left in Belsen a rump community of some 8000 Polish Jews who chose not to return to Poland.[2]

It was unfortunate, from the British point of view, that the Belsen survivors quickly produced from their midst formidable leaders. A few days after the liberation of the camp, a group of Polish Jews in the Panzer Training School responded to the shooting of a Jewish prisoner by a Hungarian guard by electing a committee to represent them to the British. Initially, there were several such bodies but with the departure of the Western Europeans in May, the Polish Jews were left as the dominant group. A survivor of Camp 1 later recalled her disbelief when she learned that a Jewish Committee had been formed because she 'simply could not imagine that there were any healthy Jews anywhere in Belsen'. This group was in comparatively good health because most of them had only arrived a week before the British, in a shipment from the Dora concentration camp, and had been installed in the Panzer Training School. They had therefore not been exposed to typhus.[3]

According to the historian Hagit Lavsky, these young men, from Polish and Lithuanian *shtetels*, 'belonged to Zionist youth movements and were preparing for a life of pioneering in Palestine'.

They could speak Hebrew and had known Hebrew songs since childhood. The spirited group had quite a significant impact on the mood in the camp. First of all they were quite numerous. Second, they were physically and mentally strong, which is probably why they survived in the first place. If anyone could organise the survivors, broken and exhausted by their ordeal, they could. Moreover, these young people had something to offer. They had a real goal. They were full of hope and their strong Zionist belief and enthusiasm transmitted itself to others. Their personal fate became inextricably linked to the fate of their own people, leading to a spontaneous decision not to return to Eastern Europe. Even before the survivors had recovered sufficiently to decide what to do next – to search for relatives, to try to build something out of the ruins, to think about the future – these young Zionists served as a compass and a guide.[4]

Dr Hadassah Bimko soon discovered that the dominant figure within this group was a Jew from Bedzin in Poland called Josef Rosensaft, 'whom everyone called Yossel'. She met him at the farewell party for Rabbi Hardman and quickly fell under his spell. 'Here was a man of small stature, but when he spoke you saw a giant,' she wrote later. 'You thought you could look through him, but after a while, you had to stop. Something told you not to go any further. I was impressed by this man's demeanour, his actions, his fast decisions, and by his Jewish pride and dignity. He had a strong will and a wonderful sense of humour'.[5]

It was a miracle that Josef Rosensaft was still alive. Born on 15 January 1911 into 'a prestigious Hasidic family', before the war he had worked in the family iron business and as a labour organiser. In July 1943 he escaped from the train taking him (and his wife and stepson) to Auschwitz, jumping into the River Vistula under machine-gun fire. After a period on the run, he was recaptured and sent to Birkenau. Transferred, after two months of stone carrying, to the labour camp at Lagisza, he escaped once more in March 1944. Again his liberty was short-lived and by the end of April he was back in Auschwitz, where he endured months of torture without revealing who had helped him escape. When Auschwitz was evacuated, Rosensaft was taken to several labour camps and finally to Dora-Mittelbau, from which he was transferred to Belsen in early April 1945.[6]

Only an extraordinary person could have come through this experience. 'This small, militant, oversensitive man' – as Derrick Sington called him – became the dominant force on the Central Committee of the liberated Jews of Belsen which was formed on 24 June 1945, but he was ably supported by other prominent Jews. Dr Bimko was invited to join the Committee and she and Josef Rosensaft were married in 1946.[7]

Much of the Committee's energy went into cultural and welfare work. In July 1945, the first Yiddish newspaper in the British Zone of Germany, *Unzer Sztyme*, appeared and in September a theatre company known as the Kazet Theater began to give performances. One American observer was struck by the 'stark realism and sheer drama' of its productions:

> Scenes with flames reaching out onto the stage depicting Jews being led to the crematoria, or showing Germans crushing the skull of a child, are commonplace . . . this is not acting but factual reproduction of what they have endured.

He also noticed that 'at the finale there never is applause, just significant and painful silence that hangs over the theatre'.

> It is not uncommon to see an audience of over 3000 persons burst into tears and hysterical sobbing throughout the production. In seeing their former miseries acted out, their lives projected onto a stage, so to speak, the displaced persons have come to regard their theatre as something a great deal more than 'entertainment'. The theatre symbolizes their will to live. It represents a culture that survived a systematic attempted extermination.[8]

In reclaiming the Jews' experience for themselves, the Committee was helped by the belated arrival in the camps of Jewish aid agencies. Until July 1945 the only Jewish people working at Belsen were the chaplains and a British welfare worker, Jane Leverson, a member of the Red Cross team, who came from a prosperous Hampstead Jewish family and had chosen not to work for a Jewish charity.[9] Meanwhile, the 'Joint' – the well-established and funded American Joint Jewish Distribution Committee – was clamouring to get into the camps but was kept out because of the military's suspicion of 'sectarian' organisations and its feeling that there were already enough fingers in the pie. After months of pressure at the highest political level, the Joint was finally able to send a team to Belsen in July, followed soon afterwards by the British Jewish Committee for Relief Abroad. When the Joint team arrived, more or less empty-handed, Rosensaft's response was 'OK, if you can't give us things, give us Yiddish typewriters so we can criticise the Joint to the Jews of the World'.[10]

That confident tone reflected Rosensaft's successes in the political arena, mainly in fighting the British. In the course of 1945, the Central Committee was engaged in more or less permanent war with the military authorities. Rosensaft, an American aid worker noted, 'has had total disregard for military law and has incurred the wrath of the military frequently who consider the Jewish Committee and their activities illegal'. Rosensaft did not endear himself to the British by regarding it as a 'matter of principle to address them in Yiddish, the language of the people he represented'.[11]

The fundamental question was whether the British would recognise Jewish survivors as Jews, rather than as Hungarians or Poles or Germans, and let them stay in the Panzer Training School, building it into a self-administered Jewish community. The British plan was, initially, to ship all those who had recovered out of Belsen to other camps and turn the place into a purely medical facility. After vociferous protests, the scheme had to be abandoned. The British also wanted to change the camp's name, from Belsen to Hohne, but the Central Committee valued the symbolism and successfully resisted that change also.[12]

The general British view was that Rosensaft and the Committee were self-appointed troublemakers. It was noted that Hungarian and Romanian Jews, who tended to be orthodox, were openly hostile to the younger and more secular Polish Zionists on the Committee, and that much of the Committee's equipment in the camp had been 'organised' from the surrounding countryside. A British Red Cross nurse noted with distaste how 'more and more as the months went by [the Jews] broke away from the other inmates and behind their strong Jewish leader they were compelled to follow his schemes and ideas. Jews who openly said they did not want to go to Palestine were ostracised and British interference was of little avail.'[13]

Rosensaft proved himself a skilful politician and consistently ran rings around the dull clods of British Military Government. But the most important battle – to secure recognition as Jews, rather than as Poles – was won for him by a group of US Army Jewish chaplains who were appalled by the way the American Army was behaving towards concentration camp survivors and brought pressure to bear in Washington, where the issue was more politically sensitive than in Britain. As a result, members of Harry Truman's Cabinet persuaded the new President to send Professor Earl G. Harrison to Europe to assess the situation. After touring the DP camps and hearing an emotional appeal from Rosensaft and a more factual one from Dr Bimko, Harrison produced a passionate, hard-hitting report which declared – with some exaggeration – 'We appear to be treating the Jews as the Nazis treated them, except that we do not exterminate them.'[14]

Harrison made immediate recommendations. He urged the United States to accept that the Jews were now a nation; to give them their own camps in Germany at once, with better food than anyone else; and to persuade the British to allow 100,000 Jews to migrate to Palestine. President Truman decided to support this – conscious that his own chances of re-election depended on Jewish support in New York and other states, but aware also that polls showed American public opinion to be overwhelmingly opposed to more Jewish immigration to the United States. In Germany, the US Army duly gave Jews their own camps.

The British, by contrast, were slow to read the new mood. They felt that to give special treatment to Jews was profoundly illiberal, to continue the work of the Nazis: 'We cannot accept the theory that the Jews are a separate race and as it was one of the principal tenets of the Nazi creed it is rather odd that they should now be trying to put it across', a British official declared. They were also determined to safeguard their Empire in the Middle East by restricting Jewish emigration to Palestine.[15]

It is beyond the scope of this book to follow in detail the extended political battle which now followed; it would last for five years and result in the creation of the state of Israel and the migration outside Europe of most of the Belsen survivors. One event though, which took place in the autumn of 1945, perhaps best expressed the transition of the Panzer Training School from British hospital into Jewish community.[16]

In the aftermath of the war, the problem of 'unaccompanied children' – orphans who had lost both parents in the camps – generated considerable attention. Welfare organisations were naturally concerned about the children's future, but there was also a political aspect to the question. Western countries which maintained strict immigration quotas might be prepared to bend the rules in the case of children, particularly if they could generate good publicity for what were essentially gestures of goodwill towards small numbers. At the same time, Jewish groups felt a particular sense of responsibility towards these unfortunate survivors.

In July 1945 both the British and Swiss governments expressed a willingness to take a certain number of orphans. As a result, the United Nations Relief and Rehabilitation Agency, UNRRA, which had by now taken over some of the 'welfare' work in Germany, was directed to drop its programme to help all DP children and focus instead on 'the difficulties of arranging the move of a relatively small group of children'. The hope originally was to send a thousand children to England and 1600 to Switzerland; but, with communication and transport still very poor, many obstacles had to be overcome before much could be achieved. Eventually, after several months' work, social workers identified between 200 and 300 Jewish children at Belsen who were eligible to go to England.

One problem lay in determining the age of children. It was quickly discovered that Jewish children who had survived European persecution for the last decade 'had done so because of their superior intelligence'. They were 'wise far beyond their years. Under subjection, they had learned that it was expedient to change their age upwards and downwards in order to live. A child of 10 years would be doomed to the crematorium. He would then say he was 14 or 16 years of age in order to be put in a work g ıg. In other circumstances, it would seem preferable to be younger and a small youth of 18 would give his age as 14 or 15 years.' Even after liberation, these children continued their pattern of lying about their age, reducing it when there were 'amenity supplies for young children', and increasing it when cigarettes were distributed to adults. Many children probably did not really know their correct age and had 'learned the hard way that proof of age was only a matter of argument and insistence. All identifying papers had long since been destroyed and there was no way by which their age could be verified.'

There were, of course, records for the period after the liberation. UNRRA workers found that 'record after record carried the tragic tale of a lone child arriving at Belsen Camp in April or May of 1945, finding an older sister, brother or parent there whom he had never expected to see again, and then losing the relative within a day or two because of typhoid or typhus, which scourges were so rampant in the camp at the time of liberation'.

The first response to the announcement of the scheme to take children to England was 'a stampede' of applicants. But there was then a long delay while the necessary logistics were organised 'at

Zone level' until finally, on 23 October 1945, 'the long-expected news was shouted over the line that two Dakota aircraft were arriving at Celle airfield on the morning of 27th October, and that 50 children should be prepared for the trip'. Work regarding the selection, documentation and arranging for medical certificates in respect of the fifty children was done by the American and British Jewish charities at Belsen, while UNRRA handled the overall organisation. Escorts for the journey were also selected. Then, a fortnight before the scheduled date of departure, the Jewish Central Committee expressed opposition to the scheme. 'They gave as their reason their doubts that the children would be placed in Jewish homes and educated as Jews.' The fact that the Jewish agencies working in Belsen approved the plan and that the Jewish Refugee Committee in England would be responsible for the children made no difference to the Committee's opposition. UNRRA workers suspected that, in addition to this reason, 'the strong Zionist element believed the chances of getting Palestinian certificates were greater if the children remained in Germany'.

As the day of departure neared, 'the Committee tried to persuade the children not to go and used all its influence with the Jewish Agencies in Belsen to stop the move. Tension in the Jewish community increased over this issue and it was not considered wise to publicise the list of the first 50 children selected until we were assured that the movement could take place at all.'

The fifty children went to England, but, 'because of the Jewish Committee's opposition, no further trips were undertaken'. The UNRRA welfare people, who had spent months organising, and tying up scarce resources, to make it possible, were understandably furious. 'Several hundred young adolescents were given hopes' which were then 'wantonly dashed by adults who certainly seemed as cruel and lacking in understanding as their oppressors', their report states. But from the Committee's perspective (and that of Zionist historians) this episode represented a triumph, a turning point on the road back to political self-government and confidence, the moment when survivors reasserted themselves and took control of their own destiny.

The end of this story, for them, came in April 1946 when Dr Hadassah Bimko accompanied the first group of Jewish children from the camps to enter Palestine.[17]

14

The Belsen Trial

THE OLD HANSEATIC town of Lüneburg lies some twenty miles to the north-east of Bergen. It enjoyed great prosperity for many centuries, mainly as a centre for the production of salt, but fell into decline early in the nineteenth century. Lüneburg's eclipse proved its salvation in the Second World War, for it saved it from the attentions of the RAF and in 1945, with the rest of northern Germany reduced to rubble, the old market town still stood – a Grimm's fairy tale of medieval bell towers, elaborately gabled façades and vast red-brick churches, in one of which Johann Sebastian Bach had sung as a chorister. The trial of Josef Kramer and forty-four others, generally known as 'the Belsen trial', began on 17 September 1945, in a converted gymnasium at No. 30 Lindenstrasse, a street of pleasant nineteenth-century villas on the outskirts of Lüneburg.

This was the first time that anyone had been prosecuted and punished for offences against international law committed in wartime. Although the Allies had repeatedly announced their intention to bring to justice those responsible for German atrocities, fear of retaliation meant that nothing was finalised until June 1945, when it was decided that 'major' war criminals like Göring would be tried before an International Military Tribunal (which sat in Nuremberg in November 1945), and lesser figures would be tried by national courts. The procedure to be followed in such trials in the British Zone was laid down by a Royal Warrant in June 1945 which explicitly limited the jurisdiction of British Military Courts to war crimes, defined as 'violations of the laws and usages of war'. The Belsen trial was like a crude amateur read-through for the much slicker productions later mounted elsewhere.[1]

The speed with which the trial was staged was undoubtedly due to the sense of outrage which coverage of the camps had generated in Britain. 'With public horror at the stories that came from Belsen went a public demand that those responsible should be punished for their deeds.' As Alan Moorehead noted, there were special reasons, quite apart from their unique awfulness, why the photographs and reports from Belsen had such an impact. 'A shudder of horror went round the world when news of the concentration camps was published,' he wrote, 'but only, I think, because of the special interest and the special moment in the war.' The timing, Moorehead believed, was crucial. 'We were engrossed with Germany and it is perhaps not too subtle to say that since Germany was manifestly beaten, people wanted to have a justification for their fight, a proof that they were engaged against evil.' And, from the German point of view, Belsen was uncovered at exactly the wrong moment. 'Worse camps like Auschwitz existed in Poland and we took no notice. Dachau was described in the late thirties and we did not want to hear. In the midst of the war three quarters of a million Indians [actually three million] starved in Bengal because shipping was wanted in other parts and we were bored.'[2]

The British public was not bored by Belsen; it was revolted and fascinated, and demanded blood: 'To many it seemed superfluous that there should be a trial at all, and the popular cry was for a summary identification and execution of the offenders.' 'I see in the papers the Belsen trial has begun. I hope they shoot the lot,' Effie Barker of the Red Cross wrote. Churchill and Eden both had some sympathy with this view, but it was eventually decided that a trial by a Military Court would be a more appropriate response.

Soon after the British had entered Belsen, a small war crimes team had begun to amass evidence from the inmates. 'There were thousands of people there and it was difficult to know where to begin,' one officer said later. They started by getting their two interpreters, the Czech Jewesses Traute Neumann and Charlotte Duchesnes, to 'bring in their friends who were in a fit condition to give evidence' and then 'got various members of different nationalities to send people along'. The process was far from perfect and the team could have done with more time. 'There were some indications of haste in the choice of evidence and in the selection of the accused', it was later conceded. 'It is possible that the delay of a further month or so would have produced a more balanced and better case.' The process was, in some ways unusual, more than half of the prosecution evidence, for example, being in the form of affidavits which, as a rule, are not allowed in criminal trials in England; but Derrick Sington, who was closely involved in the process, felt that 'a serious effort had been made to observe standards in selecting witnesses such as would have prevailed in a criminal investigation in Britain. The investigators were experienced lawyers and policemen who knew that the case they prepared . . . would have to stand up in a court that would be adhering pretty closely to normal English legal procedure.' Much evidence was 'rejected as unreliable because of obviously wild statement or hysterical attitudes'.

It quickly became apparent to the investigators that several of the defendants, such as the camp commandant Josef Kramer and Dr Fritz Klein, had worked at Auschwitz as well as at Belsen, and that specific war crimes charges were more likely to stick in the case of the former rather than the latter. 'The accused were charged with having either personally killed or ill-treated Allied nationals, or with having been concerned with such killing or ill-treatment as to share the responsibility for it,' a barrister at the

The 'Human Laundry'. Survivors being washed and disinfected by German nurses in a converted stable in the Panzer Training School.

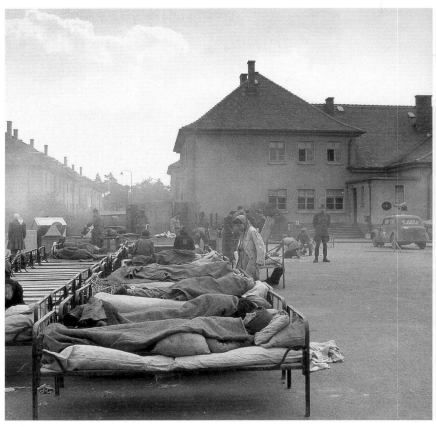

Newly evacuated patients from Camp 1 in a temporary 'ward' in one of the squares of the Panzer Training School, 27 April 1945. Over the next few weeks, the buildings around were converted into the largest hospital in Europe.

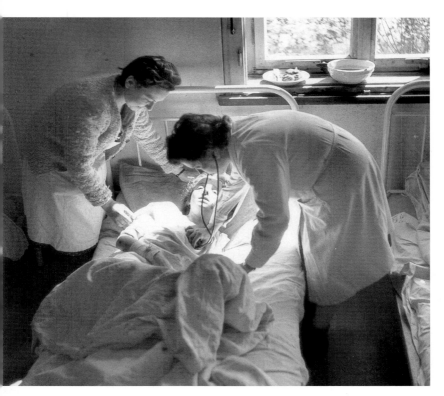

A patient is treated in the new hospital, 25 April 1945. A carefully back-lit shot giving an idealised picture of conditions at the time.

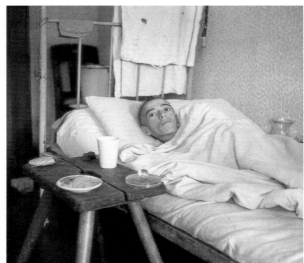

Three months after the liberation, Konrad Herschel, a thirteen year-old Czech boy, is still recovering from malnutrition. 20 July 1945.

A British soldier sprays a prisoner with DDT. The newly developed chemical was the principal weapon against typhus.

The British medical students shortly before their return to England, 25 May 1945.

The burgomasters of the neighbouring towns watching a mass burial for the benefit of *Movietone News*. 24 April 1945. It was important in propaganda terms to implicate German civilians in what was found at Belsen.

'The mad doctor of Belsen'. Dr Fritz Klein, who had worked at Auschwitz and, briefly, at Belsen, posed in one of the mass graves. 24 April 1945.

Rabbi Leslie Hardman reads the *kaddish* over a mass grave at Belsen, 21 April 1945.

'And then we all celebrated'; the last hut in Camp 1 is ceremonially burnt, 21 May 1945.

19 May 1945. Leslie Hardman conducts an open-air service in one of the squares of the Panzer Training School, soon to become 'Belsen Displaced Persons Camp'.

A year later.
Two former inmates weep over one of the Belsen mass graves. 14 April 1946.

trial wrote. 'On the Auschwitz charge the question of responsibility was directed to the gas chambers and crematoria; while on the Belsen charge the more difficult question was raised as to responsibility for conditions which had arisen by callous neglect.' So the British yoked the two together. But, although they used Auschwitz to bolster their case, the indictment said nothing about Nazi genocide in general or its anti-Semitic character in particular.[3]

The second major difficulty was that the forty accused were of three different types and had performed different functions at the camp. There were men like Kramer and Klein, who had headed the administration of the camp; less important members of the SS who had performed comparatively humble duties in the camp, such as those of cooks and clerks; and a number of Kapos (many of them Poles) who had started as prisoners of the Germans and, having been 'promoted', ended up alongside them in the dock.[4]

Although the British manipulated the judicial process to get the convictions they wanted – just as they did in the case of William Joyce (better known as Lord Haw-Haw), the American-born Irishman who broadcast for the Germans – they were also careful to maintain the forms of the English criminal trial and to ensure that court procedures should be seen to be fair. To that end, each defendant was represented by a qualified lawyer – albeit one chosen by the arbitrary traditions of British military justice. In July 1945, an Artillery officer called Major Winwood saw a notice from British Army Headquarters in Germany requesting the names of serving officers who were qualified as barristers or solicitors. Winwood had qualified as a solicitor in 1938 and – breaking the first rule of army life – 'Never volunteer' – he submitted his name. Two months later he was ordered to report the following day at RAF Headquarters at Celle. No explanation was given.

The next day he was greeted by a Staff Officer who said, 'Well, as you are the first to arrive, you had better take the first four on my list.' Only then did it emerge that Winwood was going to be required to defend SS personnel from Belsen, in a war crimes trial due to start in two to three weeks' time, the accused having all opted to be represented by British lawyers. His four clients were to be Kramer himself, Dr Klein and two SS guards. Meanwhile, Captain Raymond Phillips, a barrister who later became a High Court judge, was given four obscure SS women to defend.

> There were immense problems facing the defence [Winwood later recalled]. The charges were heinous, time was short and pressure came from the British Government to get the trial over before the Americans got going at Nuremberg . . . We had little time to formulate a coherent defence policy beyond agreeing that we would put forward a joint objection to the jurisdiction.[5]

The official plan nearly went awry, however. In an excess of professional diligence, the defence team departed from the script and went about their work with skill and devotion – 'we were determined to do our best for our clients,' Winwood wrote. Not only did one counsel cause international outrage by referring to Belsen's inmates as 'the dregs of the ghettoes of Eastern Europe', the defence produced as an expert witness a former Law Professor at London University who proceeded to fire heavy legal salvoes at the court's jurisdiction. Under international law as it stood at the date of the alleged offences, Professor Smith argued, concentration camps existed in peacetime and therefore had nothing to do with the waging of war, so that whatever took place in them was not a war crime. What was more, he said, under German law, 'the annexation of occupied countries, the establishment of concentration camps, the confinement therein of prisoners, and the construction and use of gas chambers was legal', so that German citizens could not be punished for what was alleged to be a breach of international law when what they had done was lawful by their own law. Smith also pointed out that the British were retrospectively applying to the accused at Lüneburg, in respect of acts they had committed in 1942 and 1943, a regulation which had only been inserted in the British Manual of Military Law in April 1944. This regulation reversed one, valid until 1944, which had rendered immune from punishment members of the armed forces violating the rules of warfare if they acted under orders. To make the new regulation apply retrospectively was, he said, similar to 'the worst features of the German system which we are trying to destroy'.[6]

In response, the main prosecution lawyer, Colonel Backhouse, relied on robust common-sense arguments. What had happened had everything to do with the war and was therefore covered by the Geneva and Hague Conventions, he said; it was not true that the internees all came from annexed countries and were therefore German nationals covered by German law; as for the argument of 'superior orders', it was for the accused to prove that 'what was done was done on orders from above'; and the version of the law amended in April 1944 was the correct one. In purely legal terms, Backhouse had the worst of it and, when the defence team made further difficulties, the President of the Court felt it necessary to call them in and warn them 'that progress had to be made'. 'He reminded us that we were still under military discipline and he expected us to comply,' Winwood later recalled.[7]

Whatever the legal niceties, the moral arguments were simple and powerful. The case against Kramer was that he had been actively involved in selections at Auschwitz, had gassed inmates at the Natzweiler concentration camp and had been primarily responsible for the criminal neglect, deliberate starvation and ill-treatment which had caused thousands of people to die at Belsen. In making its indictment stick, the prosecution relied heavily on its star witness, Dr Hadassah Bimko. On 21 September 1945, she described life in the Belsen and Auschwitz camps and then, in 'the biggest moment of the trial', identified fifteen of the accused as persons concerned in the running of the camps, including Kramer and Klein.

The witness . . . who told the court that her father, mother, brother, and six year-old son had all perished in Auschwitz, left her seat in the witness box and walked forward into the body of the court [*The Times* reported]. Three thousand watt lamps, hanging from the ceiling, were switched on over the dock, heightening the effect. The doctor, a square-built, dark-haired woman of about 30, was wearing a dark blue dress. Behind her walked a tall lance-corporal of the ATS police, and at her side was an interpreter in the field-service dress of a British officer. For five days we had been listening to the horrors of these camps. Now we might hear the first definite evidence linking the accused with the deliberate, savage murders carried out on such a scale that Dr Bimko has estimated that her fellow prisoners calculated that 4,000,0000 Jews had died in Auschwitz alone.

Here was one of the very few who had survived, coming forward to enact the scene of which those murdered millions must have dreamed ceaselessly during the last years of their lives – when a force even stronger than Hitler's Reich would learn of these iniquities, bring them to an end, and seek out and punish, the guilty.

There was no sign of bitterness, exultation, hatred, or vengeance in the young woman's bearing – but a simple dignity which the spectators felt was the same bearing she had maintained during her 18 months of imprisonment.[8]

Dr Bimko said that Klein had conducted selections at Auschwitz, while Kramer and another SS officer called Hoessler had attended a parade in the hospital and had both taken part actively during the selections.[9]

In defending Kramer, Major Winwood relied on the line that his client had only been following 'superior orders', which in Kramer's case was more credible than it would later become with more intelligent defenders like Eichmann. Winwood argued, too, that as commandant of the Birkenau camp, Kramer had been present at, but not complicit in, selections: 'his duty was analogous to a Battalion Commander in whose area is a prison, the orders for which come from battalion Headquarters'. Turning to the last days at Belsen, he claimed that 'there was insufficient evidence to warrant the Court finding that there was any deliberate attempt on the part of Kramer, or his staff, to ill-treat the internees who were in their charge'. Kramer's response to Glyn Hughes's charge, that he was 'unashamed' of what was found there, was that 'he had carried out his orders as a German' and 'had done all he could under the circumstances'. Then Major Winwood, the obscure solicitor given his big day in court, launched into his peroration. 'Finally, in the last days,' he declared, 'Kramer stood completely alone, deserted by his superiors, while these waves of circumstances beat around him.' Far from being the 'beast of Belsen', he was in truth the 'Scapegoat of Belsen, the scapegoat for the man Heinrich Himmler, whose bones are rotting on Lüneburg Heath not very far from here, and . . . the scapegoat for the whole National Socialist system'.[10]

Some of the exchanges brought out Kramer's closed and limited world; revealed that he was one of those SS men who 'saw themselves as soldiers doing their duty, and [had] no concept of having committed a great moral wrong as individuals', as one Auschwitz survivor later put it.

Did you watch these people slowly starving and dying [at Belsen]? – Yes. That is to say, I did not look at it, but I saw from the daily reports how many people were dying every day.

Did you see these people gradually dying of starvation and thirst? – Yes, I mentioned these facts in my letter [of 1 March 1945].[11]

Kramer was also asked why he had not gone to the army officers at the nearby barracks and obtained food from their bakery, capable of making 60,000 loaves a day.

Do you not think that the General or any other decent person would have helped you with food if you had told them of the way in which these people were dying and shown them the living skeletons that were in your camp? – The General could not have helped me as the food that was in the stores could only have been obtained by means of special indents and I could only get my food from the civilian administration. He was not allowed to give me anything.

Did you ever ask him? – No, the food that was stored there was only for the Wehrmacht . . .

Is not the truth of the matter that you never tried in any way to help these people at all? – That is not true. I have written to several firms to get additional food.[12]

Dr Fritz Klein did not try to disguise the fact that he had conducted selections at Auschwitz, but he had not been at Belsen very long and claimed to have tried to get something done when he took over as doctor right at the end. The general view among inmate doctors was that he had tried to save his own neck by ostentatiously distributing medicine when he knew the British were coming.

Much of the press reporting of the trial, however, focused not on Kramer or Klein but on the SS women who were put on trial and, in particular, on the young and very pretty Irma Grese. 'The newspapers of the victor countries had indeed seized on the value to their circulation of her ringlets and her pretty blue eyes,' Derrick Sington wrote. 'For weeks in scores of screaming headlines Irma Grese had been the "blonde beastess" . . . The deep, primeval revenge-instinct had been tended and canalised by the popular press of Britain and the United States, given its outlet and shown its quarry, which was not less "juicy" and satisfying for being young, handsome and a girl.' Although there was ample evidence of her brutality towards prisoners, it was her role in selections at Auschwitz which doomed her.[13]

Reflecting on the case a decade later, Sington argued that, while Grese was clearly guilty, there were strong extenuating circumstances. She was a young, impressionable girl who had emerged from a 'childhood in the floodtide of Nazism' to work in her teens at the SS Hospital at Hohenlychen, 'with its atmosphere of clinical Valhalla', before being sent to Ravensbrück, where she was conditioned in brutality, and then to Auschwitz. 'By 1943,' Sington wrote, 'Irma Grese had become a creature with none of what we call conscience, with no pity and no fear either.'

Sington's was, however, very much a minority view in 1945. On 16 November, the court adjourned and, after deliberating for six hours and eight minutes, returned with its verdicts. Most of the main defendants were convicted, but some of the lesser characters were acquitted. Eleven people, including Kramer, Klein and Irma Grese, were sentenced to death. Kramer's appeal to General Montgomery was rejected but Dr Klein refused to appeal, saying (his lawyer recalled) that his part in the 'Final Solution' 'was such that he was not fit to live'.[14]

Britain's most experienced hangman, Albert Pierrepoint, was flown over to carry out the executions. He duly set about weighing and measuring the eleven condemned prisoners and, on 12 December 1945, Kramer, Klein, Grese and the remaining eight were hanged.

15

Afterlives

ONE OF THE FIRST detailed accounts of the medical effort at Belsen, written by the Irish paediatrician Bob Collis, ended with a powerful rhetorical appeal:

> The problem of what to do with these forsaken, almost lost, souls is immense, but one which if not tackled and solved will make all our efforts here [a] mere waste of time, for then it were kinder to have let them die than to have brought them back to mere existence and more suffering in a hostile world where they have no longer even a hope of being able to compete in the struggle of the survival of the fittest, and must inevitably go down.[1]

Some modern readers might dismiss this as blarney; others might recoil from the direct language Collis used. Probably, too, many of the inmates of Belsen DP camp who organised themselves into a strong and self-confident community and agitated to go to Palestine would have proudly rejected Collis's characterisation of them as 'forsaken, almost lost, souls' and his assumption that without help they were doomed. Yet an important study of camp survivors published in 1964 argued that Collis's words 'contain[ed] a deep prophetic truth'.[2]

The questions Collis posed in 1945 still remain valid. Was the effort made at Belsen a waste of time? Were these people irreversibly damaged? Or did the doctors' work enable many people to go back into the world and live fulfilling and productive lives? One cannot, of course, answer Collis's questions with scientific exactitude now. Nobody conducted elaborate follow-up surveys, revisiting former inmates over the years. At the time, everyone simply wanted to get on with their lives and start afresh, and most of the Belsen inmates mentioned in contemporary accounts disappear into the crowd. What, for example, happened to the author of a very moving letter sent to the British Red Cross sister Muriel Blackman late in 1945?

Shurly you are very astonished to get a letter from Holland. Do you remember Lies and Jenny Durnbusch at Bergen? That is Lies who wright you now. I promised to wright you and so I do.

In meantime there happened many things. In June we came to Holland with an airoplane. Here we stayed in a hospital for two month, people were very nice and good for us and so we both are now in good health. When we were here for two weeks I heard that my husband lives, he was in Praag at last after a terrible time in many German camps. End of July he came to Holland, you understand that we are both very happy. My lungs are good and I am very thick. From the whole family of my husband and my is nobody back and it is very difficult for us to begin with nothing. Holland is a poor country after the war, they were without money and food and today all things are very dear. Fortunately I have a sister in the USA and she helps us with sending packages. Naturally we want to go to USA but it is very difficult and takes along time before we get a Visum. I think there is many people that wish to get away from Europe . . . I will be very glad to see you back. The thank is for you that I am in live.[3]

How did Lies and her husband get on in the years that followed? Did they get to the United States? Alas, I have not been able to find anything more about her.

There are, however, two major sources from which we can get some sort of answer to Collis's questions – psychiatric case histories and survivors' books and interviews. Before looking at this material, there are a few general points to bear in mind. No demographic profile of Belsen survivors has been published, but a substantial number of them were Jewish women who owed their lives to their youth and strength and the fact that it served the Germans' purpose to keep them alive as slave workers. While it is known that about 14,000 people died in the first five weeks after the liberation, there are no figures for the numbers dying later, so we cannot therefore reach any firm conclusions about the life span of survivors. Some lived to a ripe old age, like the woman who was able to tell *Newsweek* magazine 'I saw Anne Frank die', after reaching her 100th birthday in 1997.[4] Clearly, however, the later you got to Belsen and the less weight loss you suffered there, the greater the likelihood that you would have been healthy afterwards.

Advances in medicine also helped some survivors to live. As we have seen, the most important killer, once typhus and starvation had been seen off, was tuberculosis, for which there was then no effective treatment: doctors expected only 20 per cent of TB survivors to enjoy a normal span of life and most to be long-term invalids. However, even as the British were entering Belsen, a miraculous new drug called streptomycin was being developed in America and, as early as March 1946, being given to patients well off enough to afford it. Streptomycin was at first only available in limited quantities and enormously expensive – a full course of treatment cost some $3500 in the US and in Britain the equivalent of about £10,000 today; it also had side effects and did not work with all patients – George Orwell died of TB in 1950 despite being given streptomycin. It was only in 1952, with the arrival of another drug, isnoniazid, that a relatively cheap treatment for tuberculosis became available. 'To millions of tuberculosis sufferers and their doctors around the world,' the historian Thomas Dormandy writes, 'this was an historic advance.'[5]

There was thus a long 'transitional period when patients continued to die' or recovered slowly in sanatoria. The American Joint Jewish Committee paid for Belsen survivors to be sent to Davos in Switzerland and in 1947 a new sanatorium was opened in Italy. However, anyone who made it to 1952 was likely to recover thereafter.[6]

One particular TB case was well documented by Robert Collis himself. It was that of Zoltan, one of the four Belsen orphans whom Collis ended up taking back to Ireland when no one came to claim them. (Actually, in Zoltan's case an elderly grandmother was eventually found, in the foothills of the Tatra mountains in northern Slovakia. Collis dutifully went to see her; she at once told him to keep the boy.) In the Belsen children's hospital, Zoltan was diagnosed with severe primary tuberculosis, but with 'good food, rest and regularity, got over the acute stage of his condition and although far from well was in no immediate danger'. Then, in Sweden, he was found to have tuberculosis of the spine which Collis attempted to treat when he got the boy back to Ireland.

> Slowly an abscess developed around the affected vertebrae and the pus crept along an intercostal nerve between the ribs, eventually forming a large, round, 'cold' abscess swelling at their edge. This we had to aspirate again and again with wide thick needles which hurt as they were pushed through the skin. Zoltan, being an extrovert, yelled wildly when it hurt but didn't hold it against us afterwards.

Zoltan would probably have died had Sir Alexander Fleming, the discoverer of penicillin, not come to Dublin and given Collis supplies of a pre-streptomycin treatment for tuberculosis he was working on at the time. Zoltan improved gradually. Then one day the matron rang Collis to say that the boy 'had a high temperature, a bad headache, a stiff neck and was holding himself in a weird way'. Collis at once suspected meningitis – 'In all probability the focus in the bone of his back had spread through the membranes and he was down with tuberculous meningitis.'

Collis had received a consignment of streptomycin ten days earlier, but had never used the drug and was unaware of its dangers. 'I gave him the drug, in probably excessively large doses, intramuscularly. It acted like a charm. All symptoms disappeared within a matter of days and in just four weeks his cerebro-spinal fluid had returned to normal.'

In 1953, however, Zoltan suffered a relapse: 'One day he brought up a pint of blood in one of the main streets of Dublin.' 'It appeared that the original tuberculous focus had broken down forming a large cavity in his left lung.' Although the latest drugs suppressed his infection, the cavity remained, so Zoltan was taken to the London Chest Hospital and operated on. 'The whole left side of the chest was filled with adhesions between the pleural lining of the lung and the heart sac. [The surgeon] had to strip these adhesions back carefully so as not to tear the adhesions below.' In a five-hour operation, the diseased part of the lung was completely removed and an intense course of chemotherapy 'eliminated any other tuberculous focus which might have been present in glands or bone'. Dr Collis died in 1975, but, nearly thirty years later, in 2003, Zoltan took part in an Irish documentary about Belsen.[7]

Obviously, Zoltan was exceptionally fortunate to have his own personal physician; his history suggests that many other TB sufferers did not come through.

A wider range of documentation is available when it comes to the mental aftereffects of the camp. We know, for example, about some of the Belsen survivors who ended up in mental hospitals. In 1964, the psychiatrist Leo Eitinger described several cases of psychosis among former inmates, all of whom had been in

Auschwitz as teenage girls and had lost members of their families there. One had been admitted to a mental hospital on her return to Budapest after the liberation, and, after being discharged, had been married briefly. She then went to Israel in 1948 and had been hospitalised in an asylum there ever since. Another woman had been 'very serious ever since the liberation, very reserved, sought very little contact with others, always preferred her own company'. Despite marrying and giving birth to a child in 1957, she became progressively more withdrawn and was finally hospitalised under the diagnosis catatonic stupor.

Eitinger also described the case of a woman who had lost her sister in Belsen and had gradually developed 'a dominating emotional instability, overactivity and persecutory paranoid delusions' centred round the Gestapo; and of another who had never really recovered from the pneumonia, typhoid fever and typhus she had contracted in Belsen – she suffered from heart trouble, headaches, poor concentration and memory, was easily tired and given to anxiety and depression.[8]

Eitinger was himself a camp survivor and, though greatly respected, was regarded as something of a pessimist. Like most Scandinavians, he tended to emphasise the physical aftereffects of the camps, whereas the other great figure in the psychiatry of survivors, the New York analyst William Niederland, though equally pessimistic, highlighted more the psychological effects. In the 1950s, Niederland examined thousands of patients in the United States who were seeking compensation from the West German government, before writing a famous paper in 1961 in which he coined the phrase the 'survivor syndrome'. In it, Niederland argued that massive psychic trauma caused 'irreversible changes' in the personality. Death camp survivors, who had been 'selected' to live by the SS and seen others (including, often, their own families) selected to die, were crippled by 'survivor guilt'. They were also prematurely aged, often confusing the present with the past and, having learned to function in a world without morality and humanity, now found it difficult to relate to ordinary people, to have normal feelings. They suffered from depression, anxiety and nightmares.[9]

If Eitinger and Niederland were very downbeat about survivors, the Israeli psychiatrist Shamai Davidson (who died prematurely in 1986) was more of an optimist. Davidson believed that the idea of the 'survivor syndrome' was simply too sweeping and determinist and, by 'focusing solely on the pathological consequences of trauma', 'obscured the remarkable potential for new adaptation, recovery and reintegration throughout the life span'. His experience suggested that most survivors could be helped by therapy; indeed, the vast majority of survivors in Israel were not psychiatric patients at all.[10]

At the opposite end of the spectrum from the psychiatric case histories are the survivors who give interviews and write books. They are very much an elite group. Indeed, after interviewing 120 survivors in the 1980s, the British writer Anton Gill was left with the dominant impression that 'the people I met looked younger than they actually were and showed far greater vitality and mental liveliness than other people of their age'. Nearly all those he spoke to had been exceptional in some respect – exceptionally lucky, exceptionally clever, exceptionally tough, exceptionally flexible and resilient or exceptionally well connected. Gill emphasised – in my view rightly – that there is no single pathway through the Holocaust experience. The history of Belsen shows, more clearly than that of any other camp, that there were many different categories of concentration camp experience, and every individual will have had different experiences and reacted to them in different ways, depending on temperament and circumstance. At the same time, Gill constantly found that for the camp survivor there could be no return to the person he or she had once been, not least because many Jewish survivors had had to make the transition to a new culture and had often in the process lost their Eastern European Jewish identity.[11]

Gill concluded that it was important not to surround survivors with too much mystique – 'having survived a concentration camp does not turn one into a saint automatically, or even at all' – and that having a good support system was probably the most important thing. 'Those who have adapted back most successfully seem to be not necessarily those who have had the most fulfilled lives in terms of careers or material success, but those who from the first have been surrounded by loving and caring people who are interested in them, and who provide a warm and secure atmosphere.'

Nearly all the Belsen inmates who worked as doctors and nurses disappeared into obscurity. 'Some of them I kept up with for quite a long time. But I think they really wanted to put it behind them,' Jane Leverson recalled in 1995. 'One doctor and nurse came over to London to see me and we were very pleased to see each other – soon after I got home. But I never heard from them again.' When, in the 1980s, Colonel James Johnston asked Dr Ruth Gutman, with whom he had worked closely at Belsen, to write something about her experiences there, she replied that she had 'forgotten it all'.[12]

There were, though, several exceptions to this – most notably Dr Hadassah Bimko. After marrying Josef Rosensaft in 1946, Dr Bimko stayed at Belsen for the next four years and made a point of giving birth to her child in the camp hospital in 1948. When the Belsen DP camp finally closed, however, she and Rosensaft did not go to Israel, but to Montreux in Switzerland and, finally, to the United States. By this stage Rosensaft had developed an international business career and had become the driving force behind the Belsen survivors' organisation. Dr Bimko did not resume her medical career but instead concentrated on bringing up her son; however, after her husband's sudden death in 1975, she returned once more to the spotlight and played an important role in the creation of the United States Holocaust Memorial Museum in Washington, DC. By the time of her death in 1997, she was 'widely regarded as one of their matriarchs by Holocaust survivors'. Her memoirs were published posthumously in 2004.[13]

There seems to have been little contact in later life between

Dr Bimko and her one-time nursing assistant, Luba Tryszynska. After escorting some of the Belsen children to Sweden, Luba emigrated to the United States in 1947 – 'Belsen Angel Here Seeking Job as Nurse', the *New York Herald Tribune* reported in January that year. There she met another survivor, Sol Frederick, married and had two children. In 1995, the Dutch children she had saved flew her to Amsterdam for a reunion and she was presented with a Silver Medal for Humanitarian Services by Queen Juliana (her unfriendly reception in 1945 now quietly forgotten). In the last few years, Luba's place as the 'Angel of Belsen' has been sealed by a memoir of one of the Dutch children and her own autobiography, in the curious form of a ghost-written book for children.[14]

How did the experience of working at Belsen affect the British doctors? We need first to remember that 1940s culture had a much more robust attitude to 'trauma' than that which is current today. It was assumed that most stable, well-adjusted people could come through any situation, no matter how awful, without lasting ill effects, provided they were properly led. Equally, you were expected to put such experiences behind you, to buck up and get on with your life. The evidence suggests that this cultural conditioning helped many people come through the experience but may have created problems in later life for others.

On her return to England in 1945, after failing to save inmates with the experimental feeding technique using hydrolysates, Janet Vaughan's feelings of horror and impotence expressed themselves in anger. Her daughter recalls that when she came back from Belsen she screamed at her children for a month. She never talked about the place thereafter and plunged back into her crowded professional life – as Mistress of Somerville College, Oxford, and a public figure. But, after her retirement, at the age of eighty-one she was interviewed for a BBC series, *Women of the Century*, and, to her daughter's amazement, spoke frankly about her experiences to 'the film man' on camera.[15] This is a variation on quite a common pattern: that memories which have been kept from the immediate circle can be spoken of to outsiders.

The medical students came back and resumed their careers. Peter Horsey got scarcely a nod of recognition at St Thomas's Hospital when he returned and there was some resentment at the media attention the students had received. Nearly half a century later, when Dr Andrew Matthews chased up members of his group from St Mary's Hospital, he concluded that 'everyone had vivid memories, but no one felt that the experience had influenced their ultimate careers'. Nonetheless, there were interesting contrasts. John McLuskie felt that 'we were emotionally immature and the horrors went over our heads' and Desmond Hawkins was 'un-affected physically and mentally by the experience, presumably due to the resilience of youth. Our contemporaries in the Armed forces were subject to far greater stress.' He had seldom thought about Belsen but it had probably influenced his attitude to life in two areas: leaving him with a wish to promote racial tolerance (especially towards the Jewish community) and 'a certain pessimism about human behaviour'. By contrast, Gerald Korn's Belsen memories were 'as clear as those of yesterday'. 'I rarely fail to recall the death of a young man found in "my" hut one morning,' he wrote. 'He was kneeling by his bed. Whenever I kneel to clean the bathtub (an agreed domestic chore), I see this young man 46 years later.'[16]

Dr Matthews downplayed the intensity of his own response. Yet, shortly before his death in 1995, he wrote privately: 'In the month of May 1945, I faced the stark reality of life for the first time. I emerged unscathed but my beliefs did not. There is no God either in spirit or substance, only a Devil and that Devil is mankind.'[17]

In 1985 Dr Alan MacAuslan denied that he was affected at all by the experience, yet his daughter recalls that he constantly talked about it throughout her childhood. In 1996 he published an autobiographical novel whose hero returns from Belsen and finds everything unreal and irrelevant. When reunited with his long-desired girlfriend he becomes numbed and paralysed and sexually impotent:

> I moored the punt, pushing the metal spike with its chain attached into the grass bank, and came to lie beside her. It was no good; I was no good, useless. After a while, Meg became rigid and upset. I could not even say sorry . . . I never saw her again; couldn't really blame her.[18]

Manny Fisher, the young soldier from the East End who worked as a radiographer in 32 Casualty Clearing Station and supervised the early hospital blocks in Camp 2, later recalled how he sat up every night writing his Belsen diary. 'It was so horrific that I thought that in years to come I would imagine that I had been imagining this,' he told an interviewer. 'I determined to write a diary and I did. Nearly every night when we got back to our tents – exhausted, completely exhausted – I didn't let myself sleep. I took a little candle stub out and lit it in the tent while everybody else was snoring.' Reflecting on the experience later, he felt that, being Jewish, he was much more affected than his fellow soldiers, who could distance themselves; and that it had been a mistake not to talk about the experience. 'I wrote a diary . . . I never used to show the document – that's why I've got this post-traumatic disorder, but I do show it now to people. I don't suppress it any more,' he said in 1995.[19]

At Belsen, Glyn Hughes and James Johnston had played complementary roles. Afterwards, though, in newspapers, at the Belsen trial, and in talks to medical groups, Hughes's was the dominant voice. Rightly so, but it was a role that he never really moved on from. He was always afterwards identified with Belsen, whereas for Johnston it was just one moment in a long career.

Johnston stayed in the army and served in several post-war colonial hot spots, including Malaya and Cyprus, before ending up as Major-General and medical chief of the British Army in

Germany. It wasn't until he was retired, in 1985, that he wrote an account of his time at Belsen, at the instigation of Dr Bimko; but he was too ill to deliver it at a conference at the Holocaust Museum in Washington. He died in 1988.[20]

Glyn Hughes adored the British Army and was always careful to give it proper credit for what it had done at Belsen. But he was not a regular soldier and, passionately though he wanted to stay in the army after the war, he was not asked to do so. There may have been a feeling that he was now too big a personality to sit comfortably in the shafts of military discipline, but it is more likely that he ran up against official pressure to curb the army's wage bill in the austere post-war climate. A noticeably dry letter from the army's Director of Medical Services informed him that 'other and similar cases' had been considered and 'in no case has a Commission been granted'. 'Policy was definitely laid down [and] any departure from that policy would create a precedent that cannot be admitted.' It concluded, 'I am sorry about it, but I am sure you will understand, and I know it will make no difference to your keenness in your new appointment.' Hughes's response is not recorded.[21]

In 1947, Hughes was appointed Senior Administrative Medical Officer for the South East Metropolitan Regional Hospital Board – he 'started from scratch by going out to buy cups and saucers'. About ten years later, he became Director of the South East London General Practitioner Centre, at Peckham in south London. He also took some part in medical politics. In 1960 he was commissioned to write a survey of the medical facilities available to the terminally ill and produced a disturbing report called *Peace At Last*, which helped to pave the way for the Hospice movement.[22]

Despite his modest later career, Hughes was a public figure. He was honoured in Israel as a friend of the Jews and remained friends with Dr Bimko and her husband – attending their son's Bar Mitzvah in 1961. He was also one of the first people chosen to appear on the popular television show *This Is Your Life* in

1959. The show's gimmick was, of course, that its subject would not know that a programme was being made about him until he was lured into the studio. In Hughes's case, he was enticed into a car by the presenter, Rex Alston, and then driven on to the stage of the BBC theatre in Shepherd's Bush. Noticing that it was decorated in pink taffeta, Hughes cried out, 'My God, Rex. You've brought me to a brothel.' The programme itself gave a revealing glimpse of how Belsen was perceived at this time as an unpleasantness best kept forgotten; and, although Hughes's public reputation rested almost entirely on his association with the camp, it was only briefly referred to, most of the airtime being given over to bland recollections of his medical, military and sporting careers.[23]

Rugby remained Hughes's other passion, and provided a suitable ending for his life. On 23 November 1973 he attended a dinner at Blackheath Rugby Club and then took the overnight sleeper to St Andrews, where, the next morning, he played a round of golf and had lunch. That afternoon he watched Scotland play Argentina at Murrayfield in Edinburgh. He attended the dinner afterwards and retired to bed at the North British Hotel. The next morning he was found dead on the bed, still in his dinner jacket.[24]

The huts in Camp 1 were burnt to the ground by the British and have never been rebuilt. But in October 1945, a British Military Government official voiced concern that, with the passage of time, the significance of the mass graves at Belsen might come to be overlooked, as there was little to show what they concealed. He therefore directed that measures be taken to 'ensure that memory of the infamy of the concentration camps does not fade' and instructed the regional government to prepare plans for the fencing of the mounds and for the setting out of a suitable garden and the erection of an appropriate memorial.

Between 1946 and 1952, this order was carried out: a cemetery was created and a wall of remembrance and stone obelisk erected. The mass graves were enclosed in stone walls, on which the numbers of the dead lying in each were carved in large numerals. Unfortunately the work was done by a local craftsman in ponderously Teutonic lettering which evokes the monuments of the Third Reich.

In April 1946, on the first anniversary of the liberation, the Jewish survivors who were then living in the nearby DP camp erected a simple but dignified stone. The Central Jewish Committee at Belsen had hoped that the site could be kept as Jewish property and insisted on erecting their own monument.

More recently, an ugly modern chapel – the 'Haus der Stille', or House of Silence – has been added. Nature, in the form of the forest, has reclaimed much of the site, while, in one area, archaeological digging has uncovered some of the foundations of the huts. Elsewhere a few wooden frames have been erected to give the visitor some sense of what the huts would have looked like.[25]

Today Belsen is something of a mess, albeit one which reflects its diverse history. The museum authority has acknowledged that the site lacks coherence and that more needs to be explained for modern, literal-minded visitors. At the time of writing, it had plans to redesign the site.[26]

16

Judgements

HOW, THEN SHOULD the British relief effort at Belsen be judged? Is it true, as Bob Collis wrote, that 'never in the history of medicine has a more gallant action been fought against disease'? Or is Rabbi Greenberg right to argue that the 'mishandling' of the medicine of liberation 'reflected Allied ignorance and failure to plan, which in turn mirrored the democracies' lack of concern for the fate of the Jews'?

It is important first to restate a central point – that the primary responsibility for every death at Belsen lay with the Germans. There has been some debate over the years as to whether a policy of deliberate starvation was pursued in the camp or whether the thousands who perished there were the victims simply of neglect or, as Kramer's defending counsel argued, of circumstance. That distinction perhaps means more to philosophers than it did to Belsen's inmates in 1945. Circumstances, in the form of RAF bombing and the wilful blindness of the SS hierarchy to what was happening in Belsen, undoubtedly did contribute to Kramer's problems; but there is also ample evidence that no serious effort was made to keep the inmates alive.

It is not necessary to reopen the question of the democracies' concern for the Jews – it has been exhaustively reviewed by recent historians. Some of those who saw Belsen were aware of its wider meaning and felt a broader moral responsibility. Alan Moorehead, for example, wrote that his first 'coherent reactions', after emerging from a hut on 24 April,

> were not of disgust or anger or even, I think, of pity. Something else filled the mind, a frantic desire to ask: Why? Why? Why? Why had it happened? With all one's soul one felt; This is not war. Nor is it anything to do with here and now, with this one place at this one moment. This is time-less and the whole world and all mankind is involved in it. This touches me and I am responsible. Why has it happened? How did we let it happen?

And, after looking at the blank, apathetic, skeletal figures in the 'human laundry', Molly Silva Jones of the Red Cross wrote that 'possibly none of us had ever been so stirred – with pity – shame – remorse – yes, because even in 1934 we had heard of these things and had not realised, had not wanted to realise that such things could happen'. But probably more typical was the response of the British officer in a letter from Belsen to his wife: 'If only for this alone the war has been just and worthwhile, and there must be others like it and worse. Every person in any way connected with it must be killed.'[1]

We have seen that the British did not expect to have to deal with Belsen, did not even know – apart from a small group in the Foreign Office – what was happening there. There were two ingredients in their unpreparedness: firstly, a simple intelligence failure, a lack of information, which is understandable if not excusable in the complex and confused situation of April 1945, when the military were preoccupied with their own prisoners of war and with the campaign itself. It may seem extraordinary today that the British were not expecting to find something like Belsen – given that the Russians had liberated Auschwitz on 27 January and the Americans had entered Buchenwald only two days before (on 11–12 April) – but armies operating in the field necessarily live in a self-enclosed world. There was, secondly, a failure of imagination, an inability to conceive of what might have been happening in the German camps.

Bernard Wasserstein has shown how the British deliberately played down the specifically anti-Jewish ingredient in German mass murder; but, equally, Yehuda Bauer has argued that the failure to imagine the unimaginable was not confined to gentile British soldiers and diplomats.

> The free world, including the Jews, had detailed information about the fate of the Jews in the concentration camps, and about the mass murder that occurred in the death camps. But there was a gap between that information and knowledge; that is, the acceptance that the information was true. One could read about what was happening in the camps in the *New York Times* or in the *Chicago Tribune*. Jewish periodicals carried further details. The World Jewish Congress did a splendid job in trying to make this information available to all and sundry. But relatively few people, especially in the US Army, actually believed the stories. Gentiles and Jews both reacted with shock, and claimed they had known nothing about what was uncovered. The reaction was generally one of enraged numbness. Did the soldiers, the politicians, the representatives of organizations which seemed to be so unprepared for what they now saw, really not know what they were about to discover? In a deeper psychological sense, they really did not know, despite all the information they had received. When a Jewish chaplain in the US Army claimed that he had not been prepared for what he saw in the camps, he was being truthful.[2]

Coming from the doyen of Holocaust historians, these words should be taken seriously.

There is a subsidiary question which is of interest here, while it does not directly concern the British: how many Jews did those who did know about the 'Final Solution' in some detail expect to be alive in April 1945? What preparations to help the survivors had they made? The evidence here is fragmentary. It seems that some British Jewish observers did not expect anyone to survive, whereas in the United States some had exaggerated hopes of the numbers still left alive. Plans were made to send in independent Jewish relief teams immediately after liberation; but they did not get very far, in the face of the military's opposition.[3]

Which brings us back to the British response to Belsen. Did the British react quickly enough and with appropriate resources? The speed of the response was pretty good, in the circumstances – the truce was brokered on 12 April, the first team went in on 15 April, food and water arrived on 16 April and medical teams began working at Belsen on 18 April. However, as was privately acknowledged at the time, the resources available were grossly inadequate. 'One would have liked to have moved up twenty 1200 bedded hospitals straightaway,' Glyn Hughes told a conference in London in June 1945, 'but they were not available and there was no transport. There had been pretty severe destruction of the Rhine bridges in the neighbourhood.' And so, Colonel Johnston and Colonel Gonin had to struggle through with their own small frontline medical units, supplemented gradually by a motley assembly of other forces – the Red Cross teams, the medical students, the Irish nurses. The inability of internee doctors and nurses to make a substantial contribution was a cruel disappointment. Only with the arrival of the German doctors and nurses, the Swiss medical teams and other reinforcements (in about the second week in May) were the medical resources remotely adequate.[4]

'The task before us was the like of which nobody had any knowledge or experience,' a British officer who worked at Belsen has recently declared.

Neither had we the slightest idea of what we were to discover. All of us were in a state of utter shock – young soldiers . . .

as well as senior officers . . . What SHOULD you do when faced by 60,000 dead, sick and dying people? We were in a war to fight a war and to beat the enemy. What we were suddenly thrust into was beyond anyone's comprehension, let alone a situation which could have been organized and effectively planned for.[5]

We have seen that the British made mistakes in the management of the medical catastrophe that faced them. The wrong food was provided at first; the muddled command structure led to delays in evacuating both the sick and the 'fit' from the 'Horror Camp'; those in charge were slow to realise that the plan drawn up on 17 April was not working and must be amended; and so on. Conversely, some of the successes were produced by people who were not part of the army – and were therefore more capable of thinking and acting independently – the two Quakers who fixed the water supply; the medical students; Rabbi Hardman, who opened the hospital in Camp 1; Captain Davis, the typhus expert. It is not hard to see an overall pattern behind these details – the inflexibility of the military mind, the lack of specialist expertise in this area of medicine, the fact that military doctors are used to dealing with fit young men, not starving women; the war-weariness from which most were suffering at this stage. Again, Glyn Hughes privately conceded some of these points. 'What is to be done in the future if we meet these problems?' he asked in London in June.

If one can have ready highly trained teams, so much the better . . . The cry is for bodies of men at the beginning, and we are very short in the RAMC. You must have everything thought out – administration, supplies, everything – and be ready to go straight in, with water and food as priorities, and with combatant troops to supervise and guard the camp. It is necessary to impound skilled and unskilled labour if you can get it, and to 'lay on' beforehand all the accessories in the way of supplies. If fighting is going on at the time it is not easy.

Against that, two fundamental points have to be stressed. Firstly, the British Army did most of the work at Belsen and, for all its faults, provided the backbone of discipline and organisation without which little would have been achieved. Secondly, it was generally agreed that Glyn Hughes did well to get as much out of the army as he did, while the war was still going on; and that James Johnston showed outstanding leadership.

The British drew on the resources of Empire and on their own particular way of engaging with foreigners. The Red Cross effort at Belsen, Effie Barker remarked, was 'a magnificent example of what can be done by ordinary people with that wonderful sense of duty combined with pig headedness and lack of imagination which makes the British race tackle any job with success'. That probably holds good for the medical relief effort as a whole.[6]

It was one of the peculiarities of the British class and educational system that the very worst jobs were often given, not as in other countries, to punishment troops or political prisoners, but to young males from the privileged elite, who alone were thought to have the sense of social responsibility, awareness of social position and strength of character to do them. This tide was beginning to ebb by the 1940s, but still flowed strongly in certain sections of British society. In the medical students' accounts of first entering 'their' hut at Belsen, there are echoes of a motif commonly heard in narratives of colonialism, the moment when the young public school boy finds himself exercising authority as District Commissioner, the only white man for miles around, protected by his aura and the colour of his skin.[7]

Many of the criticisms of the British were first heard at the time. 'The internees are waking from a bad dream – they are remembering the comparative comfort of their "pre-lager" life,' Jane Leverson reported on 6 May 1945.

They are very often not grateful for that which is done for them. They are extremely fussy about the clothes with which they are issued. They grumble about their food; they complain if they are asked to eat their meat and vegetable course from their soup plates. They will not take 'no' for an answer and will beg in an irritatingly 'whiney' voice for a preferential treatment; they will bribe one in a most pathetic way. (One patient offered me three cigarettes if I would trace her little boy for her.) If they are like this now, so soon after liberation, one wonders how they will react when once again they are really free.

She found the 'better-educated and more intellectual' internees very critical of the British. Jane did not speak German, so she was almost certainly referring to the French.

They criticise the fact that the British Army here eats white bread, whilst the patients are given rye bread, which they find very unpalatable. They criticise the fact that their own doctors were not consulted before German doctors and nurses were introduced into the camp. They criticise the fact that the British military commander drove round Camp 1 on the first day of liberation, in the same car as the German military commander, 'for all the world as though we were an exhibition'. Criticism is healthy – and the British must expect it – but praise is unfortunately scarce. Considering the immensity of the task here, my own view is that, although there are small ways in which the British might have done better, on the whole, and within a very short period, the British have brought a remarkable amount of order into this area of chaos.[8]

There was an element of irrationality about some of the criticism. Then and later, internees were reluctant to accept that one of the main causes of death at Belsen was the hoarding of food by prisoners themselves; or that internee doctors were ineffective. The introduction of German medical personnel could have been more diplomatically handled, but it undoubtedly had to be done. It was a particular source of grievance that the British retained the 2000-odd Hungarian guards at Belsen and, in effect, allowed most of them to work their passage on to the Allied side and avoid prosecution. Some of the Hungarians were brutal and sadistic – and several of them were indeed later prosecuted – but without the Hungarians very little would have been achieved at Belsen: they did all the work – the digging of graves, the clearing out of water tanks, the cleaning of wards, the carrying away of the dead every night, the spraying with DDT. They even put on white jackets and waited on tables in the 'Coco-nut Grove' nightclub.

If Belsen was uncovered today, what would be done differently? Dr John Seaman, who spent many years working on famine in Africa for the Save the Children Fund, had some initial difficulty in responding to that question: 'Modern relief is such a different animal,' he said. 'The problem is different. The general circumstances are very different. The technology has shifted.' Seaman was, however, envious of one aspect of the Belsen operation, the numbers of aid workers employed by the British. To him, it was 'astonishing to have so many – some 3000'. In the equivalent modern situation, you would be lucky to have twenty or thirty people and would probably have to use local helpers who would first have to be trained up. As to the organisational problems at Belsen, he felt that 'very little has changed'.

Seaman emphasises that 'walking in on that number of starving people is a tremendous problem'. 'It is not easy to impose order on chaos. It is an intellectual problem – you have to pull the order out of what confronts you, armed with only a few facts.' When you are doing your first famine – as Johnston and Hughes were in 1945 – you don't know how to read it and, if you have never dealt with this before, it is very hard to handle. In the 1940s there was no established clinical approach to dealing with very thin and starving people; there was an element of make it up as you go along – in the circumstances, the use of the Bengal Famine Mixture was a sensible piece of improvisation. However, there has been one major shift in thinking. Whereas in the 1940s, protein (and vitamins) were the hot topics in nutrition, today there is more emphasis on energy. The special feeds given at Belsen were, by modern standards, low on energy and high on protein; now it is the other way round.[9]

Seaman is most critical of the use of protein hydrolysates. The 1943 Indian paper, he argues, 'provided no evidence at all that the hydrolysates were actually useful – merely a clinical impression and that, it seems, at second hand. All it showed was that these mixtures could be given to humans without obvious ill effect'. He finds the alacrity with which this untried technique was taken up by the Medical Research Council puzzling and the design of the trial carried out at Belsen primitive by modern standards. On the other hand, Seaman could find little evidence that the hydrolysates actually 'knocked people off' – killed people who might otherwise have lived; by and large they failed to save already moribund people.[10]

The psychological programme at Belsen in April 1945 was crude and ineffective. But here too it is important to remember that this was still completely uncharted territory in 1945, and we should be wary of assuming that the problem would be tackled better today.

One of the tenets of the 'Trauma Movement' which developed in the United States in the 1980s, in the wake of Vietnam and feminism, was that victims of traumatic events, such as natural disasters, acts of genocide, torture or rape, should be 'debriefed' by counsellors in the immediate aftermath of the 'event', to prevent traumatic memories developing. Further than that, it was argued that it was possible for foreign aid workers to assess the levels of Post-Traumatic Stress Disorder after natural disasters and acts of atrocity by giving victims questionnaires designed by American psychologists such as the 'Impact of Events Scale' and the 'Grief

Reaction Inventory'. By the early 1990s, it was standard practice to send 'trauma teams' to places like Rwanda and Bosnia to do this.

Critics of the American trauma movement argued, however, that it was not necessarily a good idea to create in peoples' minds the quasi-medical concept of 'trauma', that experience in the military showed that the most effective treatment in acute situations was simple and practical, and that it was an act of grotesque arrogance to imagine that 'war collapses down in the head of an individual survivor to a discrete mental entity, "the trauma", that can be meaningfully addressed by Western counselling or other talk therapy'.[11]

Over the last decade numerous research studies and practical experience, especially in New York after 11 September 2001, have shown that 'debriefing' soon after a traumatic 'event' is not usually effective; and that it is better to give trauma survivors a secure environment, minister to their practical needs and concerns, and leave them to cope in their own ways. This does not exclude psychotherapy later, should it be necessary. It has also become clear that there are severe limits to what outside trauma counsellors can hope to achieve, working through interpreters in a culture they do not share.[12]

In many ways, we have simply been relearning something that was found out at Belsen in the 1940s. As we have seen, there was an ascending scale of cultural contact among helpers in the camps. The first relief workers were nearly all British gentiles who did not speak Yiddish – many did even not speak German; then came Jewish volunteers from Britain and the United States; and, finally, volunteers from Palestine who shared both language and culture with the survivors. Contemporaries were in no doubt at all that the last group were by far the most effective in helping survivors. By 1946, the agencies were primarily looking for volunteers who spoke Yiddish and came from Eastern Europe.[13]

Ultimately, though, there can never be answers to such questions. We must accept that Belsen will always transcend rational historical enquiry; that there will always be multiple truths about such an event. In 1957, in a book published in Tel Aviv, Dr Hadassah Bimko wrote that 'the work of the doctors and nurses who came to us from the British Army and from voluntary organisations will for ever remain a ray of light in those dark and tragic days . . . those who recovered are everlastingly grateful for the human service rendered them so generously'. In the same volume, her husband Josef Rosensaft recalled his disagreements with the British but also paid tribute to the 'selfless devotion' of Drs Hughes, Johnston and Meiklejohn. 'It must be admitted,' he added, 'that the British did, on the whole, show much good will, deep human sympathy, and even friendship . . . [They] did everything in their power, both materially and administratively, to help and ease the physical suffering and mental anguish.' These tributes would be repeated several times. But in the year 2000, Menachem Rosensaft – the son born to Hadassah Bimko and Josef Rosensaft in Belsen in 1948 – edited for the US Holocaust Memorial Museum a volume in which Rabbi Greenberg declared that the death of 14,000 people at Belsen revealed British mismanagement born of indifference.[14]

How do we account for the change in tone? In part, the younger Rosensaft reflects growing awareness of the callous attitude of British officialdom to the Holocaust as a whole. But there is also the question of *ownership* – a feeling that Belsen belongs to the survivors (and, now, to their children) and that everyone else, whatever their motives, was simply an intruder – and therefore, by extension, a transgressor.

Perhaps, in the circumstances, that is inevitable.

APPENDIX ONE: THE DEATH RATE AT BELSEN

THE OBVIOUS WAY to measure what was happening at Belsen and the effectiveness of the British medical effort is by the death rate. Most accounts of working in the camp are peppered with such statistics. For example, on 9 May the medical student Alex Paton was told by 'a Brigadier and staff' that 'the death rate had fallen from about 500 a day to 100, which if it is due to us is certainly encouraging'.[1] Unfortunately, these death rates are often mutually incompatible, unreliable or incomplete. Donnison's generally reliable account states that 'the death rate steadily fell from 500 per day on liberation to 300 a day by the end of April. On 11 May the death rate fell below 100 for the first time'.[2] This suggests that the death rate fell steadily once the British arrived; it did not.

The most authoritative figures are those given by Eberhard Kolb in 1962. Kolb emphasises that the British found terrible conditions in the camp and that, despite all their efforts to give life to the liberated, it took several weeks to bring the death rate right down. It remained very high after the liberation and in some days at the end of April reached 1000 a day. 'It may seem surprising that the death rate was no better after 15 April but was in fact much worse. But when one considers what chaotic conditions had developed in the April days, when one considers that the English did not use a card index and that only at the end of April was the clearing of the Horror Camp begun, this is less surprising.'

Kolb gives an overall figure of the number of camp inmates dying after 15 April, numbered at about 14,000, made up as follows:

19–30 April	8992
May	4531
1–20 June	421
Total	13,944

Kolb's figures for the daily death rate are printed below, with (in square brackets in the last column) my rough estimate of the population of Camp 1 at that time. If we assume that 500 a day died between 15 and 19 April, then Camp 1's population fell over that period by at least 2000, and by 19 April was 42,000

Month	Day	Cases of death	Evacuated	Whole camp	Camp 1 (est.)
April	19	825		60,985	[41,175]
April	20	696		60,289	[40,479]
April	21	400		59,889	[40,079]
April	22	1250		58,639	[38,829]
April	23	1700		56,939	[37,129]
April	24	1200		55,739	[35,929]
April	25	785		54,954	[35,144]
April	26	343		54,611	[34,801]
April	27	496		54,115	[34,305]
April	28	421		53,694	[33,884]
April	29	326		53,368	[33,558]

Month	Day	Cases of death	Evacuated	Whole camp	Camp 1 (est.)
April	30	600		52,768	[32,958]
May	1	410		52,358	[32,548]
May	2	449	4177	47,732	[32,099]
May	3	373	733	46,626	[31,726]
May	4	317	98	46,211	[31,409]
May	5	209	9559	36,443	[31,200]

These figures come from a copy of a summary produced by the Colonel Commanding 102 Control Section, Second Army. Kolb says that in the absence of anything to compare them with it is impossible to know if these figures are accurate, but that they seem pretty accurate.[3]

Documents in the Public Record Office in London give other figures. For example, the report by Major Miles of 224 Military Government Detachment (PRO: WO 171/7950):

Month	Day	Cases of death	Sick evacuated from Camp 1 to hospital in Camp 2	Fit evacuated
April	18			
April	20			
April	21	320		
April	22	520		
April	23	344		
April	24	618	23	
April	25	68	512	
April	26	301	603	616
April	27	281		596

Month	Day	Cases of death	Sick evacuated from Camp 1 to hospital in Camp 2	Fit evacuated
April	28	304	637	533
April	29	259	724	902
April	30*	360	633	998

* Improvement in condition of camp now noticeable.

At this point the terminology changes:

Month	Date	Buried	Evacuated
May	1		
May	2	325	1290
May	3	223	1734
May	4	216	831
May	5	45	790
May	6	186	1042
May	7	162	966
May	8	100	1525
May	9	118	1285
May	10	118	580
May	11	61	364
May	12	60	50
May	13	45	75
May	14	47	Nil
May	15	30	Nil

Month	Date	Buried	Evacuated
May	16	30	746
May	17	14	477
May	18	2	73
May	19	1	421

19 May was the last day of evacuation from Camp 1. The final hut was burned on 21 May 1945.

According to the *British Zone Review*, the officer commanding 113 LAA Regt took control of burials on 24 April 'when the organization for food and water was beginning to work smoothly'. 'Up to that time it had only been possible to put one officer in charge of this task . . . The numbers buried were checked instead of being estimated.' This suggests that the numbers for the early period must be very insecure. *BZR* estimates that 'the death-rate among inmates as at the time of entry approximated 500 a day'.

By 15 May the death rate had decreased to eighty-eight per day and up to that time approximately 23,000 inmates of the KZ proper had been buried since its liberation.

APPENDIX TWO:
EXTERNAL EVACUATION FROM BELSEN*

Date	From	To	Total	Nationality
April 1945				
24	No. 2 Camp	DP Route	1164	French/Dutch
25	"	"	1130	Belgian
30	"	Prison Celle	26	German
May 1945				
1	"	Homes	30	German
1	"	POW	33	German
	"	Celle	30	Czech
2	"	Fallingbostel	2468	Russian
	"	POW	37	German
4	"	Celle	433	Italian and Yugoslav
5	"	Celle	413	Czech
	"	Celle	80	Gypsy

Date	From	To	Total	Nationality
6	"	Celle	4984	Pole
7	"	Celle	162	Pole
8	"	Fallingbostel	18	Russian
12	No. 3 Camp	Marienburg	61	Yugoslav
15	"	Lüneburg	760	Russian
17	No. 2 Camp	Soltau	7	Spaniard (accepted by French LO)
	"	Soltau	2	Luxembourg
	"	Soltau	27	Belgian
	"	Soltau	114	French
	No. 3 Camp	Soltau	301	French
	"	Soltau	63	Belgian
	"	Soltau	39	Dutch
18	"	Celle	76	Czech
20	"	Marienburg	70	Yugoslav
21	"	Barum	2186	Russian
22	"	Celle	22	Russian
	"	Celle	42	Greek
	"	Celle	1194	Czech
	"	Celle	52	Greek and Romanian
	"	Celle	34	Italian
	"	Celle	5	Lett [Latvian]
	No. 4 Camp	F.B.	501	Russian

Date	From	To	Total	Nationality
	"	Celle	49	Mixed
23	No. 2 Camp	Barduwick	201	Pole
	No. 3 Camp	Barduwick	911	Pole
	No. 4 Camp	Barduwick	72	Pole
24	No. 2 Camp	Lingen	81	Stateless
	No. 3 Camp	Lingen	596	Stateless
	No. 4 Camp	Lingen	343	Stateless

Source: 'Military Government Report on the Clearing of Belsen Concentration Camp', PRO: WO 219/3944A.
*Terminology as in the original.

NOTES

The following appear frequently in the Notes and are therefore abbreviated for easier reference:

BMJ	*British Medical Journal*
BT	R. Phillips (ed.), *Trial of Josef Kramer and Forty-Four Others (The Belsen Trial)*
BU	D. Sington, *Belsen Uncovered*
BZR	'Belsen. An account, based on Official Reports, of the uncovering by the British Army of the Belsen Concentration Camp and of the action taken during the vital days to minimise the suffering of the 60,000 inmates', *British Zone Review*, December 945
CMAC	Contemporary Medical Archive Centre, Wellcome Library, London
10GR	10 Garrison Report on work at Belsen. PRO: WO 219/3944A
Gonin	Lt. Col. M. V. Gonin, 'The RAMC at Belsen Concentration Camp' (n.d. c. 1946), IWM (D)
GW	R. Pearce (ed.), *Patrick Gordon Walker: Political Diaries 1932–1971*
Hardman	L. H. Hardman and C. Goodman, *The Survivors: The Story of the Belsen Remnant*
IAC	Sir H. L. Tidy (ed.) *Inter-Allied Conferences on War Medicine*
IWM	Imperial War Museum
JR	J. A. D. Johnston, 'The Relief of Belsen Concentration Camp. Recollections and Reflections of a British Army

Doctor'. Rosensaft Papers, United States Holocaust Memorial Museum, Washington, DC

JMP   J. A. D. Johnston, 'Medical appreciation, Belsen Concentration Camp', 18 April; 'Medical Progress Reports', 23 April, 2 May, 10 May and 20 May. PRO: WO 177/669

Kolb (1962)   E. Kolb, *Bergen-Belsen. Geschichte des 'Aufenthaltslagers' 1943–1945*

Kolb (1986)   E. Kolb, *Bergen-Belsen: From 'Detention Camp' to 'Concentration Camp'*

Nolte   H-H. Nolte (ed.), *Häftlinge aus der UdSSR in Bergen-Belsen. Dokumentation der Errinerungen*

KZBB   R. Keller et al., *Konzentrationslager Bergen-Belsen. Berichte und Dokumente*

LHCMA   Liddell Hart Centre for Military Archives, King's College, London

MGR   Military Government Report on the Clearing of Belsen Concentration Camp. PRO WO 219/3944A

RAMC   Royal Army Medical Corps

PRO   The National Archives, Public Record Office, Kew

Reilly   J. Reilly, *Belsen: The Liberation of a Concentration Camp*

Reilly et al.   J. Reilly et al. (eds), *Belsen in History and Memory*

SO   R. Collis and H. Hogerzeil, *Straight On*

Sutters   Friends Relief Service. Reports on Team 100 at Belsen Camp. June 1945. Reprinted in J. Sutters (ed.), *Archives of the Holocaust*, Volume 12: *American Friends Service Committee, Philadelphia*

Trepman   E. Trepman, 'Rescue of the Remnants: The British Emergency Medical Relief Operation in Belsen Camp 1945', *Journal of the Royal Army Medical Corps*, 147 (2001), pp. 281–93

USHMM   United States Holocaust Memorial Museum, Washington, DC

Wenck   A.-E. Wenck, *Zwischen Menschenhandel und 'Endlösung': Das Konzentrationslager Bergen-Belsen*

WL, RHP   Wiener Library London, Rose Henriques Papers

Yesterday   Hadassah [Bimko] Rosensaft, *Yesterday: My Story*

INTRODUCTION (PP. 3–6)

1.   Dimbleby, *Richard Dimbleby*, pp. 188–93.
2.   *SO*, p. 53;
3.   I. Greenberg, 'Preface' to M. Z. Rosensaft (ed.), *Life Reborn*, p. 1.
4.   *BU*, p. 7.
5.   Reilly, 'Cleaner, carer', in Reilly et al., *Belsen*, p. 159.

PROLOGUE (PP. 7–8)

1. PRO: WO 171/4184 11th Armoured Division. G; PRO: WO 177/343, DDMS 8 Corps.
2. 'Belsen Concentration Camp' (13 April 1945); Appendix A. 'Agreement with regard to Belsen Concentration Camp made by Chief of Staff, 1 Para Army, Military Commandant Bergen and BGS, 8 Corps.' Barnett Papers, LHCMA.
3. Roberts, *From the Desert*, p. 236; Delaforce, *Black Bull*, pp. 234–6; Anon., 'Taurus Pursuant', p. 104.

ONE. THE APPROACHING END (PP. 9–23)

1. Lévy-Hass, p. 10.
2. Gilbert, *Hitler Directs*, pp. 4–16; Warlimont, *Inside Hitler's Headquarters*, pp. 267–309; von Below, *At Hitler's Side*, pp. 128–65; Padfield, *Himmler*, p. 408.
3. Hilberg, *Destruction*, passim; Roseman, *The Villa*.
4. Witte, *Die Dienstkalendar*, pp. 635–42; Bauer, *Jews for Sale?*, pp. 102–3; Breitman, 'Himmler and Belsen'; Kolb (1986), pp. 20–1; Oppenheim, *Chosen People*, pp. 76–7.
5. Kolb (1986), pp. 21–4; Bauer, *Jews for Sale?*, p. 103.
6. The first group to reach the camp, in mid-July 1943, was made up of about 2500 Polish Jews who had acquired South American papers on the black market and from cynical diplomats. They thought they had bought exemption but, by the time they reached Belsen, the SS had decided not to honour such documents. After being held for several months, while their papers were closely scrutinised, about 1700 of them were shipped to Auschwitz. According to Kolb ((1986), p. 25), 'When the deportees realised on the Birkenau ramp that they had been deceived and that they were in fact in an extermination camp, one woman snatched a revolver from an SS man, shot him, and severely wounded another. Other women attacked the SS men with their bare hands.' Reinforcements were quickly called in, some of the prisoners were shot on the spot; others were killed by grenades or sent to the gas chambers. No one from this transport escaped. Another such transport followed, leaving some 350 Poles remaining at Belsen – they possessed a more potent means of immunity – they were on the 'Palestine list'.

  The next contingent consisted of Jews from Greece. Between March and August 1943, in an operation of horrible efficiency, the Jewish population of the Greek city of Salonika was briskly dispatched to the ovens at Auschwitz. Of the 46,000 Jews deported, only 74 Greek Jews and 367 'Spagnioles' (Sephardic Jews holding Spanish nationality) were sent to Belsen (Kolb (1986), pp. 25–6; Hilberg, *Destruction*, pp. 738–55).

  Then it was the turn of the Dutch. Of the 105,000 Jews from

Holland to be deported, some 3670 'exchange Jews' reached Belsen in eight transports between January and September 1944. They escaped either because they were thought to have exchange value, were 'Jews of merit' selected by the Jewish Council, or were still economically useful to the Germans, the last group being mainly diamond merchants. A few wealthy individuals were also able to buy their way out. A German Jewish industrialist who had fled to Holland in 1936, and built up a successful business there, paid the equivalent of 80,000 Dutch guilders to make sure that, after a year spent in Westerbork detention camp, his family was sent to Belsen rather than to Auschwitz: a tough and resourceful man, he 'knew that trains to the East were hopeless' (Kolb (1986), p. 26; Moore, *Victims*; Oppenheim, *Chosen People*).

The Hungarians who arrived in July 1944 were the beneficiaries of an extraordinary initiative launched by elements in the Budapest Jewish community when deportations to Auschwitz began in the spring of that year. Their approach to a group of SS officers, including Adolf Eichmann, produced the famous 'Jews for trucks' offer – a German suggestion that a million Jews might be saved in exchange for 10,000 trucks and other supplies from the West (intended to sow mistrust between the Western Allies and the Soviet Union) – and a German promise that a certain number of rich and prominent Hungarian Jews would be allowed to leave, on payment of a ransom of $1000 a head. A small committee then faced the dilemma of selecting 'from the 750,000 doomed Hungarian Jews 1600 who were to live'. Ultimately a group consisting of 'wealthy people who were able to contribute to the ransom, prominent figures from political, religious and cultural life, and some ordinary individuals, who somehow managed to gatecrash' boarded a special train in Budapest on 30 June and arrived at Belsen on 8 July 1944. After further negotiations, 318 members of this group reached Switzerland on 21 August and the remaining 1368 followed on 7 December 1944 (Löb, 'Introduction'; Cesarani, *Genocide and Rescue*).

The Hungarians apart, only 358 of the prisoners at Belsen were exchanged. The third exchange, between German nationals in Palestine and European Jews with certificates to emigrate to Palestine, finally took place in July 1944, after almost a year of negotiations. The number of parties involved, the difficulty of wartime communications, and the fact that most of the Jews entitled to go to Palestine had already been murdered, all complicated the process. Eventually, the British were persuaded to accept substitutes nominated by the Jewish Agency for Palestine, and the group of 222 people which, after many false starts, much raising and falling of hopes, and much packing and unpacking of luggage, reached Turkey (and ultimately Palestine) consisted of 'veteran

Zionists and rabbis'. Another 136 got to Switzerland in January 1945 (Oppenheim, *Chosen People*).

7.   Lévy-Hass, *Inside Belsen*, p. 15.
8.   Herzberg, *Between Two Streams*.
9.   Kolb (1986), pp. 31–8; Lee, *Otto Frank*, pp. 151–65; Fénelon, *Musicians*, pp. 235–49; Ferderber-Salz, *And the Sun*, pp. 139–50; Lévy-Hass, *Inside Belsen*, p. 51.
10. Kolb (1986), pp. 37–48; Segev, *Soldiers of Evil*, pp. 21–2, 67–73; Lévy-Hass, *Inside Belsen*, pp. 38–69; *BT*, pp. 122–3, 156–63, 731–7. 'The belly of a corpse was cut open and the liver turn[ed] out. Five or six cases of the same kind followed in the next few days. And then it began in the rest of the camp. From the bodies lying in front of, or inside the huts, they cut off the ears, the skin of the cheeks, then as this no longer sufficed for the eaters of human flesh, also pieces of arm, leg and buttock muscle. Even the genitals were cut off.' A Polish woman turned up at a door in Camp 1 selling a heart, which was almost certainly human. Verolme, *Children's House*, p. 248. According to one British account, 'the only eatable portions were the kidneys, livers, and heart'. Gonin, p. 3.
11. JR, p. 4.
12. T–543, Marian L., Fortunoff VideoArchive for Holocaust Testimonies, Yale University Library.
13. Lévy-Hass, *Inside Belsen*, p. 59; 'Berthe, who will later become our friend, treats them with respect. "You are really very nice," the brothel keeper said to Berthe one day. "When the war's over, send your husband round. I'll give him the prettiest girl in the house." Berthe said thank you.' Kroh, *Lucien's Story*, p. 22.
14. SO, pp. 32–57; McCann/Tryszynska-Frederick, *Luba*; *BT*, pp. 691–2; 'Kamenets, Belarus', internet – ww2.jewushfgen.org/yizkor/ Kamenets/ kam117.html; Verolme, *Children's House*.
15. H. Rosensaft, *Yesterday*, pp. 1–49; *BT*, pp. 66–78, 740–1; H. Rosensaft, 'Children of Belsen'.
16. Verolme, *Children's House*, pp. 167–71. The children themselves were largely unaware of Dr Bimko's role and identified only with 'Sister Luba' and 'Sister Hermina'. Accounts vary as to how food was obtained. In Dr Bimko's version (H. Rosensaft, *Yesterday*, p. 45), 'Jewish men who worked in the SS food depot . . . risked their lives daily to steal food and pass it to us under the barbed wire'; whereas in all the other accounts food is procured by Luba Tryszynska from her network of contacts among the SS guards, on daily victualling expeditions through the camp. Medicine for the children was obtained by Dr Bimko. 'Thanks to [Hadassah] nearly all of them survived, although in the Lager itself, hundreds of people died. At that time she was chief doctor in the Lager hospital, but she stayed with us and the children.' Hela Los Jafe in Ritvo and Plotkin, *Sisters in Sorrow*, p. 182.
17. Lee, *Otto Frank*, pp. 151–2.

18. Internet – www.holocaust.com.au/lb/r_letter.htm.
19. Fénelon, *Musicians*, p. 254.
20. *BT*, pp. 163–6. Some doubts were later expressed about the authenticity of this letter. *KZBB* and Wenck (pp. 363–4) accept it as genuine.
21. Dr Leo, *BT*, p. 123; *BT*, p. 167.
22. Wenck, pp. 369–71; Oppenheimer, *From Belsen*, pp. 137–43; Hardman, p. 43.
23. Fried, *Fragments*, p. 157
24. Padfield, *Himmler*, pp. 562–612.
25. Breitman, 'Himmler and Belsen', in Reilly et al., pp. 78–81.
26. For what follows: Bernadotte, *Fall of the Curtain*; Kersten, *Memoirs*; Persson, 'Folke Bernadotte', in Cesarini and Levine, *Bystanders*; Breitman, 'Himmler and Belsen'; Bauer, *Jews for Sale?*
27. Kersten, *Memoirs*, p. 276; Weindling, *Epidemics and Genocide*.
28. Kersten, *Memoirs*, pp. 276–8.
29. Ibid, p. 282.
30. Persson, 'Folke Bernadotte', in Cesarini and Levine, *Bystanders*, p. 258.
31. On Becher: Bauer, *Jews for Sale?*; Kolb (1962), pp. 157–64; Wenck, pp. 371–82.
32. He was accompanied by Dr Rudolf Kasztner, the Zionist journalist who had brokered the 1944 deal to save some Hungarian Jews. It is unclear where Kasztner was living at this time or what general role he was playing. Kasztner, who was assassinated in Israel in 1957, remains a mysterious and controversial figure (Bauer, *Jews for Sale?*; Cesarani, *Genocide and Rescue*).
33. Clara Greenbaum's account: Bridgman, *End of the Holocaust*, pp. 123–32. Valentina Gureeva, then a twenty-year-old forced labourer from Donets in the Soviet Union, remembered the white star painted on the tanks. 'They looked at us from the tanks and we looked at them from outside. They stood for a long time and then they drove away.' Nolte, p. 126.

TWO. WHAT WAS KNOWN (PP. 24–32)

1. *Hansard*, 17 December 1942, columns 2082–7.
2. Channon's diaries and Eden's *Memoirs*, quoted in Wasserstein, *Britain and the Jews*, pp. 155–6.
3. London, *Whitehall*, p. 191. Historians also agree that 'no pressure of any significance was ever exerted upon the British Government' by Britain's divided Jewish community (Alderman, *Modern British Jewry*, p. 302). Alderman continues: 'There were of course numerous appeals to the Government to admit more refugees into Britain, and Palestine, and to grant a measure of British protection to Jewish refugees in neutral countries. There was an impressive gathering at the Albert Hall on 29 October 1942 to protest against Nazi persecution. But in relation to the failure of the British

Government to take active steps to rescue European Jewry there was never a mass lobby, or a public demonstration. It was never suggested – at least in any public forum – that the British Government might actually not care very much about the fate of European Jewry. What was suggested was that the patriotic duty of British Jews was to support the war effort, and the priorities therewith as laid down by the Government, and that to challenge these priorities was to endanger the good name of the community.' 'It was simply not evident to most British Jews that they could act any differently . . .' writes Richard Bolchover, *British Jewry and the Holocaust*, p. 156; the Jewish community was 'paralysed', Reilly, *Belsen*, pp. 118–34.

4. Breitman, *Official Secrets*, sets out what the British knew and when. However, Wasserstein (*Britain and the Jews*, p. 149) makes the important point that while Churchill would have seen the decrypts of Einsatzgruppen messages, 'many of the politicians and officials who dealt with the Jewish question had no access to such intelligence material and depended largely on diplomatic and press reports'. 'Sorry to bother you': Breitman, *Official Secrets*, p. 189.

5. Wasserstein, *Britain and the Jews*; London, *Whitehall and the Jews*; Feingold, *Politics of Rescue*.

6. Raoul Wallenberg (1912–?) was a businessman from a prominent Swedish family who agreed to go to Budapest in July 1944 as the representative of the War Refugee Board. Working out of the Swedish Delegation, he used American money and Swedish diplomatic cover to save Hungarian Jews – more than 20,000 of them according to W. Laqueur and J. Tydor Baumel (eds), *The Holocaust Encyclopedia*, pp. 669–73; he may also have acted as an agent for American intelligence. When the Russians entered Budapest in January 1945, they arrested Wallenberg and he disappeared into the Gulag. His fate remains uncertain, though he may still have been alive as late as 1989.

7. Feingold, *Politics of Rescue*; Rubinstein, *Myth of Rescue*; Marrus, *Unwanted*; Niewyk and Nicosia, *Columbia Guide*, pp. 123–4.

8. Bombing Auschwitz: inter alia, Gilbert, *Auschwitz and the Allies*; and Rubinstein, *Myth of Rescue*.

9. Novick, *Holocaust*, p. 20. 'The "Holocaust" began to be widely used in connection with the Nazi murder programme in the 1960s, not as the result of a Gentile plot, but as an import from Israel. Large numbers of American journalists, covering the Eichmann trial, learned to use the word that Israelis had for many years chosen to translate "shoah" into English' (ibid., p. 133). 'While it is true that the Eichmann trial was the first time that the American public was presented with the Holocaust as a distinct – and distinctively Jewish – entity, it was as yet by no means *as* distinct, or as distinctly *Jewish*, as it was later to become' (ibid., p. 134). A

Foreign Office official wrote in January 1945 that Jewish accounts 'are only sometimes reliable and not seldom highly coloured'. An infamous Ministry of Information memorandum laid down that, in British propaganda, 'horror stuff . . . must be used very sparingly and must deal always with treatment of indisputably innocent people. Not with violent opponents. And not with Jews.' PRO: INF 1/251 Part 4. Plan to combat the apathetic attitude of 'What have I got to lose even if Germany wins?' Quoted in Caven, 'Horror in our time', p. 229

10. Donnison, *Civil Affairs*, pp. 345–6. Many of the major charities in Britain had other preoccupations; most notably, with the consequences of the Allied policy of blockade – which prevented food aid from reaching German-occupied Europe, in the mistaken belief that, by letting millions of Europeans starve, the German war economy would be weakened. OXFAM, the Oxford Committee for Famine Relief, was founded in 1942 especially to lobby the British government to change its blockade policy but, although an exception was made in the case of Greece after some half a million Greeks had died of starvation, Churchill and his ministers refused to change tack. The Jewish community in Britain, unlike its equivalent in the United States, did not have a tradition of foreign aid work and when General Eisenhower insisted that the foreign aid agencies band together into a single unit, under the banner of the Red Cross, no Jewish organisations were involved.

11. Fisher, *Raphael Cilento*, pp. 185–200; Moorehead, *Dunant's Dream*, pp. 411–99.

12. Hughes, 'Normandy to the Baltic from a Medical Angle', CMAC RAMC, 1218/2/18; 'Germany'. Fisher Papers, IWM (D).

13. SHAEF, *Basic Handbook. KLs. Axis concentration camps and detention centres reported as such in Europe*; PRO: WO 177/322; Zweig, 'Feeding the camps', p. 844. This document 'strongly suggested that conditions in the camps were improving as the war came to an end . . . An endless stream of captured German POW interrogations, and reports from liberated Allied personnel, provided much additional information on the brutal regime in the camps and the conditions of the surviving inmates. None of this material, however, made its way into the report.' Loc. cit.

14. Oppenheim, *Chosen People*, has a detailed account.

15. PRO: FO 916/847.

16. PRO: FO 916/1163. For Levy's later account of life in the Neutrals' camp: *KZBB*, pp. 61, 72–3, 82–5.

17. The fact that the Royal Air Force photographed Belsen from the air in September 1944 is sometimes seen as evidence that the British 'knew about Belsen'. It is not clear whether the camp's function was understood by the RAF or whether this photograph was ever seen by other branches of the bureaucracy.

THREE. 'YOU ARE FREE': 12–16 APRIL 1945 (PP. 33–42)

1. This chapter is largely based on D. Sington, *Belsen Uncovered* (*BU*); D. Sington, 'Belsen Camp No. 1' [30 April 1945] in Champion Papers, IWM (D); Lt. Col. R. I. G. Taylor, 'Report on Belsen Camp', Barnett Papers, LHCMA; W. E. Roach, 'The first four days in Belsen' [n.d. c. 1965] – with thanks to Graham Parmenter; W. R. Williams, [Belsen testimony] in Reilly et al., *Belsen*, pp. 244–9

2. Playfair and Sington, *The Offenders*, pp. 146–56.

3. 'Those who were still more or less healthy ran behind the car, kissed the tracks, the tyre tracks of the car or the car itself, but somehow there was no reaction, neither tears nor joy', a Russian woman, taken by the Germans for slave labour, later remembered. Nolte, pp. 140–1.

4. Gilbert, *Never Again*, p. 153.

5. Although both Sington and Glyn Hughes would later be described as 'the first man into Belsen', the first British soldiers to arrive at Belsen, according to Paul Kemp (Reilly et al., *Belsen*, p. 135), 'were members of the 1st Special Air Service (SAS). Although the majority of 1st SAS were engaged in providing a reconnaissance screen for the 6th Airborne Division, a section under the command of Major Harry Poat was in the 11th Armoured Division area to check if any members of the regiment or any other allied POWs were incarcerated there. It is not clear when the SAS reached the camp, but they did so before the arrival of a group of staff officers from HQ 8 Corps [tea-time, 15 April 1945].' According to Anthony Kemp, *The SAS at War* (London, 1993), pp. 218–19, 'All those I have spoken to in 1 SAS who were with Frankforce remember having gone into the concentration camp before it was properly liberated and there are photographs to prove this . . . they were issued with yellow armbands and inoculated against infectious diseases, with specific orders to hold the area after the German troops pulled back.' A claim by Lance-Corporal Hull, the driver of the famous SAS officer Paddy Mayne, to have shot some of the guards, is, however, 'difficult to account for as Mayne's unit at the time was sixty-odd miles away to the west. Whatever the truth of the liberation of Belsen, the SAS were not there for long as their job was to move on towards Lüneburg.' Colonel Taylor of 63rd Anti-Tank Regiment reported that on the afternoon of 15 April, while he was talking to Oberst Harries at the Panzer Training School – before, that is, Taylor himself had entered Camp 1 – an SAS officer reported to him 'that he had found a soldier of his unit who was a prisoner in Camp 1. He was given permission to remove this man, by name Jenkinson, and later reported that he had done so.' Taylor, 'Report on Belsen Camp', Barnett Papers, LHCMA.

6. Handwritten notes by Barnett. Barnett Papers, LHCMA.

7. Hughes, PRO: WO 222/201.
8. Kolb (1986), p. 48; Abisch, IWM (S).
9. Roach, 'First four days'.
10. *BU*, pp. 37–40
11. Ibid., pp. 37–40; Williams, [Belsen testimony] in Reilly et al.,
    Belsen; Ellis, *Sharp End*, pp. 275–6.
12. Baneth, IWM (S); Fried, *Fragments*, pp. 171–2; Bick-Berkovitz,
    Where Are My Brothers?, p. 11.
13. Fink, IWM (S); Knoller, IWM (S).
14. Gill, *Journey Back*, pp. 429–30; Edith (Hoffman) Birkin remem-
    bered being given macaroni milk pudding herself. It agreed with
    her; 'and that's what I feed to my family every year on 15 April,'
    she said in 1990.
15. Walker, 'The feeding problem'. See the death-rate figures in
    Appendix I. 'How should a normal soldier know our past and
    what's right?' a former inmate later asked. 'They done their best.
    But really it was the worst thing ever could have been done.' Baneth
    (IWM) (S). One British officer 'had read somewhere that starving
    people should not eat too much at once – a surfeit could be
    dangerous. As there was no one to advise me I decided to simply
    double the ration of potatoes and bread and add some meat from
    the SS stores to improve the soup.' Roach, 'First four days'.

FOUR. THE PLAN (PP. 43–53)

1. Quoted in Kemp, *Relief of Belsen*.
2. Moorehead, 'Belsen', in Connolly, *The Golden 'Horizon'*; Gonin,
    p. 5.
3. *The Times*, 26 November 1973; Hughes Papers, CMAC, RAMC
    1218; [unknown] 'The man in his time'; conversation with Mrs
    Jean Smart, 29 January 2004.
4. Carl Aarvold, tribute at Hughes's memorial service, 9 January
    1974. With thanks to Mrs Smart.
5. 'Medical report on Belsen Concentration Camp by DDMS Second
    Army' [15–19 April 1945] PRO: WO 235/19; *BT*, pp. 30–44. Other
    British accounts give higher figures for Belsen's population, as much
    as 46,685 for Camp 1 and 27,000 for Camp 2. (Trepman, p. 281)
6. Another estimate was that at least 20,000 in the 'Horror Camp'
    'required urgent hospital treatment'; while the remaining 20,000
    'might not die if they were not doctored but . . . would most
    certainly die if they were not fed and removed from the horror
    camp' – because inside the huts the dead and the dying lay cheek
    by jowl with the sick and the well. JMP, 18 April 1945.
7. H. Rosensaft, 'Children of Belsen', p. 104.
8. PRO: WO 222/201. Paper on Belsen given by Glyn Hughes to a
    conference in London in June 1945. The version published in *IAC*
    omits some of his more frank remarks.

9.   Gonin, p. 2.
10.   JR, p. 1.
11.   Johnston and Gonin both held the rank of Lt. Colonel. For brevity's sake, they are referred to hereon as Colonel Johnston and Colonel Gonin.
12.   *Daily Telegraph*, 20 May 1988; Jackson, *Thirty Seconds at Quetta*; SO, p. 56.
13.   JR, p. 8.
14.   JR, pp. 5–6; Gonin, p. 6.
15.   PRO: WO 222/201.
16.   Gonin, p. 5.
17.   Fisher, 'A soldier's diary' IWM (D); Simpson IWM (S).
18.   Warren, IWM (S); Riches, IWM (S).

FIVE. FRUSTRATIONS: 18–23 APRIL 1945 (PP. 54–67)

1.   *BU*, p. 85; Fisher, 'A soldier's diary', IWM (D).
2.   *BZR*, p. 5.
3.   *GW*, p. 146; JMP, 23 April 1945. JR, p. 10. On 20 April, 50,000 blankets arrived from the British Army and were being laundered *GW*, p. 147.
4.   10GR; Lewis, IWM (S); Taylor Report, Barnett Papers, LHCMA.
5.   JR, p. 11.
6.   Ibid.; Gonin, p. 7; Towers and Kenny, 'Belsen'; Riches, IWM (S).
7.   'There were 50 naked women, so emaciated you could have cut yourself on their ribs, being scrubbed down by these German girls just as if they were a lot of cattle, there were men of every description, ambulance drivers, stretcher bearers, etc, all walking in and out but these poor things have been so humiliated the last few years they thought nothing of this.' J. Rudman, 9 BGH, letter, 14 May 1945. IWM (D)
8.   Silva Jones, IWM (D). An American ambulance man compared it to 'a Hollywood conception of the Last Day of Judgment'. Unidentified AFS driver, May 1945. AFS Archives, New York.
9.   Gonin, pp. 8–9; Davis, 'Typhus at Belsen', p. 77.
10.   PRO: WO 171/7950, War Diary, 224 Mil Gov Det.
11.   PRO: WO 219/3944A – italics added; WO 177/669.
12.   *GW*, pp. 152–3. Patrick Gordon Walker (1907–80) was an Oxford don in the 1930s, worked for the BBC and Radio Luxembourg in the war, became a Labour MP in 1945 and was briefly British Foreign Secretary in the Wilson government in 1964. He had no medical or military experience himself; the value of his diaries lies in what he recorded from talking to others at Belsen.
13.   *BU*, p. 54.
14.   PRO: WO 219/3944A. PRO: WO 177/322, report by Major Waldron. A visiting Quaker relief worker thought that 'coordination between the Mil Gov Det and the medical staff' needed to be

improved. M. Gardiner, Friends Ambulance Unit, 23 April. Barker Papers, IWM (D); General Templer, the Director of Civil Affairs and Military Government at 21 Army Group HQ, 'was one of the first visitors' to Belsen and 'got the very best teams of his POW and DP Section to work there'. Cloake, *Templer*, p. 153.

15. BU, pp. 65–9.
16. Ferderber-Salz, *And the Sun*, pp. 15–17, 165.
17. 'There were no doctors, paramedical aid was not provided, and very little food was supplied. The only thing that was done for us was that barrels of water containing a yellow liquid were placed all over the camp, a few steps away from one another, and we were told through loudspeakers that we should drink that water as often as possible.' Ibid. PRO: WO 177/322; WO 219/3944A.
18. JMP, 23 April 1945; JR, p. 5. 'The smell inside these huts was indescribable. When we started to work in them we found it difficult to do so for more than ten minutes or so at a time without being physically sick.' GW, p. 153.
19. BT, pp. 53–4.
20. Kirill Norchenko, in Nolte, p. 136. It was generally agreed that Russian prisoners, both male and female, retained a spirit of mutual assistance more successfully than any other group. Norchenko describes how his group would not let the British take a very ill young Russian lad to hospital. 'If they had taken him with them, God knows what might have happened to him. The comrades wouldn't let me in the hospital either.' PRO: WO 219/3944A
21. Gonin, p. 5. Glyn Hughes did his best to keep up morale. 'He used to turn up in the middle of our nightly conferences with a grin all over his face usually tired out from having been in the battle all day,' Gonin wrote. 'With a large whisky in his hand he'd lay down the law as to how things should be done and he was always right', ibid., p. 10; Levy, *Witness*, p. 11; M. Gardner of FAU, Barker Papers, IWM (D); J. Leverson, Letter 25 April, WL, RHP

SIX. THE CHAPLAIN'S TALE (PP. 68–73)

1. Hardman, pp. 1–3, 9–15.
2. Hardman, IWM (S).
3. Hardman, pp. 16–28.
4. GW, pp 143–9; Hardman, pp. 36–7.
5. Levy, *Witness*, p. 15.
6. Hardman, pp. 35–41.
7. BU, pp. 63–9.
8. Hardman, pp. 39–40.
9. Levy, *Witness*, pp. 13–14; Hardman, p. 48.
10. Hardman, p. 31.
11. R. H. S. Crossman, *Palestine Mission* (London, 1946), quoted in Wasserstein, *Vanishing Diaspora*, p. 3.

SEVEN. REINFORCEMENTS: CAMP 1, 24–30 APRIL 1945 (PP. 74–89)

1. Movietone, Belsen, 23–24 April 1945: IWM, Department of Film; Wyand, *Useless if Delayed*, pp. 164–5; *BU*, pp. 87–90.
2. MGR; Moorehead, 'Belsen', in Connolly, *The Golden 'Horizon'*, p. 104. Hardman (p. 47) recalls that one burgomaster was a woman, which seems unlikely. He may have meant the SS women who were also present.
3. Moorehead, 'Belsen', in Connolly, *The Golden 'Horizon'*, p. 104; MGR. On 22 April, a 'new organization [was] set up to deal with the accumulation of dead in Camp 1 under Captain Pares'. On 26 April, the War Diary of 13th LAA Regt, RA, records: '8000 bodies buried since arrival'. PRO: WO 171/4957
4. V. A. Harden, 'Typhus, Epidemic', in Kiple, *Cambridge World History of Human Disease*; Porter, *Greatest Benefit*; McNeill, *Plagues and Peoples*; Weindling, *Epidemics and Genocide*.
5. Harrison, *Medicine and Victory*, pp. 136–7.
6. 'The Conquest of Typhus', *New York Times*, 1944 (Fred L. Soper Papers, National Library of Medicine).
7. A. MacAuslan, telephone interview, October 2004. Paton, 'Belsen'. Paton's entry continues, '[He] gave us a superb talk, [but] I rather thought he overestimated the [value of vaccination] and didn't take enough account of the fact that people who had mild attacks of typhus had not only been vaccinated but were comparatively fit men.'
8. Davis, 'Typhus at Belsen', pp. 66–83.
9. Ibid.
10. *Munk's Roll*, 6, pp. 295–7; CMAC, RAMC 792/2/3; *IAC*, pp. 462–5. One medical student described Lipscomb as 'a bit of a dry old prune' and a 'boring old gentleman'. Bradford, 'Expedition', pp. 7, 12.
11. JR, p. 7; MGR Appendix 1.
12. Drummond, 'Notes on Feeding Problems . . . at Belsen Camp', PRO: FD 1/ 142. Chief Scientific Adviser to the Ministry of Food, Drummond had been sent to Holland to advise on measures against starvation. According to his report, the death rate at Belsen on 29 April was of the order of 300–400 a day, having been 500–600 a day previously. These figures were probably underestimates. Drummond and Wilbraham, *Englishman's Food*.
13. JR, p. 7; Drummond, PRO: FD 1/ 142. What effect this had on the Russian survival rate, Western sources do not reveal. Another problem was the monotony of the food. Some of the first people evacuated out of Camp 1 were found, 'shortly after arrival, to be picking dandelion leaves for salads'. 10GR.
14. Cambray and Briggs, *Red Cross and St John*, pp. 506–7; Sutters, p. 550; Beardwell, *Aftermath*, pp. 34–7. The team of forty-eight women and twenty-four men was made up of six units – from the

Red Cross itself, the Friends' Relief Service (Quakers), Salvation
Army, and other organisations, serving under the collective Red
Cross umbrella. The surviving accounts are nearly all drawn from
the Red Cross and Quaker units. I have found little trace of the
Irish nurses.

15. Sutters, pp. 558–9
16. Gonin, pp. 9–10.
17. Beardwell, *Aftermath*, pp. 38–40; McFarlane, 'April 19th . . .'. By
the end of April, 'floods of visitors' had begun to descend on
Belsen, 'mostly', the army complained irritably, 'without authority
or clear purpose'. Some were sightseers from the Allied forces, like
the Church of England padre who took one look and refused to
get out of his car or the group of Canadian airmen who walked
halfway up the main road in Camp 1, threw up and fled. Others
were liberated prisoners of war who came to the camp hoping to
find relatives, only to be treated with brutal bureaucratic unhelp-
fulness. MGR; 10GR.
18. Leverson, IWM (S); Leverson did later work in Camp 1, helping
Leslie Hardman, in early May of 1945.
19. Cambray and Briggs, *Red Cross and St John*, p. 506; Collis, 'Belsen
camp'.
20. For what follows, *BU*, pp. 92–8.
21. MGR; IWM (F) A 70/311/4 & 5 (Sgt Lawrie).
22. *BU*, pp. 92–8; Sington had to leave Belsen on 29 April, to rejoin
8 Corps. He returned to the camp on 13 May.
23. Ehrlich, IWM (S)
24. IWM (F) A 70/311/5. Dope Sheets. Notes by cameraman William
Lawrie.
25. JMP, 2 May 1945.

EIGHT. 'WOULD WE MIND?' (PP. 90–104)

1. Paton, 'Belsen'. For general accounts of the medical students, see
Vella, Reilly and Trepman.
2. Dixey, IWM (S); Hargrave, 'Diary'.
3. Bradford, 'Expedition'; Hargrave, 'Diary'; Paton, 'Belsen'; Horsey,
'Record', Kidd; 'Diary'.
4. Dixey, IWM (S).
5. Horsey, IWM (S).
6. Proctor, IWM (S); MacAuslan, 'Belsen, May 1945'; Bradford,
'Expedition'.
7. Dossetor, IWM (S); Raymond, IWM (S).
8. Paton, 'Belsen'; Raperport, 'Expedition'; Bradford, 'Expedition'.
One student, A. T. Cook, IWM (S), later remembered the initiative to create the hospital in Camp 1 as coming wholly from the
students themselves, but contemporary accounts stress the role of
Captain Gluck.

9.   Horsey, 'Record'; Horsey, IWM (S); interview with Dr Peter Horsey, August 2004.
10.   Towers and Kenny, 'Belsen'; Dixey, IWM (S); Paton, 'Belsen'.
11.   Gibson, 'Belsen 1945'; Bradford, 'Expedition'; Dixey, IWM (S); Hargrave, 'Diary'.
12.   'To suddenly change one's occupation from that of firing a field gun to running six huge kitchens is a feat to be proud of' Coigley, 'Letter'; Dixey, 'Belsen'. One of the students later recalled that 'the food . . . delivered to his hut consisted of fresh milk in churns, which when inadvertently left outside in the hot weather rapidly went sour. And the patients discovering sour milk, became very enthusiastic about it and the first day or so sour milk was the staple diet.' A. T. Cook, IWM (S).
13.   Raymond, IWM (S); Trimmer, IWM (S).
14.   Aykroyd, *Conquest of Famine*, is a classic account by a British doctor in India. The figure for deaths is much disputed. The excellent summary, 'Famine in Bengal. Report of the Inquiry', *Lancet* (1945), i, pp. 731–2, states that '1.5 million deaths occurred as a direct result of the famine and of the epidemics which followed in its train'. Aykroyd (p. 77) has a frank account of the process by which this figure was arrived at and admits that it was an underestimate, but also thinks that the figure of 3–4 million, commonly used by modern authorities such as Sen, is too high.
15.   Sen, *Poverty and Famines*. A number of factors conspired to make things worse: the governor of Bengal was dying; the local provincial government was incompetent and corrupt; a black market in food developed; the Viceroy, Lord Linlithgow, refused to take much interest; in London, the India Office tried to pretend there was simply a 'food shortage'. The result was that, instead of the famine problem being promptly recognised and efficiently addressed in the traditional manner, it was denied and ignored. It then turned out that Churchill's decision earlier in the year to divert shipping from the Indian Ocean to the Mediterranean (in order to attack Italy) had removed much of the transport needed to bring relief supplies from abroad. See N. Mansergh, *Transfer of Power*. Volume 4. *The Bengal Famine and the New Viceroyalty, 15 June to 31 August 1944* (London, 1973); J. Whitehead, *Famine Inquiry Commission. Report on Bengal* (New Delhi, 1945); and K. S. Fitch, *The Medical History of the Indian Famine, 1943–1944* (Calcutta, 1947).
16.   'Treatment and management of starving sick destitutes', Prepared by the Committee of Enquiry into effects of starvation, Indian Research Fund Association' (Calcutta, n.d., c. 1944); K. V. Krishnan et al., 'Protein hydrolysates in the treatment of inanition', *Indian Medical Gazette*, 79 (1944), pp. 160–4.
17.   CMAC, RAMC [Lipscomb Papers]: 'It would appear,' he continued, 'that when the loss of body protein has reached a

dangerous degree, recovery can be induced, or at least much accel-
erated, by the use of mixtures of amino acids (protein hydrolysates)
either by intravenous injection, by nasal tube or by spoon feeding.'
Report of MRC Protein Requirements Committee. PRO: FD
1/6346; Janet Vaughan to George Minot, 27 May 1945, Vaughan
Papers, Somerville College, Oxford.

18. Horsey, 'Record'; Dixey, 'Belsen'; Hardman, p. 49. Alex Paton
wrote on 5 May: 'We now take a firm hand with those who refuse
to drink the Bengal Famine Mixture and treat it like medicine,
making them drink one cup.'

19. Kidd, 'Diary'; Dixey, 'Belsen'; Horsey, 'Report'. Nearly all the
students reported similar findings. However, James Gowans 'saw
a small number of marked improvements in starving but not moribund patients treated with hydrolysate . . . the best results were
seen in uncomplicated cases of starvation with oedema on which
the patients were unable to take solid food by mouth but who
could drink the hydrolysate'. He felt the hydrolysates deserved
further trials, and considered 'its complete condemnation by some
workers hasty and unjustified'. Gowans, 'Clinical observations'.

20. Janet Vaughan to George Minot, 12 and 25 May 1945. Vaughan
Papers, Somerville College, Oxford. Owen, 'Janet Vaughan'; Doll,
'Janet Vaughan'.

21. Paton, 'Belsen'.

22. Weindling argues that 'The camp inmates became in effect experimental material for nutritionists [Jack Drummond and V. P.
Sydenstricker] who visited the camp to evaluate feeding methods
and take blood profiles before entering the starvation areas of the
Netherlands. Vaughan realised the difficulties of her position and
some British doctors criticised such opportunistic experimentation'
(*Epidemics and Genocide*, pp. 395–6). This ignores the fact that
most of the MRC nutritionists had already been in Holland before
going to Belsen.

23. E. Cole, 7 May 1945, AFS Archives, New York; Oakes, IWM (S);
Reilly, pp. 29–30.

24. MacAuslan, IWM (S); *The Times*, 3 July 2002.

25. Bradford, 'Expedition'. The cinema's manager turned out to be
Marlene Dietrich's brother-in-law. There was huge excitement
when the star herself appeared, to be reunited with her sister.

26. Moorehead, 'Belsen', in Connolly, *The Golden 'Horizon'*; Lawrie,
IWM (S); Lewis, IWM (S); Oakes, IWM (S); IWM, Film Dope Sheets.

27. 'This unit carried out magnificent work,' Lt. Col. Gonin wrote
(*BMJ* (1945), ii, p. 65). 'Nothing was too big for them, and I
have never known men so hungry for work or more willing to co-
operate in any task'; Rock, *History of the American Field Service*,
pp. 420–5.

28. McFarlane, 'April 19th'; Russian prisoner Viktor Mamontov recalls
that 'The English Army had a holiday for the whole week. They

said to us we must have patience for the whole week. But how can one speak of patience when every day without stopping people were dying.' Nolte, pp. 129–30.

29.   MacAuslan, 'Belsen'.

30.   Paton, 'Belsen'; Raperport, 'Expedition'.

NINE. THE HOSPITAL: CAMP 2, 21 APRIL – 21 MAY 1945 (PP. 105–22)

1.   Fisher, 'A soldier's diary', IWM (D).

2.   Ibid.

3.   Fisher, IWM (S); *Jewish Chronicle*, 17 August 2001.

4.   JMP, 23 April 1945.

5.   Silva Jones, 'From a Diary'.

6.   'Fisher, 'A soldier's diary', IWM (D).

7.   Ibid.

8.   Bark, *No Time*, p. 51; McFarlane, 'April 19th', IWM (D), pp. 9–10. Before the war Jean McFarlane had been the captain of the English lacrosse team.

9.   Ibid.

10.   *IAC*, p. 461. 4 June 1945.

11.   Fisher, 'A soldier's diary'; Silva Jones, 'From a diary'; Blackman, Papers, IWM (D).

12.   Leverson acknowledged, however, that much 'organising' of food was going on; Jane Leverson to Jewish Committee for Relief Abroad, 6 May 1945. WL, RHP. She 'spent two days on registration, was then transferred to the hospital when the staff shortage became acute, and then to clothing distribution'. Sutters, p. 551. According to Sylva Jones, internee women doctors received two sets of under-clothes, one pair of shoes, one dress and one coat.

13.   Abadi, *Terre de Détresse*, pp. 157–8. Odette's response may have been coloured by traditional Anglo-Gallic animosities, which were certainly present at Belsen – see for example, the views of Simone Weil in Wieviorka, 'French internees', in Reilly et al.: 'We had the feeling that our lives did not mean much, though the number of survivors was already very small.' At the same time, several British officers met French friends in the camp – Colonel Taylor recognised a French girl he had known before the war and a French Resistance fighter turned out to have taught at Manchester Grammar School before the war. Barnett Papers, LHCMA; Lauth, IWM (S)

14.   PRO: WO 177/669. According to Dr R. Collis (*BMJ* (1945), ii, p. 303), Johnston, although confronted by 'a great lack of nursing personnel', was 'against handing the people over to German nurses' and got Collis to write an article on Belsen for the *BMJ*, 'with the object of rousing public opinion and getting nurses from home'. However, 'high command' had already 'decided on a different policy and hence cut out certain parts of the original article' (which finally appeared in the *BMJ* on 9 June 1945). Bark, *No*

Time, p. 51. Undated letter from Sister Lottie Burns, a German nurse at Belsen, Doherty, *Letters from Belsen*, pp. 102–4.

15. Bark, *No Time*, p. 52; M. W. Ward, 'Belsen Papers', British Red Cross Archives; Charters, Letters, 12 June, IWM (D). 'They worked extremely hard and seemed shocked by what they saw,' Dixey, 'Belsen'. For similar judgements see Towers and Kenny and several AFS drivers.

16. H. Rosensaft, *Yesterday*, p. 58; JR, p. 11; Ward, 'Belsen Papers'. There were sixty German doctors on 3 May (Bradford, 'Expedition', p. 6). On 10 May, Johnston requested a further forty German doctors and 400 nurses or nursing orderlies. 'All the doctors and 200 nursing orderlies were provided from PW. Mil Gov arranged for 299 female civilian nurses from Hamburg to arrive at Belsen in detachments of 50 daily, commencing 13 May.' PRO: FO 1010/ 1.

17. JMP, 10 May 1945.

18. JMP, 19 May 1945; PRO: WO 177/753; WO 177/672; WO 177/1152; WO 177/1257; Elvidge, Letter, IWM (D); McFarlane, 'April 19th'.

19. Green, letter to *IWM* Review, June 1992; Trepman, p. 283; Cloake, *Templer*, p. 153.

20. SO, p. 73.

21. Internet – www.holocaust.com.au/lb/r_letter.htm. The original was in Czech; Salt, IWM (S).

22. Blackman, IWM (D).

23. Colonel Johnston rescued Jean McFarlane from her nursing work by asking her to open a hospital office – she admired his 'clear concise instructions and the friendly rather charming manner, also his extremely clear picture of Belsen and the way he intended to cope with it'. She began working in Dr Bimko's office – 'small and nearly always overflowing with humanity' – where she discovered that two internee girls were 'attempting some sort of registration and were getting lists daily of the deaths. This was something but not enough since nothing was alphabetical, only names listed according to the blocks.'

It wasn't easy to monitor the hospital population. 'The Internee patients and empty beds were next door to impossible to count,' Jean McFarlane complained. 'No sooner had everything been checked than it was found that one or more of the former, plus blankets, had absconded, and with regard to the latter, it was quite normal to find a bed or even beds which had been empty a short while ago, complete with patients.'

Realising that 'working in Dr Bimko's office was an impossibility', Jean soon got Johnston's officers to clear a ward for a new office, recruited more staff and 'started on the enormous task of getting name, Christian name, town of birth, date of birth, last known address, next of kin and religion from all patients in the square for which they were responsible'. By the second week in May, Jean wrote, 'there was certain amount of system working – Proformae had been evolved sufficiently to simplify the nightmare Bed and Staff States which, with the cooperation of Sisters and RAMC sergeants, came in by 1600 hours; they were legible and in English. Deaths, Admissions and Transfer Proformae also existed and these Returns arrived at the same time. Deaths were listed alphabetically and as the Cardex was nearing completion it seemed that the registration and personnel really had got somewhere, and on 29th May, the day 29 (Br) General Hospital took over, approximately 10,000 patients had been registered, no mean achievement considering there were 22 nationalities and several thousand very sick people in the Hospital area.' She makes no mention of Leslie Hardman's efforts to register Belsen's population; there would continue to be duplication of administration in this area for some time to come. McFarlane, '19th April'.

24. Letters to Muriel Blackman: Blackman Papers, IWM (D),
25. Clarkson, in Sutters, pp. 553–5.
26. SO, p. 73–4; Charters, IWM (D), Letter, 12 June; Sutters, pp. 553–5.
27. JMP, 10 May 1945. Sington thought 'it may have been delayed reaction to the long strain, or the effect of a sudden "let up" on overwrought nerves, or an onset of anxiety and helplessness in face of an uncertain future' (BU, p. 152).
28. JMP, 10 May 1945.
29. Johnston told the medical students on 9 May that the 'original scheme broke down owing to the fact that the "fit" people in Camp III were going down like flies and Camp II was coming to resemble Camp I'. Hargrave, 'Diary'. He did not address this issue in the long paper he wrote in the 1980s (JR).
30 Baneth (Fuchs), IWM (S). In her powerful, five-hour interview, conducted in 1997, Mrs Baneth recalled with affection a Frenchman – a complete stranger – who kissed her through the wire at Neuengamme camp. 'This communication with people you get only when people are very down . . . why can't we be all our lives like that?' she asked.

TEN. BURNING THE HUTS (PP. 123–32)

1. N. Kunkel, Letters, AFS Archives, New York.
2. BZR, 7; IWM (F) A 70/337 & A 70/338.
3. SO, pp 90–1.; BU, pp. 148–51; McFarlane, '19th April'; Gibson, 'Belsen, 1945'; Forsdick, 'Another letter'.
4. Forsdick, 'Another letter'; Hargrave, 'Diary'; H. Rosensaft, 'Children of Belsen'.
5. McFarlane, 'April 19th', p. 16. The nightclub was created by 'Frosty' Winterbotham, the anaesthetist to 32 CCS.

6.   JR, p. 4.
7.   Horsey, 'Report'; Gibson, 'Belsen'.
8.   Hargrave, 'Diary'.
9.   Coigley and Stephenson, 'Starvation and its treatment'; A. P. Prior, 'Medical aspects of Belsen', letter, *Lancet* (1945), ii, p. 512.
10.   Dixey, 'Belsen'.
11.   Matthews, 'The Belsen Experience'; Hargrave, 'Diary'.
12.   Gibson, 'Belsen'. Some of the students did manage to organise primitive nursing care by the fitter inmates, who were usually pregnant girls. 'The fitter patients . . . were mostly pregnant', MacAuslan, 'Belsen, May 1945', p. 105. The women helping A. T. Cook 'were all pregnant . . . inmates who'd received good treatment in return for sexual favours' (IWM (S)). According to an AFS driver, '75% of the women that are well are pregnant by the Germans because they are at least 4 months gone' (Kunkel, AFS, 18 May); while a British Red Cross official noticed 'girls of twelve and thirteen in advanced stages of pregnancy' (Bark, *No Time*, p. 59). On 17 May, a British Army film projectionist was 'awakened by the shrill wild Russian song' of two women on their way to collect potatoes. All day yesterday an international procession walked back and forth to a fair sized potato patch, digging them up with their hands and carrying their precious potatoes back to the camp. Over 80% of the women are pregnant.' Charters, IWM (D).
13.   Kidd, 'Diary', Horsey, 'Record'. The Matron of 29th British General Hospital, Myrtle Beardwell remembered, 'scorned our grey blankets and sheetless beds, and said that they would, of course, bring in their nice blue blankets. I quietly asked her if she has enough for 11,960 beds, and she glared at me and did not reply.' When Beardwell drew her attention to a young girl making a coat out of her (grey) blanket, no more was said. Beardwell, *Aftermath*, pp. 45–6. According to Dr Fritz Leo, the British sisters did not handle any patients. They simply went from bed to bed with a tray of medicines and a glass of water. Two were sent home for drunkenness. Nearly all the Belsen diarists are hostile to the army nurses, perhaps unfairly.
14.   'Account of the activities of the London Medical Students at Belsen Concentration Camp', UNRRA Press Conference, London, 7 June 1945. CMAC RAMC 792; Hughes: *Lancet* (1945), i, p. 769 (16 June 1945); *Lancet* (1945), i, p. 739 (9 June 1945).
15.   'Belsen camp'. Letter from Major Hilda Roberts, RAMC, and Captain Petronella Potter, RAMC, *BMJ* (1945), ii, p. 100.

ELEVEN. THE 'HOLIDAY CAMP' (PP. 133–46)

1.   Gonin, p. 11.
2.   *BU*, pp. 151–61.

3. Barker, Papers, IWM (D); Dope Sheets IWM (F); unidentified AFS driver, Belsen, May 1945. AFS Archives, New York.

4. Dr Nerson, 'Report on the situation at the Bergen-Belsen camp [31 August 1945], in OSE, *Report on the Situation of the Jews*, p. 51.

5. Forsdick, 'Another letter'; Levy, *Witness*, p. 13.

6. *BU*, p. 152; 'Psychological Problems of Displaced Persons', Report for UNRRA European Regional Office, June 1945. S 518–0363. PAG 4/ 1. 13. 5.6.0. 129. UN Archives. See also 'Special needs of women and girls during repatriation and rehabilitation', S-0520-0252. PAG 1.3.11.21.1.

7. *BU*, p. 155.

8. 'Report on Belsen Concentration Camp. 31 May 1945 by R. J. Phillips, Adviser in Psychiatry to Second Army.' CMAC, RAMC 1218/2/14. 'It is not considered that psychosis will, as was first thought, prove to be much of a problem in the future,' Colonel Johnston wrote in late May. 'Providing rehabilitation is carried out energetically, the majority of patients should be mentally stable, in my opinion, within a month.' JMP, c. 18 May 1945. According to Colonel Lipscomb, 'Return to normal behaviour as bodily health improved was often surprisingly rapid, leaving only a feeling akin to that of having experienced a bad dream, but the resumption of normal manners was not always accompanied by return of willpower and initiative', *Lancet* (1945), ii, p. 315; 'The sight of all the fat, sunburnt inhabitants is staggering. The interesting fact is that the very large percentage contrary to all expectations are regaining their mental balance' (Effie Barker, Letter, 28 July. Barker Papers IWM (D)).

9. Niremberski, 'Psychological investigation'.

10. Reilly, p. 159. 'It is very hard to convey the warmth that comes into the voice when a woman survivor speaks of, as one of them put it, "my returning womanhood".' Gill, *Journey Back*, p. 105; Polina Tikhovskaya, a Russian woman taken to Germany for forced labour and then sent to Ravensbrück (and, in January 1945, to Belsen) for belonging to a French anti-Fascist group, was evacuated to Fallingbostel transit camp soon after the liberation. On 20 May she was sent across the River Elbe to Russian-occupied territory. There her menstruation suddenly returned 'in a torrent. We began then to associate with young guys, with our soldiers. And at this moment, I lay for twelve days and twelve nights in a suspension device. I had such a strong flow of blood.' Nolte, p. 139.

11. *SO*, pp. 74–5; Bick-Berkowitz, *Where Are My Brothers?*, pp. 114–19. While serving nearby as the Intelligence Officer of the 7th Somerset Light Infantry in August 1945, Richard Wollheim was ordered by High Command to put on a dance at Belsen, in order to solve the two problems of British soldier's dissatisfaction with 'non-fraternisation' and the women survivors of Belsen's need for male company. The dance soon degenerated into a fight. Wollheim's

experience, if correctly recalled, was untypical. *London Review of Books*, 4 December 2003.

12. Magda Herzberger [i/v, 1993], in Ritvo and Plotkin, *Sisters in Sorrow*, p. 231.

13. Abadi, *Terre de Détresse*, p. 158; Perl, *I Was a Doctor*, p. 182; Hardman, pp. 58–65; *SO*, p. 67. Most of Dr Perl's patients were already pregnant when the British came. Pregnant Jewish women and later all others were brought to Belsen to starve after the gassings in Auschwitz had been stopped and in early 1945 pregnant women in the Buchenwald network of camps were sent there too. There were more than 100 births in Belsen in the early months of 1945. Most of the babies died. Rahe, 'Ich wusste . . .'. On Dr Perl, see Rittner and Roth, *Different Voices*, pp. 104–5.

14. Knoller, IWM (S); Ferderber-Salz, *And the Sun*, pp. 172–80; Fischer, internet – www.holocaust.com.au/lb/r letter. htm.

15. Perl, *I Was a Doctor*, pp. 187–9; Hardman, pp. 66–73.

16. Verolme, *Children's House*, pp. 243, 257. Years later, two Quaker relief workers remembered Luba. 'We didn't see anything wrong with the children [in the home]', Marjorie Ashbery IWM (S). 'A Russian woman, in her thirties perhaps, she was rather handsome, well dressed and obviously well fed and she had a way obviously – she got stuff from the [Germans] to feed the children . . . there weren't any starving children there . . . This Russian woman managed to get all that was necessary for the children, as far as I can gather. We think that she got everything by barter. She had a great drawer of watches.' The children 'were sort of like normal children'. Beth Dearden, IWM (S): 'The unaccompanied children . . . were being looked after by a remarkable Polish woman called Luba who gathered several helpers together and they must have done a remarkable job for those children keeping them in a group and caring for them . . . The powers that be thought that they ought to be looked after by English welfare officers. So all welfare officers were told that they were to look after the children. Of course we couldn't speak their language, they didn't know us, it wasn't really a very bright idea and fortunately after only about 24 hours that was realised and they had one or two welfare officers attached to them and the rest of us went off to do jobs in the hospital.' On 23 April, M. Gardiner, FAU (Barker, Papers, IWM): 'The Welfare workers are busy with 160 children orphaned since their arrival who have been brought to Camp 2.'

17. *Munk's Roll*, 6, pp. 108–9; *SO*; Collis, *To Be a Pilgrim*. Collis's charm created its own problems: at Belsen, he became involved with a beautiful young Dutch relief worker, Han Hogerzeil, who eventually became his second wife in 1957. Nor did everyone get on with him. Collis adored James Johnston, but had a tense relationship with Glyn Hughes, possibly because his own career both as a rugby player and doctor was much more distinguished.

18. *SO*, p. 74.
19. Beardwell, *Aftermath*, p. 47.
20. Parkinson, IWM (D); *SO*, pp. 96–7; note by Lt. Col. Champion, 14 July 1945; Champion Papers, IWM (D). Mounted on one of the Hungarians' horses, Collis won a steeplechase race that was staged at Belsen in June.
21. Barker, Papers, IWM (D); 'Effie Barker recalls Stanlake'. Effie's father hunted with British generals like Wavell and Alan Cunningham. She went to Belsen to get away from her dying mother and did not return for the funeral. To her father, she explained why she could not leave. 'The last three weeks have taught me that there are only two things really worth possessing, i.e. kindness and devotion,' she wrote. 'I have been through a very great and somewhat shattering experience here – an unforgettable one . . . We work from 7 a.m. to midnight and out of hopeless misery is coming life to these poor wretches.' To her brother she added, 'Naturally I felt deeply sad when I heard the news but getting it amongst this atmosphere of such suffering and hard work, somehow took the edge off it' (Letters, 21 May 1945).
22. Barker, 21 May. IWM (D).
23. *BU*, pp. 161–70.
24. Pfirter, 'Diary' (CMAC, RAMC, 1218); J. Parkinson, in Hall Williams Papers, IWM (D).
25. Barker Papers, IWM (D).

TWELVE. 'OUR NORTHERN HOSTS' (PP. 147–55)

1. *SO*, p. 93.
2. *SO*, pp. 140, 155–77; Klemme, *Inside Story*, pp. 86–110. Seventy-two people died on the way to the ships and were buried in the ancient Jewish cemetery in Lübeck. H. Rosensaft, *Yesterday*, p. 58. Most of the 'liberated doctors and nurses' went to Sweden with the transports of the sick. J. Rosensaft, 'Our Belsen', p. 26.
3. Fried, *Fragments*, pp. 169–76.
4. PRO: WO 177/1257; Klemme, *Inside Story*, pp. 86–110; McQuillin, IWM (D).
5. Klemme, *Inside Story*, pp. 86–110.
6. Koblik, *Stones Cry Out*; Levine, in Cesarani and Levine, *Bystanders*; Bauer, *Jews for Sale?*
7. Persson, 'Folke Bernadotte', in Cesarini and Levine, *Bystanders*.
8. H. Trevor-Roper, Foreword to Kersten, *The Kersten Memoirs*; see also Koblik, *Stones Cry Out*, and Persson, 'Folke Bernadotte', in Cesarini and Levine, *Bystanders*.
9. Grunberg, IWM (D); Quint, IWM (S). Once, while staying in a Displaced Persons Camp in Sweden, she stole apples from a farmer who ran after her. In a panic, she rushed into the outside lavatory and threw the apples into the bowl. They would not flush away

and remained there for days. It was 'this terrible fear that someone's going to kill you or someone's going to do something to you . . . It was such a stupid thing to have done and I was so angry with myself for such a long time afterwards.'

10. Gill, *Journey Back*, pp. 234–5.
11. T–567. Charlotte R., Fortunoff VideoArchive for Holocaust Testimonies, Yale University Library.
12. Gill, *Journey Back*, p. 235; Fried, *Fragments*, p. 176.
13. Fried, *Fragments*, pp. 183–5.
14. Conversation with Mrs Eva Fried, Hedi Fried's (née Szmuk) daughter-in-law, August 2004.
15. Gill, *Journey Back*, p. 263. 'Life in Sweden is quiet,' a Belsen survivor told a visitor in 1955. 'Here a child does not cry, a rooster does not crow, a tramway does not ring, and people do not talk. We live a quiet life.' H. Rosensaft, *Yesterday*, p. 133.
16. T–50. Testimony of Renée H., Fortunoff VideoArchive for Holocaust Testimonies, Yale University Library. T–4100. Hertha M., Fortunoff VideoArchive for Holocaust Testimonies, Yale University Library.

THIRTEEN. DIVISIONS (PP. 156–65)

1. *BU*, pp. 202–6; Lavsky, *New Beginnings*, pp. 58–60. On Belsen as a DP camp, see also Somers and Kok, *Jewish Displaced Persons*; and M. Z. Rosensaft, *Life Reborn*.
2. Leverson, WL, RHP.
3. H. Rosensaft, *Yesterday*, p. 61.
4. Lavsky, *New Beginnings*, p. 66. There was also, for over a year, a Polish DP camp of about 8000 people on the Belsen site.
5. H. Rosensaft, *Yesterday*, p. 62. According to Levy, *Witness*, p. 18, 'After a protracted stay in the camp, the strain became evident to such an extent that Leslie Hardman was advised to leave and serve in a quieter area within the zone of occupation. He was posted to Lübeck, where he continued with dedication to look after a group of Jews who had been found there.'
6. H. Rosensaft, *Yesterday*, pp. 62–6; Lavsky, *New Beginnings*, pp. 66–7; Levy, *Witness*, p. 47.
7. *BU*, p. 191.
8. Rahe, 'Social Life', in Somers and Kok, *Jewish Displaced Persons*, pp. 76–8.
9. Jane Leverson was born in 1917, the daughter of a tobacco importer, and 'brought up in a perfectly comfortable way as someone of Jewish faith in an English environment', in a large house in Fitzjohns Avenue, Hampstead, 'with a nanny and, I think, an under-nurse, and lots of maids and cooks and things'. She went to Roedean, the elite girls' boarding school, and studied Social Science at the London School of Economics. After accompanying children evacuated to Canada,

she became Chief Welfare Officer for the Air Raid Shelters in Bethnal Green – organising social life in the big public shelters. Towards the end of the war she decided she wanted to do relief work in Europe, but chose to join the well-established Quaker Friends Relief Service because she didn't 'want to work exclusively with Jews and [was] very happy to work with everyone else'. Although she had been involved with Jewish refugee children before the war, 'I had somehow thought that perhaps the Jews were exaggerating their situation'. She wasn't an orthodox Jew, knew no Yiddish, belonged to the liberal synagogue and rejected Zionism. But when she got to Belsen she began to think again. Jane worked first in the hospital in Camp 2, but early in May went into Camp 1 to help the Jewish chaplain, Leslie Hardman. She was then the only Jewish woman working in the camp and wore a Mogun David, or Star of David. Consequently she became the focus for requests from Jewish internees. In her letters to the Jewish Committee for Relief Abroad (for whom she was now also working), she asked them to send religious materials requested by the Jews in Belsen – 'an enormous number of Jewish things like Mizziza – the badges that . . . which don't seem important to me, we hadn't got one on our house. But they were important to these people and all sorts of things were important too – that I understood . . . Tallises are prayer shawls . . . One family, one house, room, had got hold of a tallis and they were using it as a table cloth, because everything was so sparse, they had nothing . . . The Yugoslav Army chaplain was furious when he saw it . . . I hadn't really understood it was holy.' [In her synagogue, the men didn't wrap themselves in tallises to pray.]

'Towards the end of my stay at Belsen,' she wrote on 15 May, 'I felt myself to be the most privileged Jewess anywhere! I was present at the evening and morning Shevuoth services, at the Sabbath service (open air – with hundreds, or maybe thousands, of people) and at a ceremony conducted by the Rabbi Hardman, at which the Zionist flag was hoisted, we believe for the first time since the Nazis' regime, on German soil. I also attended a Hebrew and Yiddish sing-song. One of the lorries in our convoy flew the Mogun David.

'As you know, I am not a Zionist, mainly because I feel that a better approach to the Jewish question is through the Christian world, and my work amongst these people here has, rather surprisingly to me, not made me change my views except, perhaps, in one respect. I now feel quite certain (whereas formerly I only wondered), that it is a crime to try to persuade people to remain in countries where they fear a growth or the existence of anti-Semitism. Now that I have seen with my own eyes, just where anti-Semitism can lead, I feel certain that those who wish to go to Palestine or elsewhere, should be helped with all one's power, to do so.

'However, to see my fellow Jews and Jewesses worshipping

together in a German camp – to see the Zionist flag hoisted on German soil – these gave me, I think, as much joy as I have ever experienced. It was an indescribable experience – (and I believe that I am not sentimental)' (Leverson, IWM (S); WL, RHP).

Leverson worked tirelessly to help the Belsen Jews. 'We used to say, "Now look here, Jane. You've had *that* for your Jews. Now you've got to leave *some* things for the others". And she was very good about it.' Marjorie Ashbery, another Quaker relief worker later recalled. Ashbery, IWM (S).

10. Bauer, *Out of the Ashes*, pp. 23–44; Milton and Bogin, *American Jewish Joint Distribution Committee*, pp. 1269–72; speech by Edward Warburg, Atlantic City, September 1945, USHMM. RG 08.002.10.

11. M. Eigen, 'Belsen Camp', 31 August 1945, in Milton and Bogin, *American Jewish Joint Distribution Committee*, pp. 1312–20; Gill, *Journey Back*, pp. 295–6.

12. H. Rosensaft, *Yesterday*, pp. 75–87; Lavsky, *New Beginnings*, pp. 63–77.

13. Beardwell, *Aftermath*, p. 48. 'People [who] were not Palestine minded were being mentally tortured into submitting to the order of the day which was "We must go to Palestine" . . . The Jews (who had by far the most and best supplies – mainly American), refused to share with other nationalities, but they expected their fair share of all other supplies. This caused much unpleasantness' (ibid., p. 51). Reilly, *Belsen*, pp. 78–117.

14. Dinnerstein, *America and the Survivors*, pp. 9–71 (the best synthesis of an enormous literature); Abzug, *Inside the Vicious Heart*, pp. 141–68; M. Z. Rosensaft, *Life Reborn*.

15. M. Z. Rosensaft, *Life Reborn*, p. 108.

16. The following related text is based on Dorothy Pearse, 'Child Welfare Services in the British Zone' [UNRRA Internal History, c. 1949]. S 0524 – Box 0106 [PAG 4/4.2; Box 82]. United Nations Archives.

17. H. Rosensaft, *Yesterday*, pp. 103–10; Lavsky, *New Beginnings*, pp. 112–13; M. Z. Rosensaft, 'Bergen-Belsen: The End and the Beginning'. (My thanks to Mr Rosensaft.)

FOURTEEN. THE BELSEN TRIAL (PP. 166–75)

1. See Bloxham, *Genocide on Trial*, for the complex background and vast literature.

2. *BT*, pp. xxiv–xxv; Moorehead, 'Belsen', in Connolly, *The Golden 'Horizon'*, p. 112.

3. Playfair and Sington, *The Offenders*, pp. 146–56; Bloxham, *Genocide on Trial*, pp. 97–101. While the indictment relied heavily on the Auschwitz evidence, press reporting emphasised the Belsen connection.

4. *BT*, pp. xxx–xxxi.
5. Winwood, 'Recollections', IWM (D).
6. *BT*, pp. xxi–xxxiii. According to Winwood, 'One solicitor had to give up his partnership in a Golders Green practice after complaints from some of their Jewish clients. I myself was strongly criticised on three occasions by (i) a question in Parliament, (ii) a leading article in *Pravda* and (iii) the British Board of Jewish Deputies. This latter occasion was upsetting because I had been working in London, Frankfurt and Vienna for Jewish refugees in 1938/39. I answered all of these by pointing out that I was not in any way expressing my own views but those of my clients.' Winwood, 'Recollections', IWM (D).
7. Winwood, 'Recollections', IWM (D).
8. *The Times*, 22 September 1945. The figure of four million deaths at Auschwitz was a substantial overestimate. 'My personal feelings,' Dr Bimko later wrote, 'were a mixture of pain, anger and satisfaction. I suffered when, as a witness, I had to identify the accused, to look at the faces of the criminals who had so sadistically maltreated us. But I also felt satisfied that some of us had survived to see them brought to justice and that for the first time the world learnt about the crimes and atrocities they had committed.' H. Rosensaft, *Yesterday*, p. 91.
9. *BT*, pp. 66–7.
10. *BT*, pp. 510–20.
11. Elie Cohen in Gill, *Journey Back*, p. 372.
12. *BT*, pp. 177–80.
13. Playfair and Sington, *Offenders*, p. 178.
14. Winwood, 'Recollections', IWM (D).

FIFTEEN. AFTERLIVES (PP. 176–89)

1. Collis, 'Belsen camp'.
2. Eitinger, *Concentration Camp Survivors*, p. 192.
3. Blackman, IWM (D).
4. Interview with Irma Sonnenberg Menkel, *Newsweek*, 21 July 1997. Frau Menkel, who lost both her husband and brother in Belsen, was a German Jewess who had migrated to Holland. She was made a block leader in Belsen and attributed her survival to the fact that the original commandant, Haas, 'was from my home town in Germany and had studied with my uncle in Strasbourg'. 'When I went in, I weighed more than 125 pounds. When I left, I weighed 78', she told the reporter.
5. *BU*, p. 156; Dormandy, *White Death*, pp. 361–75.
6. Somers and Kok, *Jewish Displaced Persons*, p. 119.
7. Collis, *To Be a Pilgrim*, pp. 107–38; 226–7. Collis was, aptly, killed while riding a horse at the age of seventy-five. He spent much of his later career in Nigeria. According to the programme

Return to Belsen (RTE, 2003), Zoltan Zin-Collis and Suzi Diamond, another Belsen child taken to Ireland, 'were asked by their adopted families never to speak about their former lives. In the light of more modern thinking, this only served to make the repressed memories even more troublesome.' 'To make a return journey to Belsen was something neither Suzi nor Zoltan would contemplate until they were approached by the *Would You Believe* team.' A third child declined to take part in the programme.

8. Eitinger, *Concentration Camp Survivors*, pp. 139–41, 157.
9. Niederland, 'Problem of the survivor'.
10. Davidson, in Dasberg, *Society and Trauma*. The literature on survivors' post-war psychological adjustment can be sampled in Niewyk and Nicosia, *Columbia Guide*, pp. 353–5.

Historians have so far focused almost exclusively on the later lives of the Jewish inmates, who made up just over half of the camp's population at the time of liberation. A pioneering attempt to find out what happened to Russian prisoners at Belsen (Nolte, ed.) reminds us that many of them, whether former POWs or forced labourers, faced years of exile and discrimination from the Soviet authorities when they returned.

11. Gill, *Journey Back*, pp. 9–16.
12. (Leverson), Levy, IWM (S); JR. p. 13.
13. M. Rosensaft, *Yesterday*, pp. 136–204.
14. Verolme, *Children's House*; McCann/Tryszynska-Frederick, *Luba*.
15. Telephone interview with Mrs Mary Park, September 2003; Caldecott, *Women of Our Century*.
16. Interview with Dr Peter Horsey, August 2004; Matthews, 'The Belsen Experience'.
17. Belton, *Good Listener*, p. 87
18. MacAuslan, *Darling, Darling Meg*, p. 168.
19. Fisher, IWM (S).
20. JR; obituary, *Daily Telegraph*, 20 May 1988.
21. CMAC, RAMC 1218.
22. *The Times*, 26 November 1973.
23. CMAC, RAMC 1218.
24. Interview, Mrs Smart, 29 January 2004.
25. *KZBB*, pp. 235–62.
26. The documentation centre which the Lower Saxony government created at Belsen in the 1980s has done a brilliant job in recording the camp's long and complex history and in balancing the needs of the different nationalities and groups with an interest in the place.

SIXTEEN. JUDGEMENTS (PP. 190–200)

1. Moorehead, 'Belsen, in Connolly, *The Golden 'Horizon'*; Sylva Jones, 'From a diary'; Gant, IWM (D).
2. Bauer, *Out of the Ashes*, p. 37.

3. Reilly, *Belsen*, p, 129; Bauer, *American Jewry*, pp. 451–2.
4. PRO: WO 222/201.
5. Lt. Col. L. Berney, 'The Liberation of Belsen Concentration Camp'. BBC WW2 People's War website. Internet – www.bbc.co.uk/dna/ww2/A2722501.[n.d.] Berney was one of the first officers into the 'Horror Camp' and returned to become commandant of the DP camp in June 1945. See *BU*.
6. Barker, letter, 21 May 1945. Barker Papers IWM (D). 'At first everything seemed terribly inefficient and confused here,' American Friends Service driver Eugene Cole wrote on 7 May 1945. 'It still seems confused. But when I realised what a huge place this is, the huge supply problems, and everything else, I decided the British have done a remarkable job.' His colleague Norman Kunkel, though, accused the British of 'trying to get by on just enough . . . in their slow way, spending as little as they can, . . . taking care of the situation.' AFS Archives, New York.
7. Working on this book, I came into contact with Dr Bernice Lerner, the daughter of a Belsen survivor, who is preparing a study of Glyn Hughes. Although Dr Lerner teaches 'character education' at Boston University, she was quite unaware of the place of 'character education' in the English public school system.
8. J. Leverson, WL, RHP.
9. Interview with John A. Seaman, 4 November 2004.
10. The paradigm shift took place in about 1974, when the American nutritionist Donald McLaren published a famous paper called 'The great protein fiasco'.
11. D. Summerfield, 'A critique of seven assumptions behind psychological trauma programmes in war-affected areas', *Social Science and Medicine*, 48 (1999), pp. 1449–62. Transposing experience in Rwanda to the Holocaust, Summerfield asked readers to imagine 'A project, planned from afar and deploying foreign conceptual frameworks and practices being mobilised in mid-1945 to come in to assist those who have just emerged alive from the concentration camps. The project leaders have often not worked in the area before, and perhaps do not know its history. The project is funded, perhaps, for one year. In that time it hopes to tackle the "trauma" of the Holocaust for survivors, not just their personal losses but their sense of what was done to their people as a people. By so doing it also expects to reduce future mental problems, and the likelihood that they will turn from victims into perpetrators who embrace violence and war. Would not such a project seem grossly simplistic and presumptuous, and throw up ethical questions?'
12. McNally et al., 'Does early psychological intervention promote recovery from posttraumatic stress?'
13. Pinson, 'Jewish life'; Sereny, *German Trauma*, pp. 25–52; Somers and Kok, *Jewish Displaced Persons*, p. 23. The reluctance of Jewish

doctors to go to Belsen caused some resentment: 'In the whole of Jewry there was not one famous children's specialist, surgeon or gynaecologist who was willing to come and work with us, even for a short time, despite all our appeals. We had to accept the help of German doctors and nurses whom the British sent into the camp . . . Free Jews could have found a way to come, if they had really wanted to . . . they did not come.' J. Rosensaft, 'Our Belsen', p. 26. 'We were hoping that some Jewish doctors in the United States would close their private practices for a while and come to help us, if only for a month. To our great disappointment, none came. I still can't understand why.' H. Rosensaft, Yesterday, p. 58

14. H. Rosensaft, 'Children of Belsen', p. 198; J. Rosensaft, 'Our Belsen', p. 31; M. Z. Rosensaft, Life Reborn.

APPENDIX ONE: THE DEATH RATE AT BELSEN (PP. 201–5)

1. A. Paton, 'Mission to Belsen', British Medical Journal (1981), ii, pp. 1656–9.
2. Donnison, Civil Affairs, p. 222.
3. Kolb (1962) pp. 308–16.

BIBLIOGRAPHY

(Unless otherwise stated, London is the place of publication)

Abadi, O., *Terre de Détresse* (Paris, 1995)

Abzug, R. H., *Inside the Vicious Heart: Americans and the Liberation of Nazi Concentration Camps* (New York, 1985)

Alderman, G., *Modern British Jewry* (Oxford, 1992)

Aykroyd, W. R., *The Conquest of Famine* (1974)

Bark, E., *No Time to Kill* (1961)

Barton, R., 'Inside the Concentration Camps', *Purnell's History of the Second World War* (1968)

Bauer, Y., *American Jewry and the Holocaust: The American Jewish Joint Distribution Committee, 1939–1945* (Detroit, 1980)

—*Out of the Ashes: The Impact of American Jews on Post-Holocaust European Jewry* (Oxford, 1989)

—*Jews for Sale? Nazi-Jewish Negotiations, 1933–1945* (New Haven, Conn., 1994)

Beardwell, M., *Aftermath* (Ilfracombe, Devon, n.d. c. 1953)

Belton, N., *The Good Listener: Helen Bamber, A Life against Cruelty* (1999)

Berenbaum, M. and Peck, A. J. (eds), *The Holocaust and History* (1998; Bloomington, Ind., 2002)

Bernadotte, F., *The Fall of the Curtain: The Last Days of the Third Reich* (1945)

Bick-Berkowitz, S., *Where Are My Brothers?* (New York, 1965)

Bloch, S. E. (ed.), *Holocaust and Rebirth: Bergen-Belsen, 1945–1965* (New York, 1965)

Bloxham, D., *Genocide on Trial* (Oxford, 2001)

Bolchover, R., *British Jewry and the Holocaust* (Cambridge, 1993)

Botting, D., *Inside the Ruins of the Reich* (1985)

Breitman, R., *Official Secrets: What the Nazis Planned, What the British and Americans Knew* (1998)

—'Himmler and Belsen', in J. Reilly et al. (eds), *Belsen in History and Memory* (1997)

Bridgman, J., *The End of the Holocaust: The Liberation of the Camps* (1990)

Caldecott, L., *Women of Our Century* (1986)

Cambray, P. G. and Briggs, G. G. B., *Red Cross and St John: The Official Record of the War Organization of the British Red Cross Society and Order of St John of Jerusalem 1939–1947* (1949)

Caven, H., 'Horror in our time: images of the concentration camps in the British media, 1945', *Historical Journal of Film, Radio and Television*, 21 (2001), pp. 205–53

Cesarani, D. (ed.), *Genocide and Rescue: The Holocaust in Hungary 1944* (Oxford, 1997)

—and Levine, P. A. (eds), *Bystanders to the Holocaust: A Re-evaluation* (2001)

Chamberlin, B. and Feldman, M. (eds), *The Liberation of the Nazi Concentration Camps, 1945. Eyewitness Accounts of the Liberators* (Washington, DC, 1987)

Cloake, J., *Templer, Tiger of Malaya* (1995)

Coigley, M. H. F. and Stephenson, J., 'Starvation and its treatment with Protein Hydrolysate', *St Thomas's Hospital Gazette*, 44 (1946), pp. 2–9

Collis, R. and Hogerzeil, H., *Straight On* (1947)

—and MacClancy, P. C., 'Some paediatric problems presented at Belsen camp', *British Medical Journal* (1946), i, pp. 273–5

Collis, W. R. F., 'Belsen camp: a preliminary report,' *British Medical Journal* (1945), i, pp. 814–16

—*The Ultimate Value* (1951)

—*To Be a Pilgrim* (1975)

Connolly, C. (ed.), *The Golden 'Horizon'* (1953)

Crew, F. A. E., *Medical History of the Second World War: Army Medical Services. Campaigns*, Vol. 4, *North-West Europe* (1962)

Dasberg, H. et al., *Society and Trauma of War* (Maastricht, 1987)

Davis, W., 'Typhus at Belsen', *American Journal of Hygiene*, 46 (1947), pp. 66–83

Dawson, J., 'Cancrum oris', *British Dental Journal*, 79 (1945), pp. 151–7

Delaforce, P., *The Black Bull: From Normandy to the Baltic with the 11th Armoured Division* (Stroud, 1994)

Des Pres, T., *The Survivor* (New York, 1976)

Dimbleby, J., *Richard Dimbleby* (1975)

Dinnerstein, L., *America and the Survivors of the Holocaust* (New York, 1982)

Dixey, J. R. B., 'Belsen', *St Bartholomew's Hospital Journal*, 49 (1945), pp. 76–82

Doherty, M. K., *Letters from Belsen: An Australian Nurse's Experiences with the Survivors of the War* (St Leonard's, New South Wales, 2000)

Doll, R., 'Janet Vaughan', in *New Oxford Dictionary of National Biography* (Oxford, 2004)

Donnison, F. S. V., *Civil Affairs and Military Government in North West Europe 1944–1946* (1961)

Dormandy, T., *The White Death: A History of Tuberculosis* (1999)

Drummond, J. C. and Wilbraham, A., *The Englishman's Food* (1939; 1994)

Eitinger, L., *Concentration Camp Survivors in Norway and Israel* (Oslo, 1964)

Ellis, J., *The Sharp End of War* 1980; 1993

Feingold, H. L., *The Politics of Rescue* (1970; New York, 1980)

Fénelon, F., *The Musicians of Auschwitz* (1977)

Ferderber-Salz, B., *And the Sun Kept Shining* (New York, 1980)

Fisher, F. G., *Sir Raphael Cilento: A Biography* (Brisbane, 1994)

Forsdick, D., 'Another letter from Belsen', *Guy's Hospital Gazette*, 59 (1946)

Fried, H., *Fragments of a Life: The Road to Auschwitz* (1990)

Gibson, T. C., 'Belsen, 1945', *The London Hospital Gazette*, 48 (1945), pp. 144–8

Gilbert, F. (ed.), *Hitler Directs His War* (New York, 1950)

Gilbert, M., *Auschwitz and the Allies* (New York, 1981)

—*The Holocaust: The Jewish Tragedy* (1986; 1987)

—*The Day the War Ended: VE-Day in Europe and Around the World* (1995)

—*The Boys* (1997)

—*Never Again: A History of the Holocaust* (2000; 2001)

Gill, A., *The Journey Back from Hell: Conversations with Concentration Camp Survivors* (1988; 1989)

Gowans, J. L., 'Clinical observations at Belsen', *King's College Hospital Gazette*, 24 (1945), pp. 13–18

Green, P. W., Letter, *Imperial War Museum Review*, June 1992

Greenspan, H., *On Listening to Holocaust Survivors* (Westport, Conn., 1998)

Hardman, L. H. and Goodman, C., *The Survivors: The Story of the Belsen Remnant* (1958)

Harrison, M., *Medicine and Victory: British Military Medicine in the Second World War* (Oxford, 2004)

Hastings, M., *Armageddon: The Battle for Germany 1944–45* (2004)

Helweg-Larsen, P. et al., 'Famine Disease in German Concentration Camps. Complications and Sequels', *Acta Medica Scandinavica*, Supplement 274 (1952)

Henke, K-D., *Die amerikanische Besetzung Deutschlands* (Munich, 1995)

Herzberg, A. J., *Between Two Streams* (1997)

Hilberg, R., *The Destruction of the European Jews* (3rd edn, New Haven, Conn., 2003)

Jackson, R., *Thirty Seconds at Quetta: The Story of an Earthquake* (1960)

Jürgens, A. and Rahe, T., 'Zur Statistik des Konzentrationslagers Bergen-Belsen', in Die Fruhen Nachkriegsprozesse. *Beiträge zur Geschcihte der nationalsozialistischen Verfolgung in Norddeutschland*, Heft 3 (Bremen, 1997) pp. 128–48

Keller, R. et al. (eds), *Konzentrationslager Bergen-Belsen: Berichte und Dokumente* (Göttingen, 1995)

Kemp, P., *The Relief of Belsen, April 1945: Eyewitness Accounts* (1991)

Kersten, F., *The Kersten Memoirs 1940–1945* (1956)

Kiple, K. F. (ed.), *The Cambridge World History of Human Disease* (Cambridge, 1993)

Klemme, M., *The Inside Story of UNRRA: An Experience in Internationalism* (New York, 1949)

Koblik, S., *The Stones Cry Out: Sweden's Response to the Persecution of the Jews 1933–1945* (New York, 1988)

Kolb, E., *Bergen-Belsen. Geschichte des 'Aufenthaltslagers' 1943–1945* (Hanover, 1962)

—*Bergen-Belsen: From 'Detention Camp' to Concentration Camp, 1943–1945* (2nd edn, Göttingen, 1986)

Konigseder, A. and Wetzel, J., *Waiting for Hope: Jewish Displaced Persons in Post World War II Germany* (Evanston, Ill., 2001)

Kroh, A., *Lucien's Story* (Evanston, Ill., 1993)

Kushner, T., *The Persistence of Prejudice: Anti-Semitism in British Society during the Second World War* (Manchester, 1989)

—*The Holocaust and the Liberal Imagination* (Oxford, 1994)

Lancaster, J. and McDonough, R., *Holocaust: Imperial War Museum Sound Archive Oral History Recordings* (2000)

Langer, L., *Holocaust Testimony: The Ruins of Memory* (1991; New Haven, Conn., 2003)

Laqueur, W. and Tydor Baumel, J., *The Holocaust Encyclopedia* (New Haven, Ct., 2001)

Lasker-Wallfisch, A., *Inherit the Truth 1939–1945* (1996)

Lavsky, H., *New Beginnings: Holocaust Survivor in Bergen-Belsen and the British Zone in Germany* (Detroit, 2002)

Lee, C.A., *The Hidden Life of Otto Frank* (2002)

Leivick, H. et al., *Belsen* (Tel Aviv, 1957)

Levy, I., *Witness to Evil: Bergen-Belsen, 1945* (1995)

Lévy-Hass, H.,*Inside Belsen* (Brighton, 1962)

Lewis, J. T., 'Medical problems at Belsen concentration camp (1945)', *Ulster Medical Journal*, 2 (1985), pp. 122–6

Lipscomb, F. M., 'Medical aspects of Belsen Concentration Camp', *Lancet* (1945), ii, pp. 313–15

Löb, L., 'Translator's Introduction' to B. Zsolt, *Nine Suitcases* (2004)

London, L., *Whitehall and the Jews, 1933–1948* (Cambridge, 2000)

MacAuslan, A., 'Belsen, May 1945', *St Thomas's Hospital Gazette*, 43 (1945), pp. 103–7

—*Darling, Darling Meg* (Edinburgh, 1996)

McCann, M. R. with Tryszynska-Frederick, L., *Luba: The Angel of Belsen* (Berkeley, Calif., 2003)

McNally, R. et al., 'Does early psychological intervention promote recovery from posttraumatic stress?' *Psychological Science in the Public Interest*, 4 (2003), pp. 45–79

McNeill, W. H., *Plagues and Peoples* (Harmondsworth, 1979)

Marcuse, H., *Legacies of Dachau: The Uses and Abuses of a Concentration Camp, 1933–2001* (Cambridge, 2001)

Marrus, M. R., *The Unwanted: European Refugees in the Twentieth Century* (New York, 1985)

Matthews, A., 'The Belsen Experience', *St Mary's Hospital Gazette* (1991)

Milton, S. and Bogin, F. D. (eds), *Archives of the Holocaust*. Volume 10. *American Jewish Joint Distribution Committee, New York*. Part 2 (New York, 1995)

Mollison, P. L., 'Observations on cases of starvation at Belsen', *British Medical Journal* (1946), i, pp. 4–8

Moore, B., *Victims and Survivors: The Nazi Persecution of the Jews in the Netherlands 1940–1945* (1997)

Moorehead, A., 'Belsen', in C. Connolly (ed.), *The Golden 'Horizon'* (1953)

Moorehead, C., *Dunant's Dream: War, Switzerland and the History of the Red Cross* (1998)

Niederland, W., 'The problem of the survivor: The psychiatric evaluation of emotional disorders in survivors of Nazi persecution', *Journal of the Hillside Hospital*, 10 (1961), pp. 223–47

Niewyk, D. (ed.), *Fresh Wounds: Early Narratives of Holocaust Survival* (Chapel Hill, NC, 1998)

—and Nicosia, F. (eds), *The Columbia Guide to the Holocaust* (New York, 2000)

Niremberski, M., 'Psychological investigation of a group of internees at Belsen camp', *Journal of Mental Science*, 91 (1946), pp. 60–74

Nolte, H-H. (ed.), *Häftlinge aus der UdSSR in Bergen-Belsen. Dokumentation der Errinerungen* (Frankfurt-am-Main, 2001)

Novick, P., *The Holocaust and Collective Memory: The American Experience* (1999)

Oppenheim, A. N., *The Chosen People: The Story of the '222' Transport from Belsen to Palestine* (1996)

Oppenheimer, P., *From Belsen to Buckingham Palace* (1996)

Owen, M., 'Janet Vaughan', *Biographical Memoirs of Fellows of the Royal Society*, 41 (1995), pp. 483–98

Padfield, P., *Himmler* (1990)

Pearce, R. (ed.), *Patrick Gordon Walker: Political Diaries 1932–1971* (1991)

Perl, G., *I Was a Doctor in Auschwitz* (New York, 1948)

Persson, S., 'Folke Bernadotte and the white buses', in Cesarani, D. and Levine, P. A. (eds), *Bystanders to the Holocaust. A Re-evaluation* (2001)

Phillips, R. (ed.), *Trial of Josef Kramer and Forty-Four Others (The Belsen Trial)* (Edinburgh, 1949)

Pinson, K. S., 'Jewish life in liberated Germany – a study of the Jewish DPs', *Jewish Social Studies*, 9 (1947), pp. 101–26

Playfair, G. and Sington, D., *The Offenders: Society and the Atrocious Crime* (1957)

Porter, R., *The Greatest Benefit to Mankind* (1997)

Rahe, T., '"Ich wusste nicht einmal, dass ich schwanger war", Geburten im KZ Bergen-Belsen', in C. Füllberg-Stollberg, *Frauen in Konzentrationslagern: Bergen-Belsen – Ravensbrück* (Bremen, 1994) pp. 147–55

Raperport, G., 'Expedition to Belsen', *Middlesex Hospital Journal*, 45 (1945), pp. 21–4

Reilly, J., *Belsen: The Liberation of a Concentration Camp* (1997)

—'Cleaner, carer and occasional dance partner? Writing women back into the liberation of Bergen-Belsen', in Reilly, J. et al. (eds), *Belsen in History and Memory* (1997)

Reilly, J. et al. (eds), *Belsen in History and Memory* (1997)

Rittner, C. and Roth, J. K. (eds), *Different Voices: Women and the Holocaust* (New York, 1993)

Ritvo, R. A. and Plotkin, D. M., *Sisters in Sorrow: Voices of Care in the Holocaust* (College Station, Texas, 1998)

Roberts, P., *From the Desert to the Baltic* (1987)

Rock, G., *The History of the American Field Service 1920–1955* (New York, 1955)

Roseman, M., *The Villa. The Lake. The Meeting* (2002)

Rosensaft, H., 'The children of Belsen', in Leivick, H. et al., *Belsen* (Tel Aviv, 1957)

—*Yesterday: My Story* (Washington, DC, 2004)

Rosensaft, J., 'Our Belsen', in Leivick, H. et al., *Belsen* (Tel Aviv, 1957)

—'Bergen-Belsen 1945–1965', in Bloch, S. E. (ed.), *Holocaust and Rebirth* (New York, 1965)

Rosensaft, M. Z. (ed.), *Life Reborn: Jewish Displaced Persons 1945–1951* (Washington, DC, 2001)

—'Bergen-Belsen; the end and the beginning', *Rayonot*, 2004

Rubinstein, W. D., *The Myth of Rescue: Why the Democracies Could Not Have Saved More Jews from the Nazis* (1997)

Segev, T., *Soldiers of Evil* (1987; 1990)

—*The Seventh Million: The Israelis and the Holocaust* (New York, 1993)

Sen, A., *Poverty and Famines* (Oxford, 1981)

Sereny, G., *The German Trauma* (2000)

Sington, D., *Belsen Uncovered* (1946)

Smith, M. J., *Dachau: The Harrowing of Hell* (1972; New York, 1995)

Somers, E. and Kok, R. (eds), *Jewish Displaced Persons in Camp Bergen-Belsen, 1945–1959* (Amsterdam, 2003)

Stein, Z. et al., *Famine and Human Development: The Dutch Hunger Winter of 1944–1945* (New York, 1975)

Sutters, J. (ed.), *Archives of the Holocaust*, Volume 12: *American Friends Service Committee, Philadelphia* (New York, 1990)

Tas, J., 'Psychical disorders among inmates of concentration camps and repatriates', *Psychiatric Quarterly* (1951), pp. 670–90

Taylor, T., *The Anatomy of the Nuremberg Trials* (New York, 1992)

Towers, J. and Kenny, A. J., 'Belsen', *King's College Hospital Gazette*, 24 (1945), pp. 1–7

Trepman, E., 'Rescue of the Remnants: The British Emergency Medical Relief Operation in Belsen Camp 1945', *Journal of the Royal Army Medical Corps*, 147 (2001), pp. 281–93

Trepman, P., *Among Men and Beasts* (New York, 1978)

Trevor-Roper, H. R., *The Last Days of Hitler* (1947; 1962)

Vella, E. E., 'Belsen: medical aspects of a World War II concentration camp', *Journal of the Royal Army Medical Corps*, 130 (1984), pp. 34–59

von Below, N., *At Hitler's Side: The Memoirs of Hitler's Adjutant* (2001)

Verolme, H., *The Children's House of Belsen* (Freemantle, Western Australia, 2000)

Walker, J. B., 'The feeding problem', *London Hospital Gazette*, 48 (1945) pp. 150–1

Warlimont, W., *Inside Hitler's Headquarters, 1939–1945* (1964)

Wasserstein, B., *Vanishing Diaspora* (Cambridge, Mass., 1996)

—*Britain and the Jews of Europe, 1939–1945* (2nd edn, Leicester, 1999)

Weindling, P. J., *Epidemics and Genocide in Eastern Europe, 1890–1945* (Oxford, 2000)

Wenck, A-E., *Zwischen Menschenhandel und 'Endlösung': Das Konzentrationslager Bergen-Belsen* (Paderborn, 2000)

Williams, E. Hall, *A Page of History in Relief* (York, 1993)

Wilson, R. C., *Quaker Relief: An Account of the Relief Work of the Society of Friends 1940–1948* (1952)

Witte, P. (ed.), *Die Dienstkalendar Heinrich Himmlers, 1941–1942* (Hamburg, 1999)

Wollheim R., 'A bed out of leaves', *London Review of Books*, 4 December 2003

Wyand, P., *Useless if Delayed* (1959)

Zweig, R., 'Feeding the camps: Allied blockade policy and the relief of concentration camps in Germany, 1944–1945, *Historical Journal*, 41 (1998), pp. 825–51

Unpublished Material (including IWM (D))

American Friends Archive [AFS], New York City

E. L. Barker, Papers, IWM (D) 01/16/1

'Effie Barker recalls Stanlake', Twyford and Ruscombe Local History Society, 1978

B. Barnett, Papers, Liddell Hart Centre for Military History, King's College, London.

M. J. Blackman, Papers, IWM (D) 01/19/1

D. Bradford, 'Expedition to Belsen', IWM (D) 86/7/1

Lieutenant-Colonel S. G. Champion Papers, IWM (D) 93/11/1

C. Charters, Letters from Belsen, IWM (D) Con Shelf

M. Coigley, 'Notebook', IWM (D) 91/6/1

M. Coigley, Letter, 5 May 1945, IWM (D) Misc. 59 (880). (Typed copy, sender's name misspelled 'Cayley'. Telephone conversation with Dr Coigley, November 2004.)

K. J. Elvidge, Letter, 26 May 1945, IWM (D) 89/10/1

E. Fisher, 'A soldier's diary of Belsen', IWM (D) 95/2/1

D. Forsdick, 'Journal to Belsen, May 1945', IWM (D) 91/6/1

Captain J. Gant, Letter, 18 April 1945, IWM (D) 99/82/1

M. W. Gonin, 'The R.A.M.C. at Belsen Concentration Camp', IWM (D) 85/38/1

P. W. Green, Papers, IWM (D), 92/28/1

B. Grunfeld, [Memoir], IWM (D) 99/3/1

M. Hargrave, 'Diary of a medical student at Belsen', IWM (D) 76/74/1

Rose Henriques, Papers Wiener Library

P. J. Horsey, 'Record of our time in Germany', IWM (D) Con Shelf

A. R. Horwell, Papers, IWM (D) 91/21/1

H. L. Glyn Hughes, Papers. Contemporary Medical Archive Centre, Wellcome Library, London

J. A. D. Johnston, 'The Relief of Belsen Concentration Camp. Recollections and Reflections of a British Army Doctor'. Rosensaft Papers, USHMM

M. Silva Jones, 'From a Diary written in Belsen', in McFarlane Papers, IWM (D) 99/86/1

H. B. Kidd, 'Diary', IWM (D) 94/26/1

Lady Limerick, 'Diaries', IWM (D) PP/MCR/162

A. MacAuslan, 'A month in Belsen', IWM (D) 95/2/1

B. McDouall, IWM (D) 89/19/ 1

J. McFarlane, 'April 19th–May 24th 1945'. McFarlane Papers, IWM (D) 99/86/1

J. McLuskie, 'Belsen. April–May 1945', IWM (D) 95/19/1

T. McQuillin, IWM (D) 91/6/1

J. Parkinson, Letters, E. Hall Williams Papers, IWM (D)

A. Paton, 'Belsen, April–May 1945'. In possession of Dr Paton.

D. Pearse, 'Child Welfare Services in the British Zone' [UNRRA Internal History, c. 1949] S. 0524 – Box 0106 [PAG 4/4. 2; Box 82] United Nations Archive, New York

A. Pfirter, 'Diary' in CMAC, RAMC, 1218

W. E. Roach, 'The first four days in Belsen', [n.d. c. 1965]. Gedenkstätte, Bergen-Belsen

G. H. Roberts, 'Lingen Camp'. E. Barker Papers, IWM (D) 1/16/1

J. Rudman, Letter, 14 May 1945, IWM (D) 94/51/1

G. Walker, Letter, May 1945, IWM (D) 84/2/1

M. W. Ward, 'Belsen papers', British Red Cross Archives

E. Hall Williams, Papers, IWM (D) 93/27/2

Major T. C. M. Winwood, 'Recollections of the Belsen trial', IWM (D) P. 419

Sound and Video Interviews (IWM (S))
H. Abisch, 9181; N. Alexander, 15441; M. Ashbery, 16631; E. Baneth (Fuchs) 17474; T. Biber, 17514; L. W. Clarke, 9182; A. T. Cook, 13758; J. R. B. Dixey, 8996; B. Dearden, 15625; M. Dessau, 9236; Z. Ehrlich (Fantlova), 8942; A. Fink, 16594, 17750; E. Fisher, 14965; L. Hardman, 17636; P. J. Horsey, 8935; W. D. Hughes, 11540; F. Knoller, 9092; A. Lasker-Wallfisch, 11914; H. Lauth, 10732; W. F. Lawrie, 7481; G. Laws, 14839; J. E. Levy (Leverson), 15626; M. Lewis, 4833; T. McQuillin, 15540; H. Oakes, 19582 [BBC, Radio 4, 1999]; J. Parkinson, 15615; I. R. Proctor, 9309; R. Quint, 16703; F. A. Riches, 9937; R. Salt, 15622; A. Sassoon, 9093; F. Simpson, 12168; E. Trimmer, 8924; L. G. R Wand, 9082; C. W. Warren, 15605; A. F. J. Wheeler, 15442; J. Hall Williams, 15323

BBC Interviews for Open Space Programme, 1985
D. Bradford, 9232; A. Dossetor, 8902; D. C. Hawkins, 8927; A. MacAuslan, 8932; M. Raymond, 8925; C. Yorke, 8931

Fortunoff Archive for Holocaust Video Testimonies, Yale University Library
Testimony of: 19 Krystyna S.; 50 Renée H.; 77 Rosita K.; 82 Joan B.; 83 Marta R.; 166 Martin R.; 169 Rachel R.; 220 Jolly Z.; 282 Alan Z.; 542 Stephen H.; 543 Marion, L.; 567 Charlotte R.; 1417 Rose C.; 1506 Joseph H.; 2028 Roman S.; 2033 Esther F.; 2092 Odette A.; 2243 Grete M.; 2482 Hilda G.; 2717 Rose M.; 2760 Isaac F.; 2760 Harry F.; 2762 Alfred F.; 2804 Anna W.; 4100 Hertha M.; 4148 Magda E.; 4257 Hugh J.; 4262 Alice F.

INDEX